When You Read This Book You Will Know That

ISLAM

IS

THE

TRUTH

I.D. Campbell

Copyright © 2008 I.D. Campbell
All rights reserved.
ISBN: 1490418148
ISBN-13: 978-1490418148

This Book is Dedicated to Yahya Luqman Saleem and L.I.N.

Bismillahi Rahmani Raheem -In the Name of Allah Most Gracious, Most Merciful

IF YOU OPEN YOUR HEART AND YOU OPEN YOUR MIND, WHEN YOU READ THIS BOOK IT WILL OPEN YOUR EYES.

"My own observation had by now convinced me that the mind of the average Westerner held an utterly distorted image of Islam. What I saw in the pages of the Koran was not a 'crudely materialistic' world view but, on the contrary, an intense God-consciousness that expressed itself in a rational acceptance of all God-created nature: a harmonious side-by-side of intellect and sensual urge, spiritual need and social demand. It was obvious to me that the decline of the Muslims was not due to any shortcomings in Islam but rather to their own failure to live up to it."

-Muhammad Asad

ACKNOWLEDGMENTS

First and foremost, ALHAMDULILLAH. ALL PRAISE IS DUE TO ALLAH. He is the source of all truth, therefore all that I convey of the truth in this book and in life are because of ALLAH, and only the mistakes are from me.

I would also like to show my gratitude to the Great champion of Islam, Ahmed Deedat. He is to Islam, what Malcolm X was to Black people. Sheikh Deedat was our international voice when we did not have one and desperately needed one. He gave Muslims all over the world a reason to hold their heads high. He left a legacy that we MUST follow. He was harsh at times, but very stern when necessary. Muslims would do Mr. Deedat, themselves and future reverts a disservice to eschew him. He is directly responsible for the conversion of countless Muslims, including myself. His volumes of books and debates will serve as reasons to revert to Islam for nonbelievers inquisitive enough to view them and as benchmarks for Muslims brave enough to follow in his footsteps. And as the Qu'ran says one who dies fighting in the cause of ALLAH is not truly dead. Ahmed Deedat is not dead. He is alive. I would also like to acknowledge the brothers Shabir Ally, Gary Miller, Jamal Badawi, Zakir Naik, Sami Zaatari, Harun Yahya, and countless others. You all have inspired this book specifically and my life in general. Shukran (Thank you).

Finally, I would like to thank my family for putting up with my relative seclusion from them while indulging in this daunting task.

MY INTENTIONS

48.28 It is He Who has sent His Messenger with Guidance and the Religion of Truth, to proclaim it over all religion: and enough is Allah for a Witness.

Islam is the truth. When I assert this, I mean to say that it is the religion, philosophy and way of life which should be followed by every person on the face of the earth. I mean that there is not a system of beliefs superior to it. By definition, if Islam is the truth, then it has conformity to facts and actuality. It is not to be accepted with blind faith, but to be so convincing that you are compelled to accept it. Truth is something universally recognizable, thus its rejection must be a conscious decision to ignore its validity. It is, however, possible to have a poor presentation, a poor representation or a poor understanding of the truth. But when truth is presented properly, it is undeniable.

At this time, there are 1.8 BILLION people on the face of the earth who bear witness that ISLAM IS THE TRUTH. Despite their varying viewpoints, they unanimously proclaim that "THERE IS NO GOD BUT ALLAH AND MUHAMMAD IS HIS MESSENGER." It is true that Christianity has more professing Christians, but the Muslim boasts that there are more practicing Muslims on earth than any other religion. Now the amount of people who believe in any particular ideology does not prove the truthfulness of the ideology. But the amount of people who believe in ISLAM along with the fact that it is the fastest growing religion in the West, in Britain, in America and in the world, does beg for an explanation. In 2007, NBC news reported that 20,000 Americans convert to Islam each year. And out of the 20,000, there are 4 times as many women than men. In the same year, CNN news reported that 1.5 million Americans converted to Islam AFTER September 11, 2001. In the midst of an onslaught of anti-Islamic news, it is amazing that Muslims would remain Muslims and it is a miracle that others would convert or revert to Islam. But this is the nature of truth. No matter how much truth is covered. It will still shine through. The negative attention geared to denounce Islam has produced some astounding results.

My book is a culmination of all the books and articles that I have read and all the lectures, debates and talks I have seen, as well as all the dialogues that I have participated in. This book is my explanation and my understanding as to why Islam is the truth. My goal is not to have you agree with my every word, but to agree with my ultimate premise, that Islam is the true way of life given to man by God Almighty. And if I fall short of convincing you, at least I can make some people a bit more sympathetic to the plight of Islam. But these are not the only reasons for writing this book. I wish this book to be a confirmation to other Muslims. Chronicling the small amount of knowledge that I have serves as a confirmation to me as well as a foundation to build upon for new Muslims.

Perhaps the most important result I wish to achieve is to light a fire under Muslims in America and in the world to stand up and propagate Islam. Whatever lessons and teachings that you know, give it to someone else. Knowledge and truth is not to be hoarded but shared. The popular saying is "people fear what they do not understand." It is up to Muslims to provide that understanding before fear turns to anger and hatred. Who better to convey the message of Islam than a Muslim? If Muslims do not teach people Islam, someone else will. There are hundreds of prejudices and false ideas about Islam permeating society already. It is difficult to expel these preconceived notions. But it is a task that we must embark upon because it is the obligation of every Muslim to invite others to the true religion from God.

I.D. Campbell

August 2007

REASON AND RELIGION

Some religious people say that religion is not based on sensible reasoning. It is not like science which is based on observations, sensible explanations and rational conclusions. They say theology is dissimilar to this, in that it doesn't make sense or it doesn't have to make sense. They believe that you get a feeling that comes over you and convinces you of the validity of a certain faith. But feelings change, the truth does not. What happens if or when the feeling of truth dissipates? Is the faith now false or less true? No matter how devoted you are and how strong the feeling is that you have, your faith is bound to waver. One morning you wake up and you are not as enthused as you normally are. And the next morning you get that feeling back. But this is not how truth works. The truth is the truth no matter how you feel.

Some people think the truth of a religion is based on the actions of its devotees. This might measure the sincerity of that person's belief, but it in no way compromises the truth. If Adolph Hitler said the earth rotates around the sun, it's the truth, right? I believe Islam is such a truth, that the most despicable, sinful Muslim on earth could convince you of its truthfulness, if he is knowledgeable. A person who was once a Muslim, but now rejects Islam has never fully understood Islam in the first place in my opinion and in my experience with them. Often times these former Muslims with a fair amount of knowledge become agnostics, doubting their faith. I find comfort in knowing that they have found no real alternative to Islam and when I delve into their actual qualms, I am excited to tell them that many of their concerns have long been answered.

It is, of course, no sin to doubt. In fact, doubt should lead to investigation, where you find the truth or at the very least, eliminate certain things as untrue. Islam and the Qur'an in particular, use reasoning to explain its content. It encourages the reader to think, research, investigate, and even ask others about its content and its level of sensibility. The idea that theology makes no sense would render any discussion of religion useless. If theology makes no sense, then how do you distinguish between two religions when neither of them makes sense? You have to distinguish using reasoning or good sense. One of the primary functions of our mind is to choose between different alternatives. I believe that when given the comprehensive explanations of the world's religion, most people will choose Islam.

TABLE OF CONTENTS

ACKNOWLEDGMENTS 5

MY INTENTIONS 6

REASON AND RELIGION 9

Chapter I - GOD 17

    Does God Exist? 17

    Evolution - Does it Substitute for God?...........28

    God - the Islamic Picture 34

    Monotheism Vs. Polytheism 38

    About Allah 46

        99 Names of Allah: 48

        Ayat Al Kursi – Verse of the Throne..........52

        Allah's Wants and Needs..................54

        God of Love 55

Chapter II - MANKIND 59

    The Soul......................59

    Morals 65

    Faith Equals Health!!!!! 69

    Getting Started 70

Revelation 71

Chapter III - AL-QUR'AN 73

The Origin of the Qur'an 74

A Message to the Scientists 78

Big Bang 78

Earth.................................80

The Sun and Moon........................81

The Sun Rotates 82

The Expanding Universe 84

Time 85

Solar and Lunar Years 85

The Existence of Subatomic Particles..............86

Mountains Are like Pegs (Stakes) 87

Barrier Between Sweet and Salt Waters..........88

Darkness in the Depths of the Ocean 89

Layers of Heaven and Earth 91

Bees ~ Female or Male? 93

Sex of Plants 93

Lack of Oxygen 94

Evolution in the Qur'an? 94

Fingertips 96

Man Is Created from Alaq 97

Man Created from a Drop Emitted Between the Back Bone and the Ribs...............98

Human Beings Created from Nutfah 99

Human Beings Created from Sulalah 99

Man Created from Nutfatun Amshaaj 100

The Sex of a Baby 100

Fetus Protected by Three Veils of Darkness.......101

Embryonic Stages 101

Embryo Partly Formed and Partly Unformed......103

Sense of Hearing and Sight 104

How Did Man Multiply? 104

Forehead Full of Lies 106

Weight of Clouds 106

Sent down Iron 107

City of Ihram 108

Haman and the Pharaoh 109

Some Scientists' Comments Regarding Qur'an.....110

Usage and Mentioning of a Word 114

Word Repetitions in the Qur'an 115

Conclusion 118

Allegations of Plagiarism...............119

Camel Through the Eye of a Needle 123

Who Will Inherit the Earth?...............123

A Mustard Seed 124

The Allegations of Plagiarism in Perspective.....127

What about Dinosaurs? 130

Abrogation? 131

Chapter IV - A CLOSER LOOK AT ISLAM 134

Why Islam? 136

The Purpose of Life 144

A Muslim and a Mu'min 146

Kafir 151

Sin 153

Love of Allah 155

Remember 157

Pilgrimage 162

Charity 163

Fasting 165

Chapter V - CONTROVERSIAL SUBJECTS......168

Misnomers 168

Sunni or Shia 170

Women................................171

Marriage................................176

Separation and Divorce 178

No Compulsion 180

    What Non-Muslims Say about the Allegation That Islam Was Spread by the Sword..........184

    Propagation 186

War......................................189

    The Legal Definition of Self-defense..........192

    Martyr (Shaheed) 196

    Peace 198

    Jihad 199

    Right Hand Possess 200

    Forgiveness 202

Prophets 204

    The Prophets' (pbuh) Enemies..............207

    Hadith.................................210

    Prophet Muhammad (pbuh) 213

    Prophet Muhammad's Wives (Allah Bless Them) .215

    What Do Non-Muslims Say about Prophet Muhammad (Pbuh)? 219

Apostasy..................................223

Death for Adultery? 226

Chapter VI - ANSWERS TO COMMON MISCONCEPTIONS ABOUT ISLAM..229

    "Nation of Islam" 229

    5 Percenters 232

ALLAH Leads People Astray 233

Auliya.....................236

Murky Water 238

Islam and Idolatry..........................240

Misinterpretations or Mistranslations of the Qur'an...244

Earth like a Carpet 245

Answering Prayers 248

Why is There Evil in the World? 249

Chapter VII - OUR FINAL DESTINATION...............250

Resurrection and Judgment 251

Hell......................256

Paradise 262

The Heights 270

Chapter VIII - THE CONCLUSION 272

GOD

As a child, I always believed in the existence of God. I was taught and came to believe that God is never vulnerable. He is almighty, he knows everything, and he can do anything (Now I have come to the conclusion that God has power over everything, not that he can do anything). I felt that God is moral, just and honest. Also God never needs anything. He is self-sustaining. As I grew older, I was exposed to both, Christianity and Islam. But one day, at my father's home (He is a Muslim), he was playing a VHS tape of Ahmed Deedat and he was discussing "Jesus: The Beloved Prophet of Islam." During his talk, he mentioned the Muslim's position on the Divinity of Jesus (pbuh), son of Mary. He maintained that Jesus (pbuh) was a human being and he could not be God. As a human being, if he was also God, he ultimately would have to suppress or relinquish some of his godly qualities.

It was as though Sheikh Deedat was speaking directly to me because he solidified the belief that I have had since I can remember, that Jesus (pbuh) was not God. His lecture was like a newly discovered treasure. I watched it over and over again. I am a cynic by nature and someone who has always seemed to go against the grain. The message that I got from the lecture was not that Islam was the Truth, but that Christianity is not true. It amazed and intrigued me that a faith in which so many people believed could possibly be false.

I immediately searched for anything from Ahmed Deedat that I could find. Being only 13 or 14 at the time, I had no money. My father had one or two little booklets by Sheikh Deedat and on the back of them was a list of other booklets that he had written or endorsed. And I ordered them all. The problem was IPCI, the propagation center which distributed the booklets, is in South Africa. The booklets were free, but they took months to come, if you don't donate any money for postage. In the meantime, I began my own search for the falsehood in all religions. As I read, if any of the qualities I had attributed to God were compromised then I concluded that the faith was false. God is the most important being in any religion in my view. He is the Supreme Being who gives man moral guidance. If the head is weak, the body is bound to have faults. Religions such as Hinduism, Buddhism, and Judaism, quickly became exclusions to me, as they portray a needy, lustful, weak god or they were a religion in which God plays a secondary role to its followers. By this time, Mr. Deedat's booklets had reached me and thoroughly convinced me that Christianity was not the path for me. To my surprise, I did find a religion which lived up to the standards to which I placed God.

In Islam I found what great honor ALLAH is held at all times by His worshipers and especially in the Qur'an, the Book of Islam. When discussing religion, one often finds a discrepancy between the God presented by followers of a particular faith and the God projected in their scriptures. He may be said to be moral, almighty and self-sufficient, but their book of authority paints quite a different picture. The Qur'anic picture of God will soon be illustrated in this book but first we must establish that He exists.

DOES GOD EXIST?

In any discussion of the religion of God, it is important to first discuss God. Increasingly, we see on television and in the newspapers the emergence of atheism. Since more and more faiths are beginning to have a more figurative view of their religion and their religious books, it has created a breeding ground for atheists to feast. Because of this loose grip on the tenants of a person's religion, the person becomes more susceptible to the onslaught of those without faith. But there is a religion and a way of life that is to be taken literally. Its members are to stand up to anyone who questions them and their God. This religion is Islam. This is why I begin with the proof of God, and then delve into the truth of His religion for mankind.

GOD

Man has understood his limited capacity to grasp the totality of numbers. He labels this totality as infinity. Infinity is not an actual number, but the term used to demonstrate that numbers are limitless, yet man's knowledge is not. So too has man used his limited knowledge to describe the limitless God. Man has deemed the infinitely powerful, and the infinitely wise being whose beginning is infinite and whose existence is eternal to be God. Though no sensible person questions the existence of infinity, there are those who question the existence of the infinite.

There have been books, articles, and interviews by atheist supposedly questioning the existence of God. I say supposedly because they are usually questioning the motives of religion and of the religious and not the actual existence of God. The atheists are questioning the existence of the God in a particular religion or text. They sometimes very crudely dismiss and dispel someone's lifelong beliefs, but they are normally careful not to definitively say, "There is no God." An atheist, by definition, is someone who denies the existence of God. It comes from the Greek word, "a-theos" which is literally "no god." Those who do not take such a staunch view are called agnostics. Agnostic has the Greek root "agnos" meaning "unknowable." And as its root suggests, an agnostic is someone who believes that it is impossible to know whether there is a God. The definition of an atheist and an agnostic implies that the person has investigated the existence of God and they have come to the conclusion that God does not exist or that it is impossible to prove that God exists. It is important to distinguish between the two.

An atheist is usually a master of words. He cannot say that an atheist is someone who BELIEVES that there is no God, because he wishes to say that atheism is not a form of belief. However, to deny God, you must be able to show that it is impossible for him to exist, which is something none of them are eager to try to prove. The agnostic position that we will never know for sure is a more honest approach than saying, I am positive "God doesn't exist." However, I would suggest that both are disingenuous.

If three jurors are all given the same evidence for a case and one person says this evidence proves that the defendant is guilty. Another juror says this evidence proves that he is innocent. And the third person says after reviewing this evidence, "I have come to the conclusion that it is impossible to determine guilt or innocent." How do we reconcile these contrasting conclusions? We must first realize that the truth is still the truth, no matter what any of them believe. In this case, the man is either guilty or innocent. In my case, there really is a God or there isn't. There are only two choices. This means that the facts were presented poorly or interpreted poorly. But how is it that it completely convinced one person of guilt and another person of innocence, especially if all of it is inconclusive as the third party has said. The answer is that there exist preconceived beliefs before the evidence was presented. They all had the answers in the back of their minds before they came to the trial and they only heard what supported their beliefs. In terms of a court proceeding, this prejudice is harmful. But in the pursuit of God, it is mostly harmful to the atheist. As Shabir Ally once said, "If the theist is right, we will soon find out. If the atheist is right, we will never find out."

Mankind is naturally inquisitive. His mind is geared to distinguish between the true and false, thus agnosticism is a result of such enquiries. Man is also designed to believe in a higher being. Even the atheist evolutionist must admit the propensity for man to worship some form of God, whether they find it impractical or not. Wherever they have found man, they have found him believing and worshiping in God(s). Those who call themselves atheists are and have always been in the extreme minority. Perhaps because they are ostracized and they are seen as an anomaly, they are so vehement in their proclamations. But I think that the scenario I mentioned about the trial and the three jurors is too small an analogy for God. Man is given his entire life to sift through the evidence and come to a verdict. I don't think there really is a such thing as an atheist or an agnostic. I think these are people who wish not to acknowledge God, giving them the right to do as they please. But if "ignorance is bliss" then "denial is hell."

The evidence for God's existence is so overwhelming that you have to ignore it to conclude that He doesn't exist or it is impossible to know whether he exists or not. I am often asked, "How do you know that there is a God?" My answer is "I know that there is a God, in the same way that you know that your great, great, great, great grandfather existed. Is it impossible to know whether your great, great, great, great grandfather existed? Given the evidence that he existed, could it be construed in any other way? One would have to consciously deny the truth or halt their investigation to conclude otherwise. In this case, it is not the presentation or a misinterpretation of the facts, but a blatant effort to ignore and avoid the facts. With my sincerest effort, I hope to present the existence of God so clearly that it is undeniable to anyone. In fact, this entire book and those done before this one is a continuation and extension of the evidence that I am about to present. If Islam and the Qur'an are from God, they too should be submitted as evidence of God's existence. To be clear, the existence of God is a thing which is to be accepted by every mentally able human being on earth. Therefore the proof of His existence should not be some intricate scheme, but something understandable to all.

The truth is God is your greatest grandfather. Not in the sense that he begot you, but that he produced you. He is the greatest grandfather for all things. If you were to think in your mind about your whole genealogy, you must realize the existence of all of your ancestors. In doing so, you must come to the conclusion that there was one man and one woman who started this list. Now the question is, "Where did they come from?" Humanity is similar to the universe, in the sense that it is expanding. There are well over 6 billion people on earth today. And scientists agree that the universe is getting larger all the time, which means at some point in history it was all one mass. The question not only is where did this one mass come from, but who set the stages in motion?

Evolutionists suggest that humanity came from ape-like ancestors, which came from some other species and so on and so on. Their conclusion is that there was a single-celled organism which evolved into a multi-cellular organism. It continued to evolve into every species of animal and insect on earth. Even if this theory is somehow proven to be true, it does not explain the appearance of the first single-celled organism. That is, scientists cannot explain the sudden appearance of LIFE. Actually they can, but they refuse to admit it. Instead they say that the universe, humanity and life in general came about by pure chance.

I suggest that a child could expose their deceit. After they tell this amazing story of our origin with loads of scientific terms, a child might ask, "What happened right before that?" What happened right before the universe became a huge mass that began to spread out? My answer would be that GOD created these gases and began the process of creation. In contrast an atheist may say "they came from nothing, it appeared from thin air." But there was no air, not even thin air. So is their answer more plausible? What happened right before there was a single-celled organism? If you think of the universe and life on earth as a balloon which is not inflated, how does it expand? If they were a set of dominoes which are to fall upon each other, how does the process begin? Some intelligent being outside of the balloon or the dominoes must cause the balloon to expand and cause the dominoes' falling process to begin. Is this not rational and logical and completely simplistic? It is irrational to think that the universe, something with no consciousness, began to expand on its own. This is far more impossible than a balloon that inflates itself, yet no one would dare believe in such foolishness.

As for the single-celled organism, it is a living thing. It is completely irrational, illogical and unscientific to believe that a living being came from something which is non-living, because before life on earth, there was nothing but inanimate objects. What is the "CHANCE" that if you have a rock for 10 million years, it will one day produce an ant? Zero %. It will never, ever happen. LIFE comes from LIFE. To say that through chance and time, an inanimate object produced LIFE is an irrational BELIEF, at best. At worst, it is a pathetic effort to support the premise that God does not exist or that the world around us can be explained without God. Atheist ridicule theists with the phrase "god of gaps," which basically means because we don't know the answer to a question or we can't explanation a phenomenon, we simply place God in the gaps of our knowledge as the explanation. However, this is obviously not true, because an intelligent being in the creation of the universe and creation of life is the ONLY answer and explanation to the question. Any other answer is nonsensical. The alternative to an intelligent life force beginning creation can only be an unintelligent explanation.

Scientists tell us that the universe came into being after an explosion called "The Big Bang." If a child asked them, where did the material which formed the explosion come from, what answer could they give? A more damaging question is what CAUSED the Big Bang? A bang or an explosion is an action and an event. This action or event had to be evoked by something outside of it. Can any action or event be uncaused? No. Every movement you make is first born in your brain. Your brain CAUSES you to run, write, read, walk or smile. Therefore, it is not improbable but impossible for a tremendous event like the BIG BANG to occur without a cause. The very people who belittle your belief in God wish you to believe that a cataclysmic event can simply occur by chance and without cause. Yet you can't smile without a cause. Who is actually the gullible person here? If someone believes in a magic trick, but not in the magician, I would say that they are the gullible ones. If you came to a magic show and you saw a woman split in half, it should be apparent to you that you missed the first act, because you have witnessed the RESULT. However it is more probable that you would stumble across a woman sawed in half, who was born split in two separate boxes, then to believe in an uncaused explosion that resulted in the formation of the entire universe.

Let us consider time. Time is an interval separating two points of a succession of events from the past through the present to the future. Some atheists suggest that time is infinite. If time went back infinitely, then an infinite amount of time would have to elapse before we arrive at this very moment. However an infinite by definition can never finish. So if time went back infinitely, then we would never reach the moment that we are at right now. Fortunately, we HAVE reached this moment. This means that the past is not infinite but finite and that time must have had a beginning. So time is like a stopwatch. How did the time start ticking, because it is apparent that it has? We can also deduce that if time had a beginning, so too did space, better yet the universe had a beginning. How did the universe begin to exist? The starting of time (the stopwatch) and start of the universe are effects. Every effect has a CAUSE says the great scientist and theist, Sir Isaac Newton. The scientific community has dubbed it the FIRST CAUSE.

10:4 It is He (Allah) Who beginneth the process of creation.

The First Cause is the someone or something that caused the existence of everything in the universe. Albert Einstein and Stephen Hawking have both acknowledged this First Cause. Of course, that First Cause is in all actuality the creator of the universe. Since the beginning of humanity, they have known this First Cause as GOD. What took great scientist years to acknowledge took the first man no time to discover, with nothing but a bit of reflection and reasoning. And as is the nature of truth, more extensive peering into the matter only makes it more luminous. This is true when we look more deeply into the idea of cause and effect.

We have found that the universe, time and space have a cause. The expansion of space and the stretching of time are causal chains. In philosophy, a causal chain is an ordered sequence of events in which any one event in the chain necessitates the next. Time is defined by past, present, and future and these dimensions move forward directly affecting each other. The future and the present are constantly changing and the past is enlarging (The past's mountaining is also indicative of its finite nature). Space is defined by length, height and depth. Expansion of any of these dimensions affects the measurement of the others. A causal chain is specifically defined as "ordered" sequence. This implies intelligence. A causal chain can only be finite, meaning that it must have a beginning. Therefore every causal chain has a first cause.

Now causes are either mechanical or personal. A mechanical cause is like a pool ball which hits another ball. This kind of cause cannot be a first cause because it has no free will. Pool balls do not hit each other by themselves. A personal cause is a cause in which something outside of the materials of a sequence of events begins the process. For instance, a MAN using his pool stick to hit the pool balls together is an example of the process of a personal cause. When we put this into the perspective of the universe it becomes apparent that universe was began by a personal cause. To be clear, the time and space that we live in necessitates an infinite personal choice, a first cause that is not caused. It is a conscious being outside the scheme of time and space and all the laws that govern the universe.

One alternative to this view is infinite regress. Infinite regress is a causal relationship transmitted through an indefinite number of terms in a series, with no term that begins the causal chain. This basically means there is no beginning. The events of the universe are seen in terms of a circular sequence, instead of a straight line. However this has already been disproved if we reaffirm the necessity for time and space to have a beginning. Scientists, today, tell us that this universe is a little under 14 billion years old. So if someone takes infinite regress as the explanation for the universe's existence, then they are now believing in something which is without evidence and is, in fact, unscientific, rendering it a religion. Belief in infinite regress is as plausible as the belief that pool balls have always existed and they have been hitting each other by themselves FOREVER. If you meet a person who entertains the idea of an infinite universe, ask them to count to three for you, using negative infinity. They will not be able to get to the number three. They will not be able to start counting at all. So if the universe's beginning was infinite, then we would never get to this moment in time right now. Another idea is that everything simply popped into existence. Neither alternative seems logical or probable in comparison to the explanation of the First Cause.

Some have said that since time is a property of the universe, the universe is not subject to time. But the actually words and definition of "Big Bang" suggests a sequence of events. If it originated as one mass and friction within it began an explosion, then there were steps before the big bang. This means that even before the universe was formed, there was time. Now we can see that the universe may not be subject to its own time, it is subject to the time before its inception. Therefore again the universe had a beginning.

Most people who believe in the Big Bang theory maintain that the early elements of the universe existed about 400,000 years before the big bang actually occurred. There was nothing but photons, electrons and baryons. Photons began interacting causing friction and heat. The heat got to a point where electrons and protons combined to form hydrogen atoms. This began the formation of the universe that we see today. Perhaps sensing the onslaught of theists' claim of a First Cause, a small group of people have suggested that the universe has always existed and during its infinite years the big bang occurred. Since the universe is made of matter and it is said that matter is neither created nor destroyed, they reason that the matter that made up the early universe has always existed.

Matter is defined as the substances in which the universe is composed. These substances are made up of atoms, which are made up of protons, neutrons and electrons. But the early universe was not made up of matter, but of the particles which are the components of matter. It was not until the big bang that these particles formed atoms, thus forming matter. Saying the universe existed forever is like saying cars have been around since the beginning of earth, since its components, metal and rubber, have been on earth from the beginning. To compound matters, it has been found that protons decay, thus they are not eternal. If matter decays, it has an ending and most likely a beginning. Matter's ending is its transformation into energy.

Energy is the capacity of a physical system to do work. Energy is an expression of matter. Therefore energy, not matter, is what cannot be created nor destroyed. So we find that matter which makes up the universe has not always existed, but energy has, which is how the elements of matter could move in the first place. Energy has differing quantities for different forms of matter. The two categories of energy are kinetic (motion) and potential energy (stored energy). Each category has different forms of energy. Electrical energy, radiant energy, thermal energy, motion energy and sound are examples of kinetic energy. Chemical energy, stored mechanical energy, nuclear energy and gravitational energy are examples of potential energy. All forms of energy are but forces which cause things to move or to stay together and in place. But force must be applied from someone or something. Force is a push or a power. This push, this power is from the source of all power and of all things (A special push, force, energy and power is bestowed upon the living of the universe, which will be address shortly). In all, we can conclude that the universe and its components did not always existence. But the powerful influence on the universe has always existed. That is the First Cause.

4:126 But to Allah belong all things in the heavens and on earth. And He it is that Encompasseth all things.

Many atheists misunderstand the explanations given of the need for a First Cause and they formulate an argument countering their own misunderstanding. They believe that the theist argument is:

"Anything complex must have been created by an intelligence being. The universe is complex, therefore it has a Creator."

Then the atheist's argument becomes, "if the universe is complex, then its creator must be complex. And if everything complex has a creator, then the creator must have a creator." Actually the refutation of the first argument only works for the atheist if you do not include the explanation of the First Cause. I can accurately state that this complex universe must be created by an even more complex First Cause, because the First Cause is OUTSIDE the laws that govern the universe. Therefore the First Cause is not subject to being caused or created as the universe is. The definition of the First Cause renders the atheist's question meaningless. It's like asking, how fast can a car fly? Or how many legs does a fish have? By definition, the being that began creation has no creator or limitations to his power over creation. The First Cause invented creation, therefore he could not have been created. Everything that is not him is an effect and it is his creation, including creation and laws of nature.

Those who insist that the creator operates in the same manner as his creation "are like those dolls that, seeing they move by springs, imagine that the human who made them must also derive his motion from the action of springs. If they were told that he is self-moved, they would retort that it is impossible for anything to move spontaneously since everything in their world moved by a spring. Just like them, you cannot imagine that God exists in his own essence with no need of an efficient cause; and this is because you see everything around you in need of such a cause." (Dr. Mostafa Mahmoud, "Dialogue with an Atheist")

Perhaps it would be advantageous to speak of God as the "Uncreated Creator" to help people understand what God is and to avoid such criticism. This title stems from another title for God, "Immovable Mover" which was introduced by Aristotle and developed by Thomas Aquinas. They deduced that the universe and everything in it was set into motion by someone who is not subject to being created or moved.

The author of the book entitled "The God Delusion," Richard Dawkins criticizes the argument that God is the answer to the explanation of a complex universe. He concludes that the cause of this universe must be simplistic, not complex. But as many theists have pointed out, the definition of the word "complex" betrays the point that he is trying to convey. The meaning of complex is a conceptual whole made up of complicated and related parts. This contradicts theists' understanding of

God because he is not made up of any material parts, as the universe is, which means he is not complex, in the physical understanding of the word. The simple explanation Dawkins believes in is "evolution" and creation by luck. Perhaps the definition of luck and evolution are quite simple, but the luck of evolution, is not simple at all.

EVOLUTION - DOES IT SUBSTITUTE FOR GOD?

Evolution is now garnered to be a fact in the way that the existence of gravity is a fact. Because it is a fact that gravity exists but there are theories as to how it works, evolutionists say that evolution's existence is a fact, but their explanation of its process is a theory. The basic meaning of evolve is to develop or gradually change in a positive direction. In this sense, probably every theist in the world believes in this. However, this is not the connotation most have of this word. They imagine that evolve means the development and gradually change of a living thing into different species. There are those who believe in evolution and they also believe that God is reason for this change. This is reasonable. But atheists like Mr. Dawkins use evolution as a method to take God out of the process of creation. This is the part that I take exception to. I believe that any explanation of creation without God is a preposterous idea. This notion is what many atheists have called religion, a fairy tale. If you ask an atheist to explain evolution to you, he will articulate terms and phrases you may not be familiar with. He may direct you to certain sites and web pages, where evolution is explained in better terms. You will find that their explanation of the alterations of animals is due to natural selection or survival of the fittest and mutation, which is a permanent change, a structural alteration, in the DNA or RNA.

Mutations can be caused by many factors including environmental assaults such as radiation and mutagenic chemicals. Mutations are sometimes attributed to random chance events. It is said that an animal first begins to mutate, and then due to natural selection, the animals not ENDOWED with this mutation become extinct. I emphasize the word "endowed" because evolutionists insist that these mutations are

BENEFICIAL. Of course, as children (and even adults) we saw cartoons or movies of "Spiderman" or "The Incredible Hulk" where radiation infects a person and mutation causes some positive effects. The problem is mutation overwhelmingly causes harmful effects or they are ineffectual. Mutations generally weaken the animal. Evolutionists admit this, but they maintain that by pure luck an infinitesimal amount of cases of mutation result in positive effects. Even if this is the case, mutation does not introduce new information to your DNA and it most certainly does not change one species of animal into another. Mutations displace, change or eliminate information from your DNA.

Examples of mutation are growing a sixth finger, growing an ear on your foot, or your mouth and nose are joined. The victims of the atomic bomb in Hiroshima and Nagasaki were exposed to an extreme and intense dosage of radiation and none of them or their offspring was positively affected by it. And none of them developed anything that a human being does not have already in his DNA. Evolutionists suggest that mutations are happening all the time. There are over six billion people on earth and none of them are evolving into another species. None of them are growing wings or antennas or tails, no matter how many chemicals they are exposed to, unless the chemical is specifically designed to have such an effect. Unless there is a mad scientist in his laboratory cooking up a serum to develop wings in humans, there is no chance that a mutation is, from pure luck, introducing new information into a human's DNA to form wings. From this I conclude that evolution or the development of any insect, reptile or animal can only be done by an INTELLIGENT BEING. I believe this argument is called "god of gaps." Evolution does not make much sense at all, unless they place God in their gaps. And they have plenty of gaps to fill. Ask an atheist evolutionist to skip the scientific terminology and explain the presence of life on earth.

He begins with once upon a time long, long ago, there was a single-celled organism. It multiplied into a multi-cellular organism. Its first habitat was the ocean, perhaps as a fish or something fishlike. Due to hunger or some other necessity, this fish developed into an animal which could live on land. When this animal lived on land, it developed into billions, even trillions of other species. Dinosaurs and snakes developed into birds. Apelike animals evolved into apes, monkeys and human beings. Then the evolutionist will provide you with a chart of a small monkey who turns into a human being and there is you have it...evolution.

Their explanation has to begin with a magic trick, with no magician. There was a black top hat, then rabbits just started coming out of it. The atheistic evolutionist makes little attempt to explain where this single-celled organism came from. He says "WE DON'T KNOW!" He proclaims his ignorance to be superior to a theist's conviction that God gave life to this earth. Also, the millions upon millions of steps missing from their explanation are telling of the story's validity. Of course, this is my rendition of their explanation, so I advise you to ask an atheist evolutionist to simplify this explanation a bit further. Take one example, the fish that began to walk unto shore or the snake that grew wings.

There was a fish. Food became scarce in the ocean. And then what? How exactly did fish grow four legs, lungs, nostrils, eyes and ears on accident? They say there was a mutation in the fish or its offspring, which began developing these organs which fish DNA does not possess information for. The problem is mutation is random, it does not occur from necessity. They also, according to evolutionists, occur all the time. They say those mutations which are advantageous to the species are carried to its offspring. Then through natural selection, those fish without this positive mutation die out. But these mutations that they speak of do not produce completely functional organs. These organs and limbs have to develop over hundreds, maybe thousands of years. But half of an eye is not advantageous. Half a leg is not advantageous. They are harmful to a fish. Also if mutations are random occurrences, it is even more impractical that all the organs necessary to live on land would form in the water and by chance.

Evolution occurs in stages, therefore there should be fish with 1/3 an ear. There should be fossils of fish with ¼ a lung and ½ of an eye. There should be fossils with a nose without nostrils and three legs. Every possible combination that you could think of should be possible to find. Not only legs, lungs, nostrils, ears and eyes, but there should be fish with antennas, wings, fur, hair, and any other characteristic of any animal you can imagine. This is because according to the evolutionist, mutations are frequent and random, thus they do not only include organs suitable for life on the land, but organs for every kind of animal as well. If it is reasonable to believe a fish grew lungs, then it's reasonable to believe he also developed a stinger like a bee and a tail like a monkey. If we are to believe that such transition happened to the billions upon billions of species of animals, insects and reptiles that have lived on earth, there should literally be trillions upon trillions of fossils to prove this fact. I should be able to go in my backyard right now and dig up one thousand fossils of these transitions. Right now!!! Even more interesting with this theory is that the new information introduced to DNA by mutation is occurring all the time. That means that of the 6.8 billion people on earth and countless people who have inhabited it for millions of years, some of them now and then had wings, or fins, or antlers. Of course this is not true, but this is how far you can go with the explanation of evolution.

Evolutionist say reptiles became birds. I would say, there was a snake that slithered to a cliff and he could not get over. Now what? Nothing. If he can't get over a cliff to get food or shelter, he will die. He will never start to grow wings and feathers. If a family of snakes lives on the top of a mountain forever, they will always be snakes. In order to explain a phenomenon, evolutionists have to use "evolution of gaps." They use evolution and all its terminology to attempt to fill the huge craters in their observations. They are in dire need of the argument used by theist, "God of gaps." In order for a snake to grow wings, he must have prayed to God to get them (a joke). Human beings are the most intelligent beings on earth, yet they cannot add new information to your DNA to give you wings. But to adequately explain how mutation became such an astronomical success, how this mutation was administered, to explain the lack of fossil records of this great multitude of change, you need an intelligent being to have CAUSED these transformations. Thus evolution if you believe it to be true, is another indication of God's existence. The Qur'an says God is the Irresistible (13:16). No matter how you try to escape him, you can never escape him. Whatever theory posed, if it is grounded in fact, it will inevitably lead you to God.

When an evolutionist says something appeared or occurred by chance, he is really saying a miracle occurred. The word is derived from the Latin word "miraculum" meaning "something wonderful." Something wonderful might be a bit ambiguous and subjective, but a miracle is more specifically, an event or effect contrary to the established constitution and course of things, or a deviation from the known laws of nature; a supernatural event, or one transcending the ordinary laws by which the universe is governed. Today, man scoffs at the idea of a miracle and anyone who admits to belief in such a thing.

His intellect gives him a false sense of pride. They turn their noses up at more primitive men, when in fact the primitive man was more intelligent than he is. The modern man has more knowledge, but the primitive man is more intelligent. Knowledge is but the acquiring of information; intelligence is the understanding and usage of knowledge to come to rational conclusions. The primitive man appreciates miracles that we take for granted every day. We think because we have more knowledge of the birth process, that perhaps it is less than a miracle. Knowledge of something's functions only demonstrates its miraculous nature. In fact, we should have even more appreciation than the primitive man. Because the more we learn about nature, the clearer it becomes that this entire universe is a miracle, from the largest planet to the smallest molecule. Those who believe the universe had a beginning believe in a miracle, because its origin could not have been governed by the laws of nature. There were no laws of nature until it began to exist. The Big Bang is the description of a miracle. Those who believe the universe always existed believe in a miracle because it is against the laws of nature to have no beginning and to have an effect without a cause. Those who believe a living organism had a non-living origin believe in a multitude of terrific miracles. Do they also believe a dead woman can become pregnant and give birth to a living baby? Those who believe a fish grew lungs or a snake grew wings by chance, really mean this happened by a miracle. Life is most certainly a miracle, perhaps the greatest miracle of all. But who performs miracles?

6:95 He is the one to cause the dead to issue from the living. That is Allah: then how are ye deluded away from the truth?

GOD

Atheists believe in a greater miracle than any theist does. Walking on water, healing the blind and resurrecting someone are child's play in comparison to the miracles they believe in. All theists start with a subject and from this subject everything came into being. With miracles, an agent is used by God to perform them. Atheists believe that there was nothing at all, and then "boom" there was something. In mathematics, the difference between nothing and 1 is infinite. In reality, it is even more astounding. If someone bottled up a heap of nothing and waited for it turn into something, we would believe it to be a futile experiment. But even more futile is to have no bottle, no top, no air, nothing and wait for something to appear. To believe a single-celled organism came from some non-living object and mutated into a human being by chance is more amazing than believing a boat left unattended at shore after thousands of years became a ship. Though the atheist will argue that a ship is an inanimate object without the functional parts of a human being, they fail to realize that their argument gives them a deeper hole to get out of. A human being, in fact, a single cell is as complex as an entire city, therefore its structure is far less likely to come from nothing. It is more probable that a ship formed itself at shore, then to believe one living cell formed from something non-living by accident.

And don't be fooled by ADAPTATION. Adaptation is when an organism already has the information in its DNA and it uses this to adapt to its environment. For instead, there are people immune to the AIDS virus. If AIDS became highly contagious through breathing or from the touch, these people would not become infected. They would naturally reproduce with other people who are also immune to the virus. These people will live for many more years to come. In this case, humanity did not evolve from mutation and natural selection.

It adapted to its environment and then natural selection took effect. Many people use false examples like this one to prove evolution, where the organism possesses the DNA already and they label this as evolution. It is evolution in the elementary sense of the word, but not in the sense which they are trying to convey. Even if a mutation like a human ear on your forehead became necessary, this is adaptation. It is not the introduction of new information or the altering of one species to another. If there is a person with a rhinoceros horn on his forehead, then they are in business.

For these reasons, I believe in Aatheism- (no, no god). I deny the existence of an atheist. I don't believe that there are people who believe that there is no God. You can only be agnostic and that is because you have not completed your research, yet you come to a conclusion that it is impossible to know God's exists. Another kind of atheist is one who has had some traumatic experience and says there is no God. This is an emotional not a rational conclusion and will probably change with time. The death of someone in a collapsing building, in no way disproves that the building was constructed nor does calamities negate God's existence. These things only show the need for God's revelation, so he can communicate with man and give him understanding of the world around him. Would not the creator be the most qualified to do this job?

GOD - THE ISLAMIC PICTURE

Up to now, all these proofs that I have presented are in support of the existence of any deity and any religion. Now I will get more specific, in terms of a Muslim's view of God as described in the Muslim's book of supreme authority, the Qur'an. The Qur'an seldom addresses directly those who do not believe in God at all. In Surah 57:8 the Qur'an asks "What is wrong with you, that you do not believe in God?"

My Aatheism comes from verses like this, which seems to suggest there may be some problem with anyone who doesn't believe in God. In most religious books, God is considered to be an axiomatic truth. Perhaps in anticipation of the atheist movement, the Qur'an seeks to convince the reader of his existence.

In the name of Allah, the Compassionate, the Merciful.

112:1 Say: He is Allah, the One and Only;

112:2 Allah, the Eternal, Absolute;

GOD

112:3 He begetteth not, nor is He begotten;

112:4 And there is none like unto Him.

Though this is only four very short verses, it has been called ¼ of the Quranic message. That is to say, a quarter of the Qur'an pertains to the Supreme Being and it is summarized in these four verses. This is a fascinating element of the Qur'an. It seems only natural that someone who is unsure of the existence of God might gravitate towards a book with such a large portion of it dedicated to God. In this chapter, the very first word of verse one is very important. The Arabic word here "Qul" means "say." It is a clear indication that the person conveying this message, Prophet Muhammad (pbuh), is having these words put into his mouth to repeat to his audience. The appearance of the word "qul" is continuous in the Qur'an as it is a direct response given to Prophet Muhammad (pbuh) to counter what others ask. The verse continues with "ALLAH is ONE." It seems rather redundant because God is already in the singular form, but there are those who claim to be monotheists, yet their doctrines leave room for pantheism or even polytheism. The Islamic understanding of ALLAH leaves no such room. In fact the Qur'an often states that "there is no God, but him!" (2:163, 3:18, 28:70). [In the Qur'an, GOD is described in anthropomorphic ways, such as using the masculine pronouns to identify him and mentioning the hands of GOD. This is a representation of the limitations of man's language in describing God. God has no gender and no physical features as we have.]

In the second verse is the Arabic word "As-Samad" which is translated eternal, absolute. This means, that he has no beginning and no ending. He is beyond the scope of time. He was not young at one time and he cannot grow old. And he has no creator. As some might ask, who created the creator? The Muslim's understanding renders this question meaningless. By definition, a creation began to exist, but ALLAH has no beginning. He is not subject to the laws he gave to his creation.

The third verse explains that he has not fathered anyone or anything and he is not the son of anyone or anything. If God did not create you but fathered you, then you would have the same attributes as he does. Because a person or animal begets his own kind. A man begets a man. A snake begets a snake, and God would beget a god. Yet this is impossible, because Verse two said God has no beginning, which means that his son would have no beginning, as well. But his son must have a beginning, if God fathered him, because the father preceded the son. Anyone and anything with a beginning cannot be God. This completely eliminates the idea that God is a human being or animal or that he became one of them.

19.88 They say: "(Allah) Most Gracious has begotten a son!"

19.89 Indeed ye have put forth a thing most monstrous!

19.90 At it the skies are ready to burst, the earth to split asunder, and the mountains to fall down in utter ruin,

19.91 That they should invoke a son for (Allah) Most Gracious.

19.92 For it is not consonant with the majesty of (Allah) Most Gracious that He should beget a son.

19.93 Not one of the beings in the heavens and the earth but must come to (Allah) Most Gracious as a servant.

The Qur'an says it does not befit the majesty of God to have a son. It is beneath God to reproduce as his creation does. When God wishes to create something, he merely wills the thing into being. He says "be and it is." (2:117).

Taking all the attributes or knowledge of God, and placing them into a human being is impossible. Can you pour an ocean into a soda bottle? A man's brain does not have the capacity to contain the knowledge of everything from past to the future.

His body cannot store the power to create the universe. If the matter and energy of your body contained enough matter and energy to create the universe, it would explode and so would everything around you. Everything on earth would explode. The earth would explode and a new universe would begin to exist. No physical material being or thing can possess such power or knowledge because they would self-destruct. The sound waves from an explosion can blow your eardrums, but sound waves over 190 decibels can actually kill you. God made these sounds. If the power of these sound waves were filtered into a human being, he would be killed instantly. I am only trying to demonstrate the impossibility of a human being becoming God. In fact, nothing material can be God because its properties will destroy itself. The earth or the universe cannot contain the power of the being which created it.

We all know that nothing in this universe is eternal, therefore the Qur'an in Chapter 112 is saying nothing in this universal is ALLAH. And if you dreamed of something which you thought might be God, verse 4 assures you that nothing is like him, just to cover all the bases. ALLAH is unlike anything that you can even imagine.

6:103 No vision can grasp Him, but His grasp is over all vision. He is above all comprehension, yet is acquainted with all things.

It is the prerogative of some people to mock those theists who worship that which they do not see and cannot fully grasp. To them I would ask, "Is it possible for a human being to know all things?" Even if all 6.8 billion people on earth gather together and exchanged all the knowledge that they have learned, no one person can grasp all of that material. Even if all those people committed to a computer disk all the information that they knew, it would be a minute fraction of all things that can be known, whether these things are from the past, present or future. A human being is not capable of knowing all things, but he is equipped with enough reasoning to understand that the creator does not have such a limitation.

Since we cannot fully grasp the truth of all things, it stands to reason that we cannot fully grasp a being who does fully grasp the truth of all things. Can a human being see everything that there is to be seen? ALLAH is also all-seeing. How can your highly limited eyesight view a being that can see everything? Man cannot see planets without a telescope or a cell without a microscope. He cannot look at the sun without harming his eyes. He can't see inside of himself without an X-ray machine. He can't see himself without a mirror. How does he think that he can view God, who created the sun, the cells, and who created him. There was a man by the name of Moses (pbuh), who wished to see God. ALLAH presented a glimpse of His glory to a mountain and the mountain crumbled to dust. At the sight of which, Moses (pbuh) fainted. When he regained consciousness, he no longer wanted to see God (7:143). The mountain crumbled to dust because the sight of God is too awesome for his creation. The sun can consume a person millions of miles away from it in seconds. Of far greater brilliance is the light of the one who created the stars and sun. ALLAH is the source of all light. Those who insist upon seeing God are described in the Qur'an as those "thinking too highly of themselves" (25:21), especially when they are those who cannot even bare the sight and sound of thunder and lightning (4:153). But ALLAH does not deprive man from viewing his illumination, but for an earthly lifetime. Just as you need special equipment to see the planets or things microscopic, you need special equipment to see God, as well. And the sight of ALLAH is the greatest reward one can achieve.

MONOTHEISM vs. POLYTHEISM

If humanity began in Africa, its religion was most likely monotheistic. Despite popular opinion and the label of pagan or heathen given to any non-Judeo-Christian faith, African religiosity is overwhelmingly monotheistic. Though they may have invoked the spirit of their ancestors or other spirits, they never worshiped these spirits. Neither did they make graven images of God. They believed God to be "unknowable," "unseen" and self-sustaining.

GOD

"The Maasai (Kenya and Tanzania) name for God, Engai means (among others) "the Unseen One, the Unknown One." Likewise, among the Tenda (Guinea), God is called Hounounga which means: "the Unknown"...The Zulu (South Africa) point this out clearly, when they call God uZivelele, which means: "He who is of himself, the Self-existent One." God is eternal, without beginning and without end, all knowing, all powerful, both distant and near... The Akan (Ghana) say: "God is not asleep." This proverb affirms the belief that God sees and knows everything; and in the case of wrongdoing, the justice of God is unfailing. The Pygmy prayer-hymn is a clear confession of monotheism, with many attributes about God. They pray-sing:

> In the beginning was God (Khmvoum).
>
> Today is God,
>
> Tomorrow will be God.
>
> Who can make an image of God?
>
> He has no body.
>
> He is as a word that comes out of your mouth.
>
> That word! It is no more,
>
> It is past, and still it lives,
>
> So is God!

(John Mbiti, "General Manifestations of African Religiosity")

This is a belief in God which was shared with Muslims 1400 years ago and today. Zoroastrianism and Judaism are also long standing religions which had some form of monotheism. Hinduism, which gave rise to Buddhism, just as Judaism did for Christianity, is often described as polytheism. Though Hindus believe in the one supreme God, who is unseen and unknown, Brahman, they, like Christians, believe the Supreme Being manifests himself into this world. They call his manifestations incarnation. As Christians believe that Jesus (pbuh) was God incarnate, the Hindu believes that a part of the Brahman godhead, Vishnu has incarnated into the world nine times, as a man, a fish, a boar, a tortoise, and even a half man/ half lion to better understand the world. These were representations of God on earth. Muslims believe God does not incarnate at all.

16:17 Is then He Who creates like one that creates not?

It is ill-befitting God to become his own creation. There is absolutely no need for such a thing in Islam. God would not incarnate in order to understand his creation. God knows what he has created. As Ahmed Deedat once said, "I do not have to become a microphone, to understand how it works." Nor does God have to lower himself to handle any of his affairs with man. If God can create the universe without being subject to its laws, he most definitely can resolve any issues without subjecting himself to his own laws of nature. If he did this, then he would no longer be unlike anything that we can imagine. God becoming a mortal is less probable than the sun becoming a period on this page. If the sun became a period on this page, would planets still orbit it? If God did incarnate as a being on earth, he would have to relinquish some of his godly qualities, like being self-sustaining and being unseen. The problem with that is God cannot do that.

It is a common mistake people make when discussing God. They are under the impression that God can do anything, which is not the case. If you assert that God can do anything then we must assert that God can do foolish things, or stupid things, as well. If God can do anything, he could make another God like him. But he cannot. The uncreated cannot create another uncreated. Also, God cannot banish you from his dominion. ALLAH is God of the entire universe. Everything besides God is his creation. That means that he is its God. Therefore there is no place he can send you that he does not rule over.

GOD

Also the premise that everything came from God confuses some people into believing that everything is God. They think, if you kill a gnat, or a grain of grass, you are killing a part of God. The Muslims says no, everything is not God, but everything is GOD'S. The apostrophe "S" makes a world of difference.

Therefore nothing that we see in this material world can be God. If God were a man, he would have to sleep, to eat and drink and ultimately die. Yet the God of Islam cannot be seized by sleep or slumber (2:255), He needs nothing, and He is eternal and absolute. If He relinquished any of these attributes then He would cease to be God. You see, God is not a title that you can take off and put back on. God is WHAT you are, not who you are. His nature makes Him God. Without His nature, He is not God.

If a square became a circle, it is no longer a square, anymore. For something to become another thing, it has to undergo some transformation into something else. If God became a man, then he is no longer God. But being God is not like the presidency, where after four years, someone new applies for the position. God is God, forever. If I could sum up the understanding of monotheism of Islam, it would be "GOD is GOD." So when I meet a theist, I can discuss the ultimate and Supreme Being, God, and when they venture off with incarnations of another man or animal or statue, I can say, no, GOD is GOD. This statement is so simple, yet man's yearning to get closer to God tempts him, time and time again, to venerate something or someone undeserving of the greatest honor.

Of course, the Qur'an says repeatedly that God is one. However, Muslims do not simply believe that there is one God because the Qur'an says so, but because of the sound reasoning in the Qur'an that God is one. Joseph (pbuh), a prophet of God, while in prison, asked two fellow prisoners if it is more preferably to worship an assortment of gods or the one true God, which encompasses the abilities of all the other gods (12:39). This is like asking, do you prefer one president or ten? The rational person would choose one. And the Qur'an provides further reasoning to why one should consider that there is but one God. In Surah 67:3-4, the harmonious nature of the universe is spoken off. It is suggested that if you constantly ponder the universe, you will be compelled to marvel at its magnificent structure and beauty. Would this universe exist as it does, with laws allowing every element of nature to correspond to each other in a staple, balanced and unchanging system, if there were more than one Almighty God?

23:91 No son did Allah beget, nor is there any god along with Him: (if there were many gods), behold, each god would have taken away what he had created, and some would have lorded it over others! Glory to Allah! (He is free) from the (sort of) things they attribute to Him!

What we call nature and its every component is following a strict order. If there were gods of equal or differing amounts of power, there would be utter chaos and confusion, suggests the Qur'an. Not to mention the fact that they would be dependent upon each other. The god of futility needs the god of love, and the god of life. The god of the earth needs the god of the sun. The existence of a smoothly running government suggests a single governor.

Polytheism or worshiping more than one God is called "shirk" in Arabic. A polytheist is called a "mushrik." In almost all instances, those who believe in many gods hold one God superior to all others. The other gods are his minions, susceptible to his punishment or recipients of his blessings. There are also man/gods or men with extraordinary powers bestowed upon them from the gods. Oftentimes, these gods and men intermingle. The gods seemingly wish to lives as humans do and humans wish to live as the gods do. There are gods with wives and children, yet they are involved in the movements of the universe and the lives of those on earth. The Qur'an points out that it is difficult to be impartial to a multitude of gods.

39:29 Allah puts forth a Parable a man belonging to many partners at variance with each other, and a man belonging entirely to one master: are those two equal in comparison? Praise be to Allah! But most of them have no knowledge.

GOD

The Qur'an frequently mentions "shirk" as associating partners with God. This is because it is clear that the polytheist believe in higher powers, but an ultimate higher power reigns over smaller gods. It is Muslim's belief that those considered as other gods are not gods at all, but merely his agents, whom he assigns duties to fulfill.

Because Islam views other religions as a result of a corruption of the true message originally revealed to a specific people, Islam equips its followers to see the truth in other religions, which is at every religion's core. Almost all religions have the same core views, goals and supreme GOD. The Qur'an encourages Muslims to come to common ground with those of different faiths (3:64). And it asks those of other faiths not to go to extremes in your religion (5:77). For example, with a Hindu, the Muslim might say, "We both believe in a supreme being which is unseen and unlike anything in our imagination. However, I do not find it incumbent of God to become a tortoise or a man and have intimate relationships with a woman." Whatever the Hindu's reason is for God to become a man, it can be answered by a Muslim that God can do all of this without becoming a sperm, an embryo, a baby, a teenage and an adult. Therefore the only reason God would have for becoming a man would be to degrade or downgrade himself. So, it is more sensible that God did not become a human being.

There are those who insist that the supreme God is accompanied by other gods with less strength and abilities. A Muslim offers that their understanding is parallel to Islam in the sense that Muslims have a belief in the supreme GOD, but those whom they call lesser gods are angels and the men with extraordinary power are prophets and all of them are subject to GOD, but none of them share his majesty or might. They only carry out his will.

The Qur'an says an oath to Muhammad (pbuh) is an oath to ALLAH (48:10). The mistake of some religions is that they look at a verse like this and assume that it means Prophet Muhammad (pbuh) is ALLAH. In the gospel of John, Jesus (pbuh) says "if you see me, you see the father." The person who would say this means Jesus (pbuh) is God, might be the very person to say that verse 48:10 means Muhammad (pbut) is God. Jesus (pbuh) also said you have never seen God or heard his voice, therefore Jesus (pbuh) could not have meant, in his first quote, that he is God. Jesus (pbuh) actually meant that he was a representative for God. The Qur'an says both these men are but servants of ALLAH (33:40, 19:30). They deliver his message as a messenger delivers the king's message to the countrymen. The king and the messenger are not the same person, but if you reject the message you reject the king. However if you kill the messenger, you are in no way harming the king.

You see, "shirk" is not merely the degradation of God, but also the degradation of man. God made man viceroy on earth and even made angels and jinn bow in obedience to him (7:1). In Islam, man is superior to angels. Therefore man worshiping something he is made to be superior to degrades him (6:165-166, 7:10). And man worshiping another man is worshiping his equal. Even if the man to be worshiped is a saint and or a martyr, this is a goal attainable by all men.

22:73 O men! Here is a parable set forth! listen to it! Those on whom, besides Allah, ye call, cannot create (even) a fly, if they all met together for the purpose! And if the fly should snatch away anything from them, they would have no power to release it from the fly. Feeble are those who petition and those whom they petition!

The Qur'an offers several objections to the deification of a man. It challenges those receiving worship to create something and cause it to reproduce. It also challenges those who worship them to contemplate how a creation of GOD can guide you to truth. It can only be that the god in which they believe has a GOD, because he is source of all guidance and truth. Again, the Qur'an says "what is wrong with you, how do you judge" (10:34-36), but this time to those who give worship to anyone other than ALLAH. It is compelling man to go straight to the source. Don't worship the messenger, worship the king. Islam is also very critical of those who worship idols and statues. It insists that man not worship anything which can not harm or benefit him. There was a young man by the name of Abraham (pbuh) who was in the midst of those who worshiped idols. One day, Abraham (pbuh) smashed all of the idols and left one remaining. The idol worshipers were beside themselves, when they discovered the broken idols. Abraham (pbuh) said, maybe the remaining statue destroyed the others. He suggested that they ask the statue what happened. The idol worshipers basically said, don't be a fool, Abraham (pbuh). These idols cannot move to smash one another. To this Abraham (pbuh) asked, then why do you worship them (21:51-66).

7:197 And those whom you call upon besides Him (Allah) are not able to help you, nor can they help themselves.

7:198 And if you invite them to guidance, they do not hear; and you see them looking towards you, yet they do not see.

This is in terms of idols, but the Qur'an speaks about the inability of anything that someone may worship to do anything without God's permission (7:191-197). Islam cuts out every middle man or mediator that can be thought of. No intermediate to God is necessary (46:28). Muslims do not worship the messengers of God or representations of God or any image of God. Muslims pray directly to God. And in Islam, worship is everything that you do. Therefore with every action and intention, you are worshiping someone or something.

36:60 Did I not enjoin on you, O ye Children of Adam, that ye should not worship Satan; for that he was to you an enemy avowed?

36:61 And that ye should worship Me, (for that) this was the Straight Way?

Worshiping satan means to obey him and live sinfully because most people don't literally worship satan. Worshiping God means to obey him and live righteously. So "shirk" is also doing anything contrary to the laws of God. When sinning, you are performing an act of worship to something other than God. The Qur'an speaks of man's vain desires, like money, power or sex, as being his god (45:23). All these things are beneficial, but none should be more important to you than obeying the commands of GOD.

ABOUT ALLAH

When speaking of GOD, the Qur'an often uses the plural pronouns, "we" and "our." This usage is prevalent in many languages, specifically Semitic languages. It is because there are two kinds of plurals in languages like Hebrew and Arabic. One is the plural of numbers and the other is a plural used to indicate royalty, sovereignty or majesty. When someone of another language encounters such a plural form, they often mistake it for a plural of numbers. This is most noticeable with Christians and their misunderstanding of the Hebrew scripture as speaking of the Trinity. Fortunately for Islam, its strict, outspoken and uncompromising message of the oneness of GOD has very seldom received such misunderstanding of its scriptures.

His proper name in the Arabic language is ALLAH. ALLAH is not another word for God, ilah, but it is the name for God used by Arab speaking people since their inception. And though they worshiped many idols, they, like the Hindus, always held as sacred and unknowable their supreme God, whom they called ALLAH. Some scholars of Arabic say that ALLAH is the contraction of the words "al" (the) and "ilah" (god). Though it is an attractive proposition and its usage is difficult to avoid in discussions (I have already used it), there is no evidence to substantiate such a claim. If the Arabs always used ALLAH as the name for the one supreme God, it is more likely that "ilah" was derived from "ALLAH" instead of the other way around. In fact the common statement of Muslims "la ilaha ilALLAH" or "there is no God by ALLAH" illustrates that ALLAH is not another word for God, thus it would translate "there is no ALLAH, but ALLAH."

Because the name for the Supreme Being in Arabic has no gender or plural form, it is to this day used by Arab speaking Christians and Jews in the place of the generic word for God, "ilah," which has "aliha" as plural form. This should be considered by those who feel "disgust" or "horror" when the name ALLAH is mentioned (39:45). And the Qur'an testifies to the fact that ALLAH is the name of God.

17:110 Say: Call upon Allah, or call upon Rahman: by whatever name ye call upon Him, (it is well): for to Him belong the Most Beautiful Names.

20:8 Allah! There is no God but He! To Him belong the most Beautiful Names.

These verses show that there is little reason to bicker over the name of God. The nature of God is what is important. Not to mention that it is unlikely that the different people of the world who worshipped ALLAH throughout history spoke Arabic. They had their own name for God. For example the Aborigines called God, "ATNATU," which literally means "without an anus" because they believe as Muslim do today that God is self-sufficient. He needs no water, no food, no shelter, and no air. He needs nothing. Therefore the Aborigines came to the conclusion that if he does not eat or drink, then he does not have a call of nature. So they would not worship anything, which needed food or water. This, of course, ruled out the worship of man and animals. Though some may call them primitive, their understanding of God is far superior to the majority of the world today. More people of the earth right now, worship a snake, a cow, or a human being than the one true God alone. There are more people who worship the creature than those who worship the creator. The Aborigines call God by ATNATU, but this is actually an attribute. The Qur'an does not use such a crude attribute, yet it has at least 99 attributes or names for ALLAH. And these attributes are in relation to his creation, which demonstrate that Islam maintains that God is a personal God. Many people assert that God exists but that he is not a God which deals with his creation. We will soon delve into this claim.

99 NAMES OF ALLAH

AR-RAHMAN – THE GRACIOUS 2:163

AR-RAHIM–THE MERCIFUL 1:1-2

AL-MALIK–THE SOVEREIGN 20:114

AL-QUDDUS–THE HOLY 59:23

AS-SALAM–THE AUTHOR OF SAFETY 59:23

AL-MUMIN–THE GIVER OF PEACE 59:23

AL-MUHAIMIN–THE PROTECTOR 59:23

AL-AZIZ–THE MIGHTY ONE 59:23

AL-JABBAR–THE COMPELLER 59:23

AL-MUTAKABBIR–THE MAJESTIC 59:23

AL-KHALIQ–THE CREATOR 59:24

AL-BARI–THE MAKER 59:24

AL-MUSAWWIR–THE FASHIONER 59:24

AL-GHAFFAR–THE GREAT FORGIVER 40:42

AL-QAHHAR–THE IRRESISTIBLE 13:16

AL-WAHHAB–THE BESTOWER 3:8

AR-RAZZAQ–THE PROVIDER 51:58

AL-FATTAH–THE JUDGE 34:26

AL-ALIM–THE ALL-KNOWING 2:115

AS-SAMI–THE ALL-HEARING 3:38

GOD

AL-BASIR~THE ALL-SEEING ONE 3:15

AL-LATIF~THE SUBTLE ONE 6:103

AL-KHABIR~THE AWARE 34:1

AL-HALIM~THE CLEMENT 17:44

AL-AZIM~THE GREAT ONE 2:255

AL-GHAFUR~THE ALL-FORGIVING 35:28

ASH-SHAKUR~THE APPRECIATIVE 35:30

AL-ALIYY~THE SUBLIME 42:4

AL-KABIR~THE MOST GREAT 34:23

AL-HAFIZ~THE PRESERVER 11:57

AL-MUQIT~ THE MAINTAINER 4:85

AL-HASIB~THE RECKONER 4:6

AL-KARIM~THE GENEROUS ONE 82:6

AL-RAQIB~THE WATCHFUL 4:1

AL-QARIB~THE NIGH 11:61

AL-MUJIB~THE RESPONSIVE 11:116

AL-WASI~ THE ALL-EMBRACING 2:247

AL-HAKIM~THE WISE 2:129

AL-WADUD~ THE LOVING 11:90

AL-MAJID~THE MOST GLORIOUS ONE 11:73

ASH-SHAHID~THE WITNESS 4:79

AL-HAQQ~THE TRUTH 22:6

AL-WAKIL--THE TRUSTEE 4:81

AL-QAWI--THE MOST STRONG 22:74

AL-MATIN--THE FIRM ONE 51:58

AL-WALI--THE PROTECTING FRIEND 2:257

AL-HAMID--THE PRAISEWORTHY 22:64

AL-HAYY--THE ALIVE 3:2

AL-QAYYUM--THE SELF-SUBSISTING 3:2

AL-WAHID--THE ONE 40:16

AL-AHAD--THE ONE 112:1

AS-SAMAD--THE ETERNAL 112:2

AL-QADIR--THE ABLE 6:65

AL-MUQTADIR--THE POWERFUL 54:42

AL-AWWAL--THE FIRST 57:3

AL-AKHIR--THE LAST 57:3

AZ-ZAHIR--THE MANIFEST 57:3

AL-BATIN--THE HIDDEN 57:3

AL-WALI--THE GOVERNOR 13:11

AL-MUTA'ALI--THE MOST EXALTED 13:9

AL-BARR--THE SOURCE OF ALL GOODNESS 52:28

AT-TAWWAB- THE ACCEPTOR OF REPENTANCE 40:3

AL-AFUW--THE PARDONER 4:149

AR-RA'UF--THE COMPASSIONATE 24:20

GOD

AL-JAME'~THE GATHER 3:9

AL-GHANI~THE SELF-SUFFICIENT 35:15

AN-NUR~THE LIGHT 24:35

AL-HADI~THE GUIDE 25:31

AL-BADI~THE ORIGINATOR 2:117

RABB~THE SUSTAINER OR LORD 3:51

MUBIN~THE MANIFEST 24:25

AL-QADIR~THE MIGHTY 16:70

AL-HAFIZ~THE PROTECTOR 12:64

AL-KAFIL~THE SURETY 16:91

ASH-SHAKIR~THE APPRECIATIVE 2:158

AL-AKRAM~THE MOST BOUNTEOUS 96:3

AL-A'LA~THE MOST HIGH 87:1

AL-KHALLAQ~THE CREATOR 15:86

AL-MAULA~THE PROTECTOR 8:40

AN-NASIR~THE HELPER 4:45

AL-ILAH~THE GOD 21:108

AL-ALLAM~THE OMNISCIENT 5:109

AL-QAHIR~THE OMNIPOTENT 6:18

AL-GHAFIR~THE FORGIVER 40:3

AL-FATIR~THE CREATOR 35:1

AL-HAFIYY~THE MOST GRACIOUS 19:47

AL-MUHIT~THE PERMEATING 41:54

AL-RAFI~THE SUBLIME 40:15

AL-KAFI~THE SUFFICIENT ONE 39:36

GHALIB~THE PREDOMINANT 12:21

AL-MANNAN~THE MOST GRACIOUS 3:164

AL-JALIL~THE GLORIOUS 55:78

AL-MUHYI~THE GIVER OF LIFE 30:50

AL-MUMIT~THE GIVER OF DEATH 7:158

AL-WARITH~THE INHERITOR 15:23

(M.I. Siddiqi, "Ninety-nine Names of Allah")

AL-BA'ITH~THE AWAKENER 22:7

DHUL-AL-JALALI-AL-IKRAM~THE LORD OF MAJESTY AND GENEROSITY 55:27

DHUL-FADL-AL-AZIM~THE LORD OF INFINITE GRACE 2:105

Muslims, when referring to the name of Allah, often use the phrase "Subhanahu wa Ta'ala," sometimes abbreviated "SWT" meaning "Glorified and Exalted is He."

AYAT AL KURSI - VERSE OF THE THRONE

2:255 Allah! There is no god but He, the Living, the Self-subsisting, Eternal. No slumber can seize Him nor sleep. His are all things in the heavens and on earth. Who is there can intercede in His presence except as He permitteth? He knoweth what (appeareth to His creatures as) before or after or behind them. Nor shall they compass aught of His knowledge except as He willeth. His Throne doth extend over the heavens and the earth, and He feeleth no fatigue in guarding and preserving them for He is the Most High, the Supreme (in glory).

While other scriptures take great pains to enumerate the lineage of people, the genealogy of a specific person or the character of a specific person, the Qur'an focuses its attention on understanding ALLAH, as the list of the 99 names and the Ayat al Kursi demonstrate. In this verse it is explained that ALLAH exists without being created. He has always lived and he will always live. He does not die (25:58) and He is always aware and conscious. He is never weary from creation (46:33, 50:38) and He never sleeps. He is the owner of everything in existence and nothing can occur without His permission. His knowledge is incomprehensible and inexhaustible.

31:27 And if all the trees on earth were pens and the ocean (were ink), with seven oceans behind it to add to its (supply), yet would not the words of Allah be exhausted (in the writing): for Allah is Exalted in Power, full of Wisdom.

As Ayat al Kursi suggests, it is ALLAH who shares this knowledge with man as he wills. ALLAH taught man what he did not know (4:113). He is the true source of knowledge, wisdom and truth. This is why further examination of scientists lead man directly to GOD, whose position is "over the heavens and the earth." This means that God is not in the realm of this universe. I have stated that it is beneath the majesty of GOD to become his creation. It is even beneath GOD to enter his creation (like a man entering his ant farm), yet he feels no fatigue while maintaining it. This short verse was a summation of this book up to this point.

ALLAH'S WANTS AND NEEDS

To put it simple, ALLAH does not need or want anything. This is documented several times in the Qur'an.

2:263 ... Allah is free of all wants,

14:8 ...yet is Allah free of all wants

35:15 ...Allah is the One Free of all wants,

47:38 ... Allah is free of all wants,

27:40 ...truly my Lord is Free of all Needs

29:6 ...Allah is free of all needs from all creation.

Needs denote a dependency on something or someone. ALLAH is truly independent. To want something suggests a yearning and a difficulty in getting that something. It leaves a possibility that your wants can be unfulfilled or your goals are unattainable. However the GOD of Islam is "the Doer of all that He intends" (85:16). This is why He does not need or want. He can do all things that he wills. But this is qualified. All that He intends is not anything that you can think of, but godly things. God cannot lie because this is something which He will never intend, because it goes against his very nature.

This is not usually discussed among theists, but I reasoned long ago that GOD could not tell a lie. It is universally accepted that lying is morally wrong in most instances. And if God promised man something and he reneged on it, who could actually call GOD on it, and how could you punish him? In discussion with a former Muslim,

GOD

now an agnostic, who was leaning towards Christianity and supporting the argument of Christianity, he surmised that God could do anything, including tell a lie. I told him that I do not believe that GOD can lie, but I had no knowledge of the Islamic understanding of this matter. I knew that ALLAH'S promise is true (3:9), meaning that he tells the truth, but I did not know if GOD had the capacity to lie. To my surprise, I found in a lecture by Dr. Gary Miller, that ALLAH has a way or path that he follows. As the Muslims follow the "Sunnah of Muhammad" which is his life and mission, ALLAH has his own Sunnah. This is GOD'S Nature and it does not change, EVER (17:77, 48:23).

This understanding about God's nature is hinted at in the Bible, as well. I found later that the agnostic with whom I was speaking, had been unaware that the Bible plainly says that GOD CANNOT LIE (Titus 1:2), which means that GOD cannot do anything after all. And James 1:13 says that God can't be tempted with evil. God can't lie and he can't even be tempted to lie. This is because his nature is righteousness. So what GOD intends is all things which are "good" and "godly." In the same vein, the Qur'an says those in heaven will get "all" that they desire (43:71). This is not pork chops and beer, but "all" that is good and godly. GOD only does godly things and he will reward you with good or godly things.

It is the same as man only doing human things, as it is his nature. A man can't barrel his way through an ant hole and God can not shrink himself into the birth canal of a woman. Since all that GOD intends is limited to godly things, the definition of omnipotent in Islam is different from some other religions. Omnipotence of ALLAH is not that he can do anything, but that he has power over all things (2:20, 2:284, 3:165), which can be agreed upon by all theists.

GOD OF LOVE

85:14 And He is the Oft-Forgiving, Full of Loving-Kindness

I want this verse to be set into people's minds because it is something that should be on the lips of every Muslim today. Almost every non-Muslim in the world today thinks of ALLAH as some tyrannical, blood craving vengeful God, when this is the furthest from the truth. Because their knowledge of Islam is from those who are already prejudice against Islam, they have a poor understand of the God of Islam. God's love is spoken of in the Qur'an as being expressed through action. It is not merely a word or a feeling. This love is personified to man through his provision to man. He does not simply provide man with the bare necessities like food and water and shelter. But to bestow man with a variety of delicious foods, fruits, vegetables, and drinks, and to illuminate the world with brilliant color and beautiful sound are things which are not necessary. Even greater proof is that God has given man the ability to love and to share with others. He has given man an appreciation for love, for great taste and for beauty. These things show that God gives man more than he needs. This is an illustration of his loving kindness.

Love is also demonstrated through ALLAH'S forgiveness, mercy and blessing that he bestows on ALL OF MANKIND, good or bad. The term "oft-forgiving" means that GOD repeatedly forgives man and his love and kindness are in great abundance. 114 times the phrase "BISMILLAHI RAHMANI RAHEEM" is repeated in the Qur'an. This is the introduction to every chapter in the Qur'an except one, Chapter nine. It means "In the name of ALLAH, MOST GRACIOUS, MOST MERCIFUL." In Arabic, the words "Rahman" and "Raheem" have the same root RHM which means love or compassion. Rahman means that ALLAH'S love is so abundant that it is given to all his creation, whether they are deserving or not. It is God's unconditional love. This mercy is given to all (7:156). Raheem is the love and mercy of ALLAH specifically given to those who earn and deserve it. Indeed ALLAH challenges man to try and count the amount of blessings that he has received (14:34).

19:96 On those who believe and work deeds of righteousness, will (Allah) Most Gracious bestow love.

GOD

Verses like these do not mean that God hates those who are not believers or righteous people, but as the name "Raheem" suggests, he gives special preference to those who believe and do righteous deeds. There are a multitude of verses in the Qur'an which say God "loves not" those who are aggressors, wasteful, treacherous, transgressors, or wrongdoers (2:190, 4:107, 5:87, 7:31). As I have mentioned God's love is shown through mercy, blessings and/or forgiveness. He bestows this love for those who perform righteous deeds. Because God is a just God, justice demands balance. So a sinful deed requires punishment. That punishment is a suspension of his love, meaning you will lose out on some of your blessings because of your sin. Is this not justice? This does not mean that he does not have compassion for you, but that he embodies both, compassion and justice which require reward and punishment. It should be pointed out also, that this love is spoken of in an abstract sense. I have done righteous deeds and sinful deeds. If taken literally, one assumes that ALLAH loves me and he does not love me, at the same time. When put into proper perspective is it clear that the deed or misdeed is being praised or abhorred, not the actual person.

Every human being on earth is blessed by God immensely with every moment of their lives. More important than the blessings of health, wealth, family, power and possessions is OPPORTUNITY. To those who are constantly sinning, and committing crimes, every moment is a chance to redeem themselves and their situation. As soon as you can understand life, you realize that it is not yours. That it is a gift which is given to you and that you have to return it someday. In the meantime, you ought to be doing all that you can to make the most of your life. And if you chose not to, you cannot say you were not afforded you every waking day and every moment of your life to change and asked for forgiveness from the "Oft-Forgiving."

The Qur'an mentions God's name, ALLAH, over 2600 times. It also describes Him as LORD (Rabb) about 950 times. This name denotes the supreme GOD, ruler and sustainer of the world. As previously mentioned, God's love, mercy and forgiveness is of great importance in the Qur'an. Different forms of God's attribute of compassion (RHM) occurs at least 560. And about 230 times the Qur'an speaks of

ALLAH's forgiveness. How obvious is it that he ordains compassion, grace and mercy for himself to give to mankind (6:12)? Yet, the good or bad deeds that you do, do not affect GOD, they affect you. He is still God, whether you worship him or not. Those who do not believe or those who turn to disbelieve "do not harm ALLAH in the least" (3:144).

MANKIND

114:1 Say: I seek refuge with the Lord and Cherisher of Mankind,

114:2 The King (or Ruler) of Mankind,

114:3 The God (or Judge) of Mankind.

THE SOUL

41:53 Soon will We show them our Signs in the (furthest) regions (of the earth), and in their own souls, until it becomes manifest to them that this is the Truth. Is it not enough that thy Lord doth witness all things?

We have discussed the explanation of the time and expansion of the universe as proof of God's existence, but we can delve a little further into this subject. Expansion, of course, is a motion in an outward direction and every motion is subject to the measurement of time. However, motion cannot be fully understood when you are connected to a certain thing that is in motion. For example, if you are on a train and it is moving at 40 mph, you can not perceive its speed unless you look at a fixed object outside of the train. This is because you are inside of the train as it is moving. If you were outside of the train, your perception of the train would be completely different. The person outside of the train, would have a far better measurement of the train's speed. Another example is an elevator. Inside of an elevator, you may feel that you have moved slowly or barely at all, when in that time you may have ascended or descended several floors. The same is true with the earth. It is in constant motion, but because we are on the earth as it is rotating, we do not perceive its motion at all. The premise is that you can't fully perceive motion if you are an integral part of a thing which is in motion. With that said, consider yourselves, when you walk, jog, run or fall out of a tree. When your body is doing all these things you can perceive the speed at which it is moving. This means that the element of man that does this perception of motion is not an integral part of the body and that this element was created outside the body. Had it developed and originated at the same time as your body was formed, you couldn't grasp the speed at which you run or jog, etc. The thing with which you perceive your motion is the SOUL (nafs).

"This is a stunning conclusion to draw and it means that part of our being is external to the framework of the temporal continuum. It is immortal, it can observe time from a point of stillness and perceive it without being implicated in it. It, therefore, neither ages nor elapses. When the body crumbles into dust, that part will remain as it is to live its own non-temporal life -that part is the spirit." (Dr. Mostafa Mahmoud, "Dialogue with an Atheist")

Of course, atheists and agnostics scoff at the idea of a soul. They say this is unscientific and impossible to prove. Unfortunately for them, I have just given one proof already and there is MORE. The reason that they can't acknowledge the existence of a soul is because it would validate the existence of things outside of the material world, the most important being GOD. This materialistic view is that if one can't see, touch, taste, smell or hear something, it is impossible to prove its existence and it is out of the realm of science. However, many material things are out of the realm of science's reach right now, meaning they have no explanation for them, yet they exist. We must remember that I have shown that the First Cause is not material, it is not of this universe, through reasoning and logic and the discoveries of science.

Science is the observation, identification, description, experimental investigation, and theoretical explanation of phenomena. Scientists make a discovery and then its implications are discerned. This is where the reasoning comes into play. For example, it is scientifically proven that we do not see with our eyes. Our eyes are but tools used to send an electrical signal to the brain and the image is seen in your brain. Also, we do not actually hear with our ears. The sounds outside of our bodies are filtered through channels in the ear and turned into electrical signals in your brain and your brain interprets these sounds. The same is true with touching, tasting and smelling. Your hands and skin, your tongue and your nose are but vessels which send an electrical signal to your brain and it interprets that signal. When you touch a hot stove, your hand does not pull away on its own. Your brain interprets the signal as pain and it signals back to your hand to move. In other words, if the signal was cut off before it got to the brain, then you would leave you hand on the hot stove. When you have a nice juicy hamburger, it is your brain which distinguishes the different smells of onions, pickles, lettuce and tomatoes; the brain is where you determine how delicious this burger is. That hamburger is nothing but an electrical signal being interpreted in your brain.

To prove that your brain is actually seeing, tasting, hearing etc, let's think about our dreams. Scenery in your dreams may be changed. You can live at your job and work at your home, but all this seems perfectly normal in your dreams. Everything that you do in real life, you can do in your dreams. You can watch a movie in your dreams, yet your eyes are closed. You can hear a parade in your dreams, yet there is no real parade going on. You can eat, sleep and even die in your dreams. And every event in your dreams is as real to you as this world around you is.

You experience this whole world and everything in it as different electrical signals interpreted in your brain. THIS IS A SCIENTIFIC FACT. No scientist on earth would refute this. It is universally accepted that you have to be pretty intelligent to be a scientist. But there is an old saying, "those blessed with great intelligence, often lack common sense." The word "intelligence" should be replaced with "knowledge" in this instance, because knowledge is simply an accumulation of facts, whereas intelligence suggests the understanding and application of knowledge. So if you understand that the five senses that we have are all being perceived in the brain as electrical signals, then you have a stupendous question to answer, HOW DOES A THREE POUND LUMP OF TISSUE PERCEIVE or interpret ANYTHING? The brain is approximately three pounds of atoms lumped together like a hunk of meat. Inside of the brain is complete darkness and complete silence, at all times.

When a person is watching a movie in the theatre or listening to their favorite band's CD, inside your brain is still complete darkness and complete silence. Let's say you have a potato chip in your hand. The nerves in your hand are sending a message to the brain that a potato chip is in your hand. It goes to the brain. At the same time, your eyes turn towards the chip in your hand and the image goes upside down through your retina and it is sent to your brain and the image is perceived right side up. Your nose smells the chip as it gets closer to your nose and mouth. The taste buds on your tongue send messages to the brain. This three pound lump of atoms then understands all of these signals?

A book is also a three pound lump of atoms, but it perceives absolutely nothing. Common sense would tell us that atoms do not feel or perceive anything. Only a conscious being perceives and feels things. That means that something else in your body is using your five senses and your brain as a tool to perceive the world around us. Something immaterial. Some scientists scoff at such a notion of "something immaterial", but this is only due to their predetermination to deny the existence of God, because they too believe in the immaterial. Do they not believe in dreams and thoughts? Dreams and thoughts are immaterial. A scientist can tell you when a thought or dream has occurred in the brain, but THEY CAN NOT TELL YOU WHAT THAT DREAM OR THOUGHT WAS. The thoughts are not susceptible to any of our five senses, therefore they are immaterial. Logically speaking, something immaterial would come from something else immaterial. The immaterial thought comes from the immaterial soul which comes from that First Cause, which is itself immaterial. The Qur'an affirms that God gives man signs of him in the universe and WITHIN man (41:52-53, 42:29, 51:41).

Theists generally believe that the reason that man is alive and different from one another is due to the spirit (ruh) from God which dwells inside of the body. This spirit is the source giving life. When it is in full effect with the human body, it is called the soul (nafs).

50:16 It was We Who created man, and We know what dark suggestions his soul makes to him: for We are nearer to him than (his) jugular vein.

MANKIND

This verse mentions the closeness of God to man. Something of God is inside of man, the soul. It is reported that Jesus (pbuh) said that God is so close to man that he counts the hairs on his head (Matthew 10:30). In another place, the Qur'an says if you sat and watched a man die, you must realize that God is nearer in proximity to the man than you are (56:83-85). The initial breathe given to man is what makes him, at birth, whole and pure because it is directly from God. And it directs him to stay this way. This predisposition towards righteousness is called "fitrah." Love and compassion are innate senses, but hatred, prejudice and dislike are learned behaviors and attitudes. According to Islam, every person is born with this positive inclination and it helps man differentiate between right and wrong. But the spirit in the body is given free will and desires, thus is it called yourself or your soul. God gave man this perfect spirit and it is his choice to purify it or corrupt it (91:7-10).

Man's body is basically made from the earth and water, the basic elements of our planet. Earth and water can be broken down further into the elements of oxygen, hydrogen, carbon and so on. But if all these elements could be fused together, they would never produce a human being. In fact, all the elements of man's body, his blood, his veins, a heart, lungs and everything else, could be surgically connected to form a human's body, but it is the soul or spirit inside of the person, which is truly alive. The body is but a car, useless without a driver. It is easy enough to determine that man came from the earth, seeing that after his death, if left unattended the body of man would become again one with the earth. This is observable from any animal or rodent decomposing. His body is seemingly draining back into the earth. This again raises the question of how inanimate objects like earth and water can obtain life and consciousness. Not only consciousness, but distinctive consciousness. If man is created from the same substances by pure chance, with no intelligent intervention, how could people possibly have different personalities? A human can make robots with different functions, but how likely is it that robots accidentally form by themselves from the same materials and they all have different functions? The soul is what makes us different.

Scientists tell us that every single atom in our bodies is replaced every seven years. When I read this fact, I immediately recalled the Qur'an when it says "see how clear WE make our signs to you." How hard is it to deduce from this knowledge that our bodies are not ourselves? If what the scientist says is true, then the bodies that we have are not the same bodies from seven years ago. If you have a car and for seven years you change every part, nut and bolt on it, it is not the same car anymore. The same thing happens to every human being on earth, with every microscopic atom of his body, yet we all are the same people. How? Because we have a soul. Your physical body does not feel regret, it does not feel love and it does not feel high or low self-esteem. YOU feel self-esteem, love, and pain. It is the soul which is experiencing this world, but how?

I was once in a debate with an atheist who explained to me the basic methods of sight. He stated that the eyes see an image, the image travels to the brain as an electrical signal and the brain produces the image. Though his explanation was a bit more intricate, this was the gist of his point. But there are two problems with this explanation. One is the brain is completely dark inside at all times. If we were able to peer into the brain at the exact moment that it was interpreting an image, we would see absolutely nothing. The other problem is if the brain formulates an image inside of it, who sees the image? You would need eyes inside of your brain to see the image made by the brain from the electric signal. Think about your computer. You type words in. A signal is given to the computer to print out the very message you typed. The printout is presented on the monitor and you view it. This is what happened inside your brain. The brain has presented the printout as an image, BUT WHO SEES THE PRINTOUT?

That something intangible inside of you is who. That something that enters you in your mother's womb which brings you to life and departs from you at the time of your death. Perhaps that is the energy, the power, the force that cannot be created nor destroyed. Maybe there is a simple energy force present in all of creation and a particular force for life. The Qur'an says ALLAH breathes his ruh (spirit) into man (15:29, 38:72, 32:9). I would suggest that that force is the breath of God in you. If you have ever seen a deceased person, you could see that the life force in that person is no longer present. A dead body is nothing but a computer turned off. The body needs a soul for it to work and the computer needs electricity. And the death of the body does not affect the soul, just as damaging the keyboard or a monitor does not affect the computer.

MANKIND

Some have suggested that this idea is stifled by those who are mentally or physically handicapped. However, these are but damage to the body and not the soul. Injury and sickness is like keys missing on your keyboard. They are a detriment to your perception of the world, just as missing keys affect your ability to use the computer, but the computer is intact. No matter your deficiency or illness, your immaterial soul is in perfect condition.

So this raises the question, what is the purpose for GOD, the First Cause, to put us in a position to perceive this world? If someone sets a stage and places you in it, they are trying to see how you behave in this setting. They are testing you. THIS WORLD IS BUT A TEST (18:7).

MORALS

29:2 Do men think that they will be left alone on saying, "We believe", and that they will not be tested?

29:3 We did test those before them, and Allah will certainly know those who are true from those who are false.

This verse speaks to theists and specifically Muslims. It stresses that belief like love is just an empty word, if it is not accompanied by actions and intentions verifying this belief. It may be that some are simply giving lip-service. Whether you believe in God or not, we are all being tested and given the opportunity to be moral and just or immoral and sinful. But if you believe in God, you must know that he knows your actions and intentions and they will be accounted for.

67:13 And whether ye hide your word or publish it, He certainly has (full) knowledge, of the secrets of (all) hearts.

67:14 Should He not know,- He that created? and He is the One that understands the finest mysteries (and) is well-acquainted (with them).

God has implanted into man a conscience. This is a moral compass towards true morality. Where does this conscience come from? It is, as the soul is, immaterial. It is that voice inside you which tells you whether your actions and intentional were malevolent or benevolent. A conscience and morality are absent in all life on earth, aside from human life. It is useless in other life forms. If the animal kingdom was moral, they would all become extinct. Since man is given dominion over this earth, he is to use his conscience to be as GOD is, merciful and gracious to all that inhabit it. The internal compass guiding man to morality and righteousness is another proof of GOD. Man is the only being on earth that is compelled to do what is right. But man's conscience alone is not enough to guide him.

In debates with people of different faiths or no faith, I often wonder what their goals for these debates are. My goal is to convince others of the validity of Islam or at least to help them better understand Islam. This has always been my aim, but my approach has definitely evolved. Ridicule and mockery were tools that I used in discussions of religion. But as I grew older and learned more about Islam, I found that this is not the proper manner to argue about something so important and powerful to other people. Nowadays, I mention to some theists that it is impolite or morally wrong to purposely belittle my beliefs, especially with no intention of enlightening me. More often than not, it seems to resonate with them. That is because they have a code formulated for them to follow which is moral. Most often my speech on morality falls on death ears when told to an atheist. This is not to say that atheists are immoral, but that there is no guide which you can point to and verify that belittling someone's belief, no matter how deserving you think it may be, is morally wrong. Their moral code is their own personal choice. I do not denounce personal choice. My personal choice is to follow the moral code I deem most accurate. I am merely saying that a moral code formulated completely by human beings is inherently flawed because man has an inclination like animals to be selfish. He makes laws and rules to accommodate himself and his agenda. His laws will naturally affect him and those whom he cares for in a positive manner. But those outside of that circle will receive less benefit, no benefit or they may even be harmed by his laws. Only God, who is neither helped nor harmed by man's actions, can best provide guidelines for man's moral code.

Morals, independent of God, can become immoral in man's view. And immorality can become first acceptable then eventually moral in the sight of man. For example, consumption of alcohol was at one time universally considered wrong but now it has slowly becoming acceptable and those opposing such immorality are criticized for their stance. As Deedat once said, "it use to be that the person who drank alcohol stuck out like a sore thumb, now the person who doesn't drink is the one frowned upon as a killjoy."

16:63 Satan made their deeds fair seeming to them.

When I was in the 10th or 11th grade a teacher/counselor came to my classroom to discuss the dangers of drugs. Being careful not to give us too much information on drugs, she spoke in vague terms, only mentioning marijuana specifically. When it was asked of the class to give their input, I raise my hand and said "I agree that we all should stay away from drugs, but I also include alcohol as a drug and dangerous intoxicate. Though alcohol is legal, I believe that what intoxicates in great quantities, should be forbidden even in small quantities (this is a saying from PROPHET MUHAMMAD peace and blessings be upon him)." The counselor was at a loss for words. I presume that she drank alcohol and she felt it was acceptable maybe in moderation, but how could she articulate that to a class full of students that she just advised not to use drugs, at all. I think I gave her a way out by not formulating my statement into a question, so she stumbled onto the next student. I believe she knew, like everyone does that alcohol is something that should be shunned. More crimes are committed involving alcohol than any other drug and it is common knowledge that abstinence is always better than drinking in moderation or the cure and treatment for alcoholism. Yet people still try to rationalize their indulgence in alcohol. This same thing is true with gambling. Most of us think it is wrong to squander money on long-shots and virtual impossibilities, but its periodic benefit allows man to bend that rule of morality.

2:219 They ask thee concerning wine and gambling. Say: "In them is great sin, and some profit, for men; but the sin is greater than the profit.

5:90 O ye who believe! Intoxicants and gambling, (dedication of) stones, and (divination by) arrows, are an abomination, of Satan's handwork: eschew such (abomination), that ye may prosper.

When an immoral act is morphed into a universally accepted norm, it is only human morality at work, justifying the sin. It is still a sin in God'S eyes. But if you reject God, you have an excuse to be as immoral as you want. Strangely, atheists take great pains to show how moral they are without God. The peculiar part about that is that if God did not create man, and you believe man is a freak accident that assembled into a complex animal, then why are you moral at all? Morality has no place in the animal kingdom and natural selection. Therefore, those who don't believe in God aught not believe in morals. If atheistic evolutionists are correct, abandonment of morals will eventually lead to man evolving into something else, bigger and better than man. In fact, the morals an atheist displays is proof of God and disproof of their religion of "chance" that many subscribe to.

It is very important to note that morality in humans is not just a proof of God, but proof of a PERSONAL GOD. Though some admit a First Cause, scientists are adamant that he is not the kind of God religious people believe in, someone who is involved with man and his relationship to others. In 1929, Einstein told Rabbi Herbert S. Goldstein "I believe in Spinoza's God, who reveals Himself in the lawful harmony of the world, not in a God Who concerns Himself with the fate and the doings of mankind." (Brian 1996, p. 127)

29:61 If indeed thou ask them who has created the heavens and the earth and subjected the sun and the moon (to His Law), they will certainly reply, "Allah." How are they then deluded away (from the truth)?

The existence of morality and how it is engrained into mankind disproves their theory of an impersonal God. He did not make man for sport (23:115). It is God'S wish for man to be righteous, gracious and merciful to everyone and everything. Man's morality also proves God'S morality. Lying, cheating, stealing and killing are wrong in man's sight, because God has deemed them wrong first. Fasting, charity and death in the cause of righteousness are all against the selfishness, instincts and desires of man. These things had to be defined by God to be deeds of righteousness and honor to be adopted by man.

FAITH EQUALS HEALTH!!!!!

The theist is comforted by the proof that man has a soul which is being tested for its moral aptitude. His faith in GOD and his moral life put him at ease. It is a fact that people of faith are less stressed and depressed merely because of their faith. To put it simple, belief in God is good for your health. This is because of the moral compass in every person. Once it leads them to the source of all morality, they live life more at ease than someone who has not found the source, or someone who is unsure or unconvinced that there is a source to begin with. When someone realizes that death is inevitable and they are under the impression that life is meaningless, it is less difficult to be stressed, depressed or to even consider expediting death. Those who understand the purpose of life are better equipped to handle the difficulties of life.

Those outside of churches, synagogues and mosques often blame their apprehension about religion on the participants of a certain religion. Perhaps if they understood that there are different kinds of believers, they would be less apprehensive about religion. A Harvard psychologist named Gordon Allport did some research in the 1950's on human prejudice and he began to categorize people's commitment to a certain religion as extrinsic religiosity and intrinsic religiosity. Extrinsic religiosity is the commitment one has to a faith based upon what the religion can do for a particular person. Their conviction may be in order to gain respect and notoriety, to elevate their social status or just to conform to the norms of society.

An intrinsically religious person is better described as a true believer. He or she sees religion as a law to govern their lives. Fulfillment of the religion's principles is their goal. They are more deeply committed to their religion. These are the people that are less stressed with difficult issues, more optimistic about their future, and less depressed because they know that God promises that he will not give man a burden which he cannot bear (2:286). He also promises relief from every burden that a man faces (94:5-6). This is perhaps the only benefit that the fanatics that call themselves Muslims have produced. Of all the prejudices that they give birth to, the one that Muslims hold a high degree of conviction about Islam, is the one belief that is true of most Muslims. We have true intrinsic religiosity. Not surprisingly, Allport also found that intrinsically religious people were not likely to be prejudice as were their counterparts were. So when those who don't subscribe to a particular religion see a so-called religious person acting inappropriately, it may be that they are not the "true believers."

GETTING STARTED

Because GOD gives man a moral compass and a soul to test his righteousness, GOD also gives man ALL the answers to the test. Actually, the discovery of the answers to the test is really why the intrinsic religious person is so at ease. Once you have studied and practiced the material, the test is a breeze. But first you must find the material. Along with your conscience, God gives man the ability to gather information, and gain knowledge. These are complimented by the ability to process that information into terms of importance, from the meaningless to what is completely essential. What things are completely essential and most important to man should be the answers to the test.

The Qur'an puts great emphasis on knowledge and the pursuit of knowledge. The actual word "ilm" or its derivative occurs in the Qur'an over 700 times. It is third only to the name of God, ALLAH, and the word for LORD, Rabb. Its number of occurrences seems to beg the reader to gain more KNOWLEDGE about the LORD who will lead you to the test's answers. The Qur'an frequently tells its reader to research a certain topic, or to ask someone of knowledge on that topic for confirmation as to what the Qur'an proclaims. It places the reader into the role of investigator. If you follow the advice of the Qur'an and research its contents to verify its truth, you are bound to open yourself to knowledge you never fathomed. But with knowledge, you need understanding. The Qur'an asks man to read (96:1) and reflect on what he has read by himself or with others (34:46). When you are in pursuit of the test's answers, you will find that GOD has provided man with everything that he needs.

REVELATION

We have established the existence of God and why it is necessary to believe in Him. Now what does he want with us? If everyone were to write down the ideal and essential aspects of religion, I think the results would only be fulfilled by the religion of Islam. For instance, it is not essential for there to be numerous gods, but it is essential to have at least one God, who is responsible for the existence of the universe in which we live. In fact, it is ideal to have only one God governing the universe.

When you consider the longevity of man's existence on earth and the multitude of people who have inhabited this planet, several questions come to mind. What belief system did they adhere to? Did God even bother communicating with these people?

Is it possible that any of the religions of today were present or even practicable at the beginning of humanity?

Man has always been concerned with the purpose of life. Did the first person or people know their purpose? Did he realize his mortality? Of course, evidence of their mortality was present through sickness, aging and death, but death is a little late to realize that you and everyone else will die one day. Yet the inevitably of death must have encouraged them to have a greater need to understand the purpose of life. The ability to understand through reasoning is an ability given exclusively to human beings on this earth. For every living thing on earth, there are provisions set aside for their needs.

In the ecosystem, we see the perfect life cycle and balance set for living animals and plants to co-exist. The sunlight and rain give life to the plants and leaves, which are eaten by the praying mantis and the praying mantis is eaten by the spider and so on. This process that we take for granted is a law invoked to provide enough sustenance for all the living creatures of the earth to live. Not only are they provided sustenance but they are given the innate ability to defend themselves, to build themselves shelter and the ability to reproduce themselves. All these things ensure their species' continued existence. Man is also a beneficiary of these laws and abilities, but he is given the gift of reasoning as well.

With reasoning comes the need to understand things. If every need of creatures on earth is provided for, it would follow that the necessity for man to understand would also be provided for. I believe this provision comes in the form of revelation. Every machine made comes with a book of instructions from the manufacturer on "how best to use this machine." So too does the complex machinery called a human being come with a book of instructions by its manufacturer of "how to properly use this machine." Because man has free will, unlike every other thing on earth, he needs an instruction manual to best utilize the tools that are God-given to him.

AL-QUR'AN

14:1 A Book which We have revealed unto thee, in order that thou mightest lead mankind out of the depths of darkness into light - by the leave of their Lord - to the Way of (Him) the Exalted in power, worthy of all praise!

The instruction manual, the centerpiece, the cornerstone of Islam is the Qur'an. To a Muslim, it is the exact words of GOD put into the mouth of Prophet Muhammad (pbuh). The Qur'an, itself makes the point that God provides for all the needs of his creation. And if you reflect on the provisions given to his creation, you will realize that man's hunger for purpose and guidance is also provided for in the words of the Qur'an (16:64-69). As the words of God, they overrule anything spoken by anyone, ever. If Prophet Muhammad (pbuh) is quoted as saying something contrary to the Qur'an, every Muslim is to ignore the quotation of Prophet Muhammad (pbuh) and obey the words of the Qur'an. I stress this point because critics frequently use sources outside of the Qur'an to denounce Islam, but in the Qur'an is Islam. Simply out of curiosity about the beliefs of over one billion people, one should at least read the Qur'an or go through the index and pick topics to read over.

THE ORIGIN OF THE QUR'AN

In about the year 610, a man went to a mountain that he frequented to meditate called Mt. Hira . While inside on the mount, he felt a presence. It grasped him tightly and said "IQRA." The man responded, "I am not learned." Again he hears "IQRA," and frightened he repeats "I am not learned." As he is still being tightly squeezed, he hears "IQRA." Iqra in Arabic means to read, to recite or to proclaim. The man had been under the impression that he was to read something, but he was illiterate. After the second time, the man realized that he was not supposed to read, as there was nothing there for him to read, but to repeat or proclaim.

96:1 Proclaim! (or read!) in the name of thy Lord and Cherisher, Who created

96:2 Created man, out of a (mere) clot of congealed blood:

96:3 Proclaim! And thy Lord is Most Bountiful,

96:4 He Who taught (the use of) the pen,

96:5 Taught man that which he knew not.

These were the first verses of the Qur'an revealed to Prophet Muhammad, by the angel Jibril (Gabriel) (peace be upon them both). (For those who find it far-fetched to believe in such a being, they need to look no further then within themselves to understand that they are spiritual beings encased in a physical body. The immaterial God used an immaterial being to speak to the immaterial part of man.) Prophet Muhammad (pbuh) repeated the words spoken to him by the angel and at that moment, he became the prophet of GOD. This occurred one night in the month of Ramadan (44:3). This night is called the NIGHT OF POWER (QADR) (97:1-4). No one knows, exactly which night it was, but Muslims pray furiously throughout the month to receive great blessings, because "The Night of Power is better than 1000 months."

After receiving this message, Prophet Muhammad (pbuh) did not know that he was a prophet. Every day on the television someone says that they have spoken to God and there is no doubt at all in their minds that this happened. But if a voice spoke to you, what is the normal response? It would probably be skepticism. And this is how Prophet Muhammad (pbuh) felt. He did not immediately believe the voice. He was frightened. He even thought that he might be going insane (68:2). He ran home to his wife, Khadijah, shivering. Khadijah consoled him and told her uncle Waraqa, an Arab Christian, about Muhammad's experience. They both convinced Muhammad (pbuh) that he was not mad, but that he had received a revelation from God. He was still in doubt. Revelation had not come to him after the first occasion in over a year. Then one night as he slept he heard.

74:1 O thou wrapped up (in the mantle)!

74:2 Arise and deliver thy warning!

74:3 And thy Lord do thou magnify!

These words are being spoken to Prophet Muhammad (pbuh) and in turn he recites them to an audience, thus it is first a command to him to get up and magnify God, then it is a command to all. The revelations were given to Prophet Muhammad (pbuh) in intervals, as situations arouse and questions were asked of him. And he would recite the verses, GOD gave him though the angel, to his audience.

25:32 Those who reject Faith say: "Why is not the Qur'an revealed to him all at once? Thus (is it revealed), that We may strengthen thy heart thereby, and We have rehearsed it to thee in slow, well-arranged stages, gradually.

Islam Is The Truth

20.114 High above all is Allah, the King, the Truth! Be not in haste with the Qur'an before its revelation to thee is completed, but say, "O my Lord! advance me in knowledge."

The verses of the Qur'an were used to encourage people to believe in it, by providing continuous truths. Instead of revealing it all at once and saying swallow this, Prophet Muhammad (pbuh) gradually intrigued people's interest with the truth of Islam, until it was embraced. And this is how Muslims are supposed to propagate Islam.

The word "Qur'an" means recitation. Prophet Muhammad (pbuh) was carrying on every day activities, all of a sudden words that were not his own came from his mouth. Jesus (pbuh), like Muhammad (pbuh), was given words to speak. He spoke of the Hebrew Scriptures, without ever being taught them (John 7:15-16). Prophet Muhammad (pbuh) did the same. Many chapters of the Qur'an begin by introducing that "this is part of the Qur'an," to inform the audience that what they are about to hear is not from Prophet Muhammad (pbuh). The verses start as declaration that this is no longer Muhammad (pbuh) speaking but the words of God, by using phrases like "this is the truth, wherein there is no doubt…"

Also the Qur'an is in a different dialect of Arabic than that spoken by Prophet Muhammad (pbuh), himself. It makes mention that he never spoke in such a poetic manner as the Qur'an does and that he had no access to the stories [like the birth of Mary, the mother of Jesus (pbuh)] that he was speaking of in the Qur'an. The Qur'an defends itself from the critics who insisted that Prophet Muhammad (pbuh) was responsible for the Qur'an's content.

All that Prophet Muhammad (pbuh) revealed and recited was devoted to memory by Muhammad (pbuh) and his devoted followers. The general population, at that time, was illiterate in Arabia, so memorization and recitation was the primary manner of learning. Their sense of memory was heighten due to this fact and their belief that they were remembering the exact words of GOD only added to the meticulous nature in which Prophet Muhammad (pbuh) and his followers kept track of the revelations. The few who could read and write put the verses down on animal skin or papyruses. The revelations continued for 23 years and in order to preserve its text, Prophet Muhammad (pbuh) recited the Qur'an back from memory to the angel Jibril (pbuh) (87:6). This may seem like a daunting task to most, but there are thousands of people walking around today that have memorized and can recite every chapter and verse of the Qur'an, including school age children. Not to mentioned that verses of the Qur'an are recited by 1.8 billion Muslims five times a day.

After Prophet Muhammad's (pbuh) death, the Qur'an was compiled into book form. Two of these Qur'ans still exist to this day as proof that the Qur'an has remained intact for 1400 years. GOD promised that he would protect it (15:9) and the sacred revelations preserved in the museums are verifiable proof to this fact. The Qur'an is the only religious book that has remained in its original form for 1400 years.

41:2 A Revelation from (Allah), Most Gracious, Most Merciful;

41:3 A Book, whereof the verses are explained in detail,- a Qur'an in Arabic, for people who understand.

Unlike most religious scriptures, the Qur'an itself claims to be the words of God, and it does so repeatedly. Many of its Surahs, or chapters are laced with such a proclamation (13:1, 14:1, 18:1, 25:1,32:2, 36:2:5, 39:1, 40:2, 45:2, 46:2, 55:1-2) and it gives evidence to support this claim. It includes a falsification test, challenging its reader to try and prove that it is not from GOD.

4:82 Do they not consider the Qur'an (with care)? Had it been from other than Allah, they would surely have found therein much discrepancy.

As Gary Miller said, "what student would turn in an exam to the teacher and dare the teacher to find a mistake in it." He suggested that the teacher would stay up all night trying to find one. And this is what ALLAH wants those who do not believe that it is from him to do. FIND A MISTAKE!!! When you cannot find one, then ask yourself, "where did this book come from?" Of course, there have been thousands of books written in attempt to discredit the Qur'an and Islam in general and despite their adamant attempts, all of their claims have been refuted by knowledgeable Muslims. Many of these false claims have already been refuted in this book and hopefully, I will dispel a few more misconceptions about Islam as I proceed. This is to show that simply because someone thinks they have found a mistake and they have cosigners to their finding, it does not necessarily mean their findings are correct. Maybe instead of presenting one's findings to people who already agree with them, they should present them to the learned men and women of Islam, where their claims can be more accurately addressed and explained. Nonetheless, the content of the Qur'an is no doubt remarkable.

A MESSAGE TO THE SCIENTISTS

3:190 Behold! in the creation of the heavens and the earth, and the alternation of night and day,- there are indeed Signs for men of understanding.

BIG BANG

21:30 Do not the Unbelievers see that the heavens and the earth were joined together (as one unit of creation), before we clove them asunder? We made from water every living thing. Will they not then believe?

MANKIND

This verse was put into Prophet Muhammad's (pbuh) mouth 1400 years ago. In 1978, Dr. Arno A. Perzias and Dr. Robert W. Wilson, were awarded the Nobel prize for physics for their discovery of cosmic microwave background radiation (CMBR). CMBR is the remnants of the cooling of the universe after a huge explosion. Cosmologist consider this to be the best evidence for the BIG BANG, which is described in the Qur'an as a singular mass which split asunder. How did Prophet Muhammad (pbuh) know something that modern science and modern technology determine just recently? Also we learn from science and the Qur'an that in the beginning of the universe everything existed in a gaseous state.

41:11 Moreover He comprehended in His design the sky, and it had been (as) smoke

If we look closer at the first verse mentioned, there is another scientific statement in the Qur'an. "We made from water every living thing." (21:30, 24:45) And more specifically the Qur'an says God made human beings from water (25:54). Ask the evolutionist where did life origin. Ask the scientist how much of our bodies are water based. Protoplasm is the "living substance" of a cell and it is made up of 70-90% water. About 60 to 70% of an adult body is water (12 gallons). The blood is about 83% water, the bones are 22% water and our muscles are 75% water. The brain is made of 70% water, the lungs are nearly 90% water and the liver is nearly 97% water.

These are scientific facts recently discovered in the last 50 or 60 years by non-Muslims. Verse 21:30 has the triple threat of two scientifically accurate statements and a recently fulfilled prophecy that non-Muslims would be the people to confirm the truth of this scripture. The verse ends with a rhetorical question. Basically asking, after finding this evidence, how can you not believe in ALLAH and the Qur'an? How did an illiterate man in the desert find out this information? How could anyone in that time and place state this with any certainty? This is the method of the Qur'an. It presents facts to you and challenges you to put them into perspective. This is a direct challenge to scientists and to those who use science as their measure of truth.

EARTH

In early times, people believed that the earth was flat. For centuries, men were afraid to venture out too far, lest they should fall off the edge. Sir Francis Drake was the first person who proved that the earth is spherical when he sailed around it in 1597. Consider the following Qur'anic verse regarding the alternation of day and night: "Seest thou not that Allah merges Night into Day And He merges Day into Night?" [Al-Qur'an 31:29]

Merging here means that the night slowly and gradually changes to day and vice versa. This phenomenon can only take place if the earth is spherical. If the earth was flat, there would have been a sudden change from night to day and from day to night. The following verse also alludes to the spherical shape of the earth:

"He created the heavens And the earth In true (proportions): He makes the Night Overlap the Day, and the Day Overlap the Night." [Al-Qur'an 39:5]

The Arabic word used here is Kawwara meaning 'to overlap' or 'to coil' – the way a turban is wound around the head. The overlapping or coiling of the day and night can only take place if the earth is spherical. The earth is not exactly round like a ball, but geo-spherical i.e. it is flattened at the poles. The following verse describes the earth's shape:

"And the earth, moreover, Hath He made egg shaped." [Al-Qur'an 79:30]

[The Arabic word dahaha has been translated as "vast expanse", which also is correct. The word dahaha also means an ostrich-egg.] The Arabic word for egg here is dahaha, which means an ostrich-egg. The shape of an ostrich-egg resembles the geo-spherical shape of the earth. Thus the Qur'an correctly describes the shape of the earth, though the prevalent notion when the Qur'an was revealed was that the earth is flat.

(Dr. Zakir Naik, "The Qur'an and Modern Science, Compatible or Incompatible?")

Another reference to the circumference of the earth is when the Qur'an speaks of the two easts and the two wests of the earth (55:17). If you go far enough to the east you will come to the west and vice versa. And as the earth rotates, from space these directions switch around. It is important to note that two norths and two souths are not mentioned as the north and south do not switch positions as the earth is rotating.

The simple statement that "(He is) Lord of the two Easts and Lord of the two Wests" bears great significance. It would have been easier to say that he was LORD of the EARTH, but these words are used to establish that the author knows that the earth is round and that it is rotating on its axis.

THE SUN AND MOON

"It was believed by earlier civilizations that the moon emanates its own light. Science now tells us that the light of the moon is reflected light. However this fact was mentioned in the Qur'an 1,400 years ago in the following verse:

"Blessed is He Who made Constellations in the skies, And placed therein a Lamp And a Moon giving light." [Al-Qur'an 25:61]

The Arabic word for the sun in the Qur'an, is shams. It is referred to as siraaj, which means a 'torch', or as wahhaaj which means 'a blazing lamp' or as diya which means 'shining glory'. All three descriptions are appropriate to the sun, since it generates intense heat and light by its internal combustion. The Arabic word for the moon is qamar and it is described in the Qur'an as muneer, which is a body that gives nur i.e. light. Again, the Quranic description matches perfectly with the true nature of the moon, which does not give off light itself and is an inert body that reflects the light of the sun. Not once in the Qur'an, is the moon mentioned as siraaj, wahhaaj or diya or the sun as nur or muneer. This implies that the Qur'an recognizes the difference between the nature of sunlight and moonlight.

Consider the following verses related to the nature of light from the sun and the moon:

"It is He who made the sun To be a shining glory And the moon to be a light (of beauty)." [Al-Qur'an 10:5]

"See ye not How Allah has created The seven heavens One above another, "And made the moon A light in their midst, and made the sun As a (Glorious) Lamp?" [Al-Qur'an 71:15-16]"

(Dr. Zakir Naik, "The Qur'an and Modern science, Compatible or Incompatible?")

There is also a verse in the Qur'an about ALLAH's light which has been used incorrectly. 24:35 ALLAH is the Light of the heavens and the earth. The Parable of His Light is as if there were a Niche and within it a Lamp: the Lamp enclosed in Glass: the glass as it were a brilliant star: Lit from a blessed Tree, an Olive, neither of the east nor of the west, whose oil is well-nigh luminous, though fire scarce touched it: Light upon Light! Allah doth guide whom He will to His Light: Allah doth set forth Parables for men: and Allah doth know all things. Some critics read part of this verse and conclude that ALLAH only has reflective light, as if he is gaining his light from some outside source. When you read the entire verse without prejudice it is clear that ALLAH is the source of light (the lamp) AND he has reflective light (the brilliant star) and he sheds light out to the niche or the universe. The universe is actually a reflection of ALLAH.

THE SUN ROTATES

"For a long time European philosophers and scientists believed that the earth stood still in the center of the universe and every other heavenly body, including the sun, moved around it. In the West, this geocentric concept of the universe was prevalent from the time of Ptolemy in the second century B.C. In 1512, Nicholas Copernicus put forward his Heliocentric Theory of Planetary Motion, which asserted that the sun is motionless at the center of the solar system with the planets revolving around it. In 1609, the German scientist Yohannus Keppler published the 'Astronomia Nova'. In this he concluded that not only do the planets move in elliptical orbits around the sun, they also rotate upon their axes at irregular speeds. With this knowledge it became possible for European scientists to explain correctly many of the mechanisms of the solar system including the sequence of night and day.

After these discoveries, it was thought that the Sun was stationary and did not rotate about its axis like the Earth. I remember having studied this fallacy from Geography books during my school days. Consider the following Quranic verse:

"It is He Who created The Night and the Day, And the sun and the moon: All (the celestial bodies) Swim along, each in its Rounded course." [Al-Qur'an 21:33]

The Arabic word used in the above verse is yasbahûn. The word yasbahûn is derived from the word sabaha. It carries with it the idea of motion that comes from any moving body. If you use the word for a man on the ground, it would not mean that he is rolling but would mean he is walking or running. If you use the word for a man in water it would not mean that he is floating but would mean that he is swimming.

Similarly, if you use the word 'yasbah' for a celestial body such as the sun it would not mean that it is only flying through space but would mean that it is also rotating as it goes through space. Most of the school textbooks have incorporated the fact that the sun rotates about its axis. The rotation of the sun about its own axis can be proved with the help of equipment that projects the image of the sun on the table top so that one can examine the image of the sun without being blinded. It is noticed that the sun has spots which complete a circular motion once every 25 days i.e. the sun takes approximately 25 days to rotate around its axis.

In fact, the sun travels through space at roughly 150 miles per second, and takes about 200 million years to complete one revolution around the center of our Milky Way Galaxy.

"It is not permitted To the Sun to catch up The Moon, nor can The Night outstrip the Day: Each (just) swims along in (its own) orbit (According to Law)." [Al-Qur'an 36:40]

This verse mentions an essential fact discovered by modern astronomy, i.e. the existence of the individual orbits of the Sun and the Moon, and their journey through space with their own motion. The 'fixed place' towards, which the sun travels, carrying with it the solar system, has been located exactly by modern astronomy. It has been given a name, the Solar Apex. The solar system is indeed moving in space towards a point situated in the constellation of Hercules (alpha Layer) whose exact location is firmly established.

The moon rotates around its axis in the same duration that it takes to revolve around the earth. It takes approximately 29½ days to complete one rotation. One cannot help but be amazed at the scientific accuracy of the Quranic verses. Should we not ponder over the question: "What was the source of knowledge contained in the Qur'an?"

(Dr. Zakir Naik, "The Qur'an and Modern science, Compatible or Incompatible?")

THE EXPANDING UNIVERSE

In 1925, an American astronomer by the name of Edwin Hubble, provided observational evidence that all galaxies are receding from one another, which implies that the universe is expanding. The expansion of the universe is now an established scientific fact. This is what Al-Qur'an says regarding the nature of the universe:

"With the power and skill did We construct The Firmament: For it is We Who create the vastness of space." [Al-Qur'an 51:47]

The Arabic word mûsi'ûn is correctly translated as 'expanding it', and it refers to the creation of the expanding vastness of the universe. Stephen Hawking, in his book, 'A Brief History of Time,' says, "The discovery that the universe is expanding was one of the great intellectual revolutions of the 20th century."

The Qur'an mentioned the expansion of the universe, before man even learned to build a telescope! Some may say that the presence of astronomical facts in the Qur'an is not surprising since the Arabs were advanced in the field of astronomy.

MANKIND

They are correct in acknowledging the advancement of the Arabs in the field of astronomy. However they fail to realize that the Qur'an was revealed centuries before the Arabs excelled in astronomy. Moreover many of the scientific facts mentioned above regarding astronomy, such as the origin of the universe with a Big Bang, were not known to the Arabs even at the peak of their scientific advancement. The scientific facts mentioned in the Qur'an are therefore not due to the Arabs' advancement in astronomy. Indeed, the reverse is true. The Arabs advanced in astronomy, because astronomy occupies a place in the Qur'an.

(Dr. Zakir Naik, "The Qur'an and Modern science, Compatible or Incompatible?")

TIME

Albert Einstein is a Nobel Prize winner and probably the most famous figure in the history of science. He gained world notoriety for his theory of relativity. One aspect of this theory is time. Time is a relative concept. It can change according to your environment. Einstein penned his theories between 1905 and 1916. However 1400 years ago, the Qur'an spoke of the relativity of time on numerous occasions. The Qur'an speaks of man perceiving his entire life to be but an hour (10:45, 46:35). As the saying goes, time flies when you are having fun. To some, one day will be like 1000 years (22:47, 32:5) and to others one day might feeling like 50,000 years (70:4). This is a demonstration that the author of this book understood that time is relative. Sadly some people like Rev. Jimmy Swaggart did not understand the relativity of time and mistakenly viewed these verses as evidence of contradictions in the Qur'an. But Einstein and everyone who is aware of relativity of time can help correct this mistake. Since Prophet Muhammad (pbuh) articulated this 1300 years before Einstein, it might be asked, "will they then not believe?"

SOLAR AND LUNAR YEARS

In the western world, time is understood in terms of the earth rotating around the sun. The solar calendar has 12 months and 365 days in one year. Many countries in the eastern society measure time by the rotation of the moon around the earth. This system uses the lunar calendar, where 12 months and 354 days are in one year. The lunar calendar is 11 days less a year than the solar calendar. In the time of Prophet Muhammad (pbuh) and until now, the people of Arabia use the lunar calendar. Interestingly enough the author of the Qur'an wishes to reveal that he is aware of both lunar and solar calendars.

18:25 So they stayed in their Cave three hundred years, and (some) add nine (more).

Surprisingly, 300 years of the solar calendar is exactly 309 years of the lunar calendar. The author of the Qur'an instead of saying 309 years decides to articulate the time 300 and add nine, to demonstrate his knowledge of both systems.

(Harun Yahya, "Miracles of the Qur'an")

THE EXISTENCE OF SUBATOMIC PARTICLES

In ancient times a well-known theory by the name of 'Theory of Atomism' was widely accepted. This theory was originally proposed by the Greeks, in particular by a man called Democritus, who lived about 23 centuries ago. Democritus and the people that came after him, assumed that the smallest unit of matter was the atom. The Arabs used to believe the same. The Arabic word dharrah most commonly meant an atom. In recent times modern science has discovered that it is possible to split even an atom. That the atom can be split further is a development of the 20th century. Fourteen centuries ago this concept would have appeared unusual even to an Arab. For him the dharrah was the limit beyond which one could not go. The following Quranic verse however, refuses to acknowledge this limit:

"The Unbelievers say, 'Never to us will come The Hour': say, 'Nay! But most surely, By my Lord, it will come Upon you - by Him Who knows the unseen - From Whom is not hidden The least little atom In the Heavens or on earth: Nor is there anything less Than that, or greater, but Is in the Record Perspicuous.'" [Al-Qur'an 34:3] [A similar message is conveyed in the Qur'an in 10:61]

This verse refers to the Omniscience of God, His knowledge of all things, hidden or apparent. It then goes further and says that God is aware of everything, including what is smaller or bigger than the atom. Thus the verse clearly shows that it is possible for something smaller than the atom to exist, a fact discovered only recently by modern science.

(Dr. Zakir Naik, "The Qur'an and Modern science, Compatible or Incompatible?")

MOUNTAINS ARE LIKE PEGS (STAKES)

In Geology, the phenomenon of 'folding' is a recently discovered fact. Folding is responsible for the formation of mountain ranges. The earth's crust, on which we live, is like a solid shell, while the deeper layers are hot and fluid, and thus inhospitable to any form of life. It is also known that the stability of the mountains is linked to the phenomenon of folding, for it was the folds that were to provide foundations for the reliefs that constitute the mountains. Geologists tell us that the radius of the Earth is about 3,750 miles and the crust on which we live is very thin, ranging between 1 to 30 miles. Since the crust is thin, it has a high possibility of shaking. Mountains act like stakes or tent pegs that hold the earth's crust and give it stability. The Qur'an contains exactly such a description in the following verse:

"Have We not made the earth as a wide expanse, and the mountains as pegs?" [Al-Qur'an 78:6-7]

The word awtad means stakes or pegs (like those used to anchor a tent); they are the deep foundations of geological folds. A book named 'Earth' is considered as a basic reference textbook on geology in many universities around the world. One of the authors of this book is Frank Press, who was the President of the Academy of Sciences in the USA for 12 years and was the Science Advisor to former US President Jimmy Carter. In this book he illustrates the mountain in a wedge-shape and the mountain itself as a small part of the whole, whose root is deeply entrenched in the ground. [Earth, Press and Siever, p. 435. Also see Earth Science, Tarbuck and Lutgens, p. 157]

According to Dr. Press, the mountains play an important role in stabilizing the crust of the earth. The Qur'an clearly mentions the function of the mountains in preventing the earth from shaking: "And We have set on the earth Mountains standing firm, Lest it should shake with them." [Al-Qur'an 21:31] The Quranic descriptions are in perfect agreement with modern geological data.

(Dr. Zakir Naik, "The Qur'an and Modern science, Compatible or Incompatible?")

BARRIER BETWEEN SWEET AND SALT WATERS

Consider the following Quranic verse:

"He has let free the two bodies of flowing water, Meeting together: Between them is a Barrier Which they do not transgress." [Al-Qur'an 55:19-20]

In the Arabic text the word barzakh means a barrier or a partition. This barrier is not a physical partition. The Arabic word maraja literally means 'they both meet and mix with each other'. Early commentators of the Qur'an were unable to explain the two opposite meanings for the two bodies of water, i.e. they meet and mix, and at the same time, there is a barrier between them. Modern Science has discovered that in the places where two different seas meet, there is a barrier between them. This barrier divides the two seas so that each sea has its own temperature, salinity and density. [Principles of Oceanography, Davis, pp. 92-93] Oceanologists are now in a better position to explain this verse. There is a slanted unseen water barrier between the two seas through which water from one sea passes to the other.

But when the water from one sea enters the other sea, it loses its distinctive characteristic and becomes homogenized with the other water. In a way this barrier serves as a transitional homogenizing area for the two waters. This scientific phenomenon mentioned in the Qur'an was also confirmed by Dr. William Hay who is a well-known marine scientist and Professor of Geological Sciences at the University of Colorado, U.S.A. The Qur'an mentions this phenomenon also in the following verse:

"And made a separating bar between the two bodies Of flowing water?" [Al-Qur'an 27:61]

This phenomenon occurs in several places, including the divider between the Mediterranean and the Atlantic Ocean at Gibraltar. But when the Qur'an speaks about the divider between fresh and salt water, it mentions the existence of "a forbidding partition" with the barrier.

"It is He Who has Let free the two bodies Of flowing water: One palatable and sweet, And the other salty and bitter; Yet has He Made a barrier between them, And a partition that is forbidden To be passed." [Al-Qur'an 25:53]

Modern science has discovered that in estuaries, where fresh (sweet) and salt-water meet, the situation is somewhat different from that found in places where two seas meet. It has been discovered that what distinguishes fresh water from salt water in estuaries is a "pycnocline zone with a marked density discontinuity separating the two layers." [Oceanography, Gross, p. 242. Also see Introductory Oceanography, Thurman, pp. 300-301.] This partition (zone of separation) has salinity different from both the fresh water and the salt water. [Oceanography, Gross, p. 244 and Introductory Oceanography, Thurman, pp. 300-301.] This phenomenon occurs in several places, including Egypt, where the river Nile flows into the Mediterranean Sea. (Dr. Zakir Naik, "The Qur'an and Modern Science, Compatible or Incompatible?")

DARKNESS IN THE DEPTHS OF THE OCEAN

Prof. Durga Rao is an expert in the field of Marine Geology and was a professor at King Abdul Aziz University in Jeddah. He was asked to comment on the following verse:

"Or (the Unbelievers' state) Is like the depths of darkness In a vast deep ocean, Overwhelmed with billow Topped by billow, Topped by (dark) clouds: Depths of darkness, one Above another: if a man Stretches out his hand, He can hardly see it! For any to whom Allah Giveth not light, there is no light!" [Al-Qur'an 24:40]

Prof. Rao said that scientists have only now been able to confirm, with the help of modern equipment that there is darkness in the depths of the ocean. Humans are unable to dive unaided underwater for more than 20 to 30 meters, and cannot survive in the deep oceanic regions at a depth of more than 200 meters. This verse does not refer to all seas because not every sea can be described as having accumulated darkness layered one over another. It refers especially to a deep sea or deep ocean, as the Qur'an says, "darkness in a vast deep ocean." This layered darkness in a deep ocean is the result of two causes:

1. A light ray is composed of seven colours. These seven colours are Violet, Indigo, Blue, Green, Yellow, Orange and Red (VIBGYOR). The light ray undergoes refraction when it hits water. The upper 10 to 15 metres of water absorb the red colour. Therefore if a diver is 25 metres under water and gets wounded, he would not be able to see the red colour of his blood, because the red colour does not reach this depth. Similarly orange rays are absorbed at 30 to 50 metres, yellow at 50 to 100 metres, green at 100 to 200 metres, and finally, blue beyond 200 metres and violet and indigo above 200 metres. Due to successive disappearance of colour, one layer after another, the ocean progressively becomes darker, i.e. darkness takes place in layers of light. Below a depth of 1000 meters there is complete darkness. [Oceans, Elder and Pernetta, p. 27]

2. The sun's rays are absorbed by clouds, which in turn scatter light rays thus causing a layer of darkness under the clouds. This is the first layer of darkness. When light rays reach the surface of the ocean they are reflected by the wave surface giving it a shiny appearance. Therefore it is the waves which reflect light and cause darkness. The unreflected light penetrates into the depths of the ocean. Therefore the ocean has two parts. The surface characterized by light and warmth and the depth characterized by darkness. The surface is further separated from the deep part of the ocean by waves.

The internal waves cover the deep waters of seas and oceans because the deep waters have a higher density than the waters above them. The darkness begins below the internal waves. Even the fish in the depths of the ocean cannot see; their only source of light is from their own bodies. The Qur'an rightly mentions: "Darkness in a vast deep ocean overwhelmed with waves topped by waves."

In other words, above these waves there are more types of waves, i.e. those found on the surface of the ocean. The Quranic verse continues, "topped by (dark) clouds; depths of darkness, one above another."

These clouds as explained are barriers one over the other that further cause darkness by absorption of colours at different levels. Prof. Durga Rao concluded by saying, "1400 years ago a normal human being could not explain this phenomenon in so much detail. Thus the information must have come from a supernatural source".

(Dr. Zakir Naik, "The Qur'an and Modern science, Compatible or Incompatible?")

As a side note consider that in 24:40, the Qur'an parallels those who are in a state of disbelief with someone in the deep sea of darkness and he can barely see his own hand. This is an insight into the Quranic definition of disbelief. Despite the level of darkness, a person knows that he has hands, whether he can see them or not. There are other senses that he can use to determine that he has hands. The Qur'an is suggesting that disbelievers are they who know the truth, but will not accept it or they are those who do not use all the means at their disposal to find the truth.

LAYERS OF HEAVEN AND EARTH

The Qur'an mentions that ALLAH created seven heavens. Many Muslim scholars have interpreted the number "seven" to be symbolic to mean numerous heavens or galaxies. However, others have suggested that the Qur'an uses this number literally, but that the word heaven(s) is used to describe two different things. Heaven may mean the entire universe, but when using the term "heavens" it is in reference to the sky above earth. This is because the Qur'an also uses the word for earth in two different perspectives. At times, it is used to describe the land and the Qur'an also says there are seven earths.

65:12 Allah is He Who created seven Firmaments and of the earth a similar number. Through the midst of them (all) descends His Command: that ye may know that Allah has power over all things, and that Allah comprehends, all things in (His) Knowledge.

The startling thing about this seven heavens and the seven earths is that it has been recently discovered that the there are seven layers of the earth's atmosphere and exactly seven layers of the earth's interior.

The Seven "Heavens" layers of our atmosphere:

troposphere

stratosphere

ozone layer

mesosphere

thermosphere

ionosphere

exosphere

The Seven layers that of the Earth:

crust

lithosphere

upper mantle

asthenosphere

lower mantle

outer core

inner core

(Harun Yahya, "Miracles of the Qur'an")

BEES – FEMALE OR MALE?

16:68 And thy Lord taught the Bee to build its cells in hills, on trees, and in (men's) habitations;

16:69 Then to eat of all the produce (of the earth), and find with skill the spacious paths of its Lord: there issues from within their bodies a drink of varying colours, wherein is healing for men: verily in this is a Sign for those who give thought.

In these verses the Qur'an uses the female gender of the words for bee (fa'slukî and kulî). Interestingly enough, it has been found that the worker bees that we see are all female, the male bees stay at the hive. It is impossible to determine the sex of a bee simply by looking at it, so how did Prophet Muhammad (pbuh) know that the worker bee was female?

(Dr. Zakir Naik, "The Qur'an and Modern Science, Compatible or Incompatible?")

SEX OF PLANTS

Speaking of determining the sex of a bee, how much more difficult must it be to determine the sex of plants. Apparently, the author of the Qur'an knew that plants can be male or female as man and animals are.

20:53 "He Who has, made for you the earth like a carpet spread out; has enabled you to go about therein by roads (and channels); and has sent down water from the sky." With it have We produced diverse pairs of plants each separate from the others.

The Qur'an also speaks of male and female fruits and vegetables, and other things which we are not aware.

36:36 Glory to Allah, Who created in pairs all things that the earth produces, as well as their own (human) kind and (other) things of which they have no knowledge.

(Dr. Zakir Naik, "The Qur'an and Modern science, Compatible or Incompatible?")

LACK OF OXYGEN

Astronauts wear space suits in order to breathe because of the lack of oxygen in outer space. Without his suit he would suffocate and die. It could be a good guess, but how would someone 1400 years ago know for certain that going into outer space effects your breathing and oxygen intake.

6:125 Those whom Allah (in His plan) willeth to guide,- He openeth their breast to Islam; those whom He willeth to leave straying,- He maketh their breast close and constricted, as if they had to climb up to the skies: thus doth Allah (heap) the penalty on those who refuse to believe.

(Harun Yahya, "Miracles of the Qur'an")

EVOLUTION IN THE QUR'AN?

Charles Darwin is a name that is revered and reviled. He is the originator of the theory of evolution, which most scientists today believe in. His theory, in a book entitled "The Origin of Species," was published in 1859. He surmised that every species on earth was created in progressive stages.

Strangely enough Prophet Muhammad (pbuh) said that man was made in stages over 1200 years before Darwin was even born. In this verse, as does others in the Qur'an, it seems to be particularly speaking to the skeptics, those who admit the existence of a First Cause, but reject a personal God.

71:13 What is the matter with you, that ye place not your hope for kindness and long-suffering in Allah

71:14 Seeing that it is He that has created you in diverse stages?

32:9 But He fashioned him in due proportion, and breathed into him something of His spirit. And He gave you (the faculties of) hearing and sight and feeling (and understanding): little thanks do ye give!

Whether you accept Darwin's theory of evolution or you do not, it is difficult to understand it without GOD. The spirit within us and our senses were given to us by GOD. They were not an accidental side effect. Life comes from life. Our spirit comes from "something of HIS spirit." That energy can't be created or destroyed, because it is not of this universe. But something of ALLAH'S spirit does not diminish his power in the less, just as the life force we used to begot our children does not diminish our strength or power. It is ALLAH who transformed man from nothing worth mentioning to who we are now. The Qur'an states that it was six days that ALLAH created the heavens and the earth and all in between them (50:38). However, this was not days as in 24 hours, but more accurately six "periods" or "stages." In Surah 32:4, the Qur'an says that creation was done in 6 days and the very next verses assert that one day can be construed as 1000 years. And the beginning of Surah al-Insan also attests to this fact, as it speaks of the long period of time in creation before man was non-existent.

76.1 Has there not been over Man a long period of Time, when he was nothing - (not even) mentioned?

76.2 Verily We created Man from a drop of mingled sperm, in order to try him: So We gave him (the gifts), of Hearing and Sight.

76.3 We showed him the Way: whether he be grateful or ungrateful (rests on his will).

FINGERTIPS

If you were watching any movie or show about murder, the first thing the detective does when he comes to the scene is have someone check for fingerprints. That is because every person has a unique fingerprint. It is every person's signature.

And the Qur'an seems to give reference to this signature. When discussing the resurrection of all of mankind for the DAY of JUDGMENT, ALLAH says that he recreate man as he were on earth.

75:3 Does man think that We cannot assemble his bones?

75:4 Nay, We are able to put together in perfect order the very tips of his fingers.

Can we believe that it is simply a coincidence that the fingerprint of man is how he is identified and the Qur'an makes mention of recreating him down to his fingerprint? Why did the Qur'an specifically mention finger tips? How would Prophet Muhammad (pbuh) know that this is an excellent way of identification?

(Dr. Zakir Naik, "The Qur'an and Modern science, Compatible or Incompatible?")

MANKIND

MAN IS CREATED FROM ALAQ (A LEECH-LIKE SUBSTANCE)

A few years ago a group of Arabs collected all information concerning embryology from the Qur'an, and followed the instruction of the Qur'an: "If ye realise this not, ask of those who possess the Message." [Al-Qur'an 16:43 & 21:7]

All the information from the Qur'an so gathered, was translated into English and presented to Prof. (Dr.) Keith Moore, who was the Professor of Embryology and Chairman of the Department of Anatomy at the University of Toronto, in Canada. At present he is one of the highest authorities in the field of Embryology. He was asked to give his opinion regarding the information present in the Qur'an concerning the field of embryology. After carefully examining the translation of the Quranic verses presented to him, Dr. Moore said that most of the information concerning embryology mentioned in the Qur'an is in perfect conformity with modern discoveries in the field of embryology and does not conflict with them in any way. He added that there were however a few verses, on whose scientific accuracy he could not comment. He could not say whether the statements were true or false, since he himself was not aware of the information contained therein. There was also no mention of this information in modern writings and studies on embryology. One such verse is:

"Proclaim! (or Read!) In the name of thy Lord and Cherisher, Who created – created man, out of a (mere) clot of congealed blood." [Al-Qur'an 96:1-2]

The word alaq besides meaning a congealed clot of blood also means something that clings, a leech-like substance. Dr. Keith Moore had no knowledge whether an embryo in the initial stages appears like a leech. To check this out he studied the initial stage of the embryo under a very powerful microscope in his laboratory and compared what he observed with a diagram of a leech and he was astonished at the striking resemblance between the two!

In the same manner, he acquired more information on embryology that was hitherto not known to him, from the Qur'an. Dr. Keith Moore answered about eighty questions dealing with embryological data mentioned in the Qur'an and Hadith. Noting that the information contained in the Qur'an and Hadith was in full agreement with the latest discoveries in the field of embryology, Prof. Moore said, "If I was asked these questions thirty years ago, I would not have been able to answer half of them for lack of scientific information"

Dr. Keith Moore had earlier authored the book, 'The Developing Human'. After acquiring new knowledge from the Qur'an, he wrote, in 1982, the 3rd edition of the same book, 'The Developing Human'. The book was the recipient of an award for the best medical book written by a single author. This book has been translated into several major languages of the world and is used as a textbook of embryology in the first year of medical studies.

In 1981, during the Seventh Medical Conference in Dammam, Saudi Arabia, Dr. Moore said, "It has been a great pleasure for me to help clarify statements in the Qur'an about human development. It is clear to me that these statements must have come to [Prophet] Muhammad (pbuh) from God or Allah, because almost all of this knowledge was not discovered until many centuries later. This proves to me that Muhammad must have been a messenger of God or Allah." [The reference for this statement is the video tape titled 'This is the Truth'. For a copy of this video tape contact the Islamic Research Foundation] Dr. Joe Leigh Simpson, Chairman of the Department of Obstetrics and Gynaecology, at the Baylor College of Medicine, Houston, U.S.A., proclaims: "...these Hadiths, sayings of [Prophet] Muhammad (pbuh) could not have been obtained on the basis of the scientific knowledge that was available at the time of the writer (7th century). It follows that not only is there no conflict between genetics and religion (Islam) but in fact religion (Islam) may guide science by adding revelation to some of the traditional scientific approaches...there exist statements in the Qur'an shown centuries later to be valid which support knowledge in the Qur'an having been derived from God."

MAN CREATED FROM A DROP EMITTED BETWEEN THE BACK BONE AND THE RIBS

MANKIND

"Now let man but think from what he is created! He is created from a drop emitted – Proceeding from between the back bone and the ribs." [Al-Qur'an 86:5-7]

In embryonic stages, the reproductive organs of the male and female, i.e., the testicles and the ovaries, begin their development near the kidney between the spinal column and the eleventh and twelfth ribs. Later they descend; the female gonads (ovaries) stop in the pelvis while the male gonads (testicles) continue their descent before birth to reach the scrotum through the inguinal canal. Even in the adult after the descent of the reproductive organ, these organs receive their nerve supply and blood supply from the Abdominal Aorta, which is in the area between the backbone (spinal column) and the ribs. Even the lymphatic drainage and the venous return go to the same area.

HUMAN BEINGS CREATED FROM NUTFAH (a minute quantity of liquid)

The Glorious Qur'an mentions no less than eleven times that the human being is created from nutfah, which means a minute quantity of liquid or a trickle of liquid which remains after emptying a cup. This is mentioned in several verses of the Qur'an including 22:5 and 23:13. [The same is also mentioned in the Qur'an in 16:4, 18:37, 35:11, 36:77, 40:67, 53:46, 75:37, 76:2 and 80:19] Science has confirmed in recent times that only one out of an average of three million sperms is required for fertilizing the ovum. This means that only a 1/three millionth part or 0.00003% of the quantity of sperms that are emitted is required for fertilization.

HUMAN BEINGS CREATED FROM SULALAH (quintessence of liquid)

"And made his progeny from a quintessence of the nature of A fluid despised." [Al-Qur'an 32:8]

The Arabic word sulâlah means quintessence or the best part of a whole. We have come to know now that only one single spermatozoon that penetrates the ovum is required for fertilization, out of the several millions produced by man. That one spermatozoon out of several millions is referred to in the Qur'an as sulâlah. Sulâlah also means gentle extraction from a fluid. The fluid refers to both male and female germinal fluids containing gametes. Both ovum and sperm are gently extracted from their environments in the process of fertilization.

MAN CREATED FROM NUTFATUN AMSHAAJ (mingled liquids)

Consider the following Quranic verse:

"Verily We created Man from a drop of mingled sperm."" [Al-Qur'an 76:2]

The Arabic word nutfatin amshaajin means mingled liquids. According to some commentators of the Qur'an, mingled liquids refers to the male or female agents or liquids. After mixture of male and female gamete, the zygote still remains nutfah. Mingled liquids can also refer to spermatic fluid that is formed of various secretions that come from various glands. Therefore nutfatin amsaj, i.e. a minute quantity of mingled fluids refers to the male and female gametes (germinal fluids or cells) and part of the surrounding fluids.

THE SEX OF A BABY

Who determines the sex of a baby, the man, the women or both? Before reading on this issue, I have no idea what the answer is? It someone without technology and science it is nothing but a guess. I have two sons and I often boasted that I am responsible for this, and it is actually true. The sex of a baby is determined by the sex chromosomes, XY chromosomes for males and XX chromosomes for females. Both the man and women chromosomes combine to make a male child or female child.

However, the women's body only contains the X chromosomes. The man's sperm contains either X or Y chromosomes, therefore whichever the man's sperm determines the sex of the child. I wonder how critics suggest Prophet Muhammad (pbuh) knew such a thing.

53:45 That He did create in pairs,- male and female,

53:46 From a seed when lodged (in its place)

FETUS PROTECTED BY THREE VEILS OF DARKNESS

"He makes you, in the wombs of your mothers, in stages, one after another, in three veils of darkness." [Al-Qur'an 39:6]

According to Prof. Keith Moore these three veils of darkness in the Qur'an refer to:

(I) anterior abdominal wall of the mother

(ii) the uterine wall

(iii) the amnio-chorionic membrane.

EMBRYONIC STAGES

"Man We did create From a quintessence (of clay); Then We placed him As (a drop of) sperm in a place of rest, firmly fixed; Then We made the sperm into a clot of congealed blood; Then of that clot We made a (foetus) lump; then We Made out of that lump Bones and clothed the bones With flesh; then We developed out of it another creature. So blessed be Allah, The Best to create!" [Al-Qur'an 23:12-14]

In this verse Allah states that man is created from a small quantity of liquid which is placed in a place of rest, firmly fixed (well established or lodged) for which the

Arabic word qarârin makîn is used. The uterus is well protected from the posterior by the spinal column supported firmly by the back muscles. The embryo is further protected by the amniotic sac containing the amniotic fluid. Thus the foetus has a well protected dwelling place. This small quantity of fluid is made into alaqah, meaning something which clings. It also means a leech-like substance. Both descriptions are scientifically acceptable as in the very early stages the foetus clings to the wall and also appears to resemble the leech in shape. It also behaves like a leech (blood sucker) and acquires its blood supply from the mother through the placenta. The third meaning of the word alaqah is a blood clot. During this alaqah stage, this spans the third and fourth week of pregnancy, the blood clots within closed vessels. Hence the embryo acquires the appearance of a blood clot in addition to acquiring the appearance of a leech. In 1677, Hamm and Leeuwenhoek were the first scientists to observe human sperm cells (spermatozoa) using a microscope. They thought that a sperm cell contained a miniature human being which grew in the uterus to form a newborn. This was known as the perforation theory. When scientists discovered that the ovum was bigger than the sperm, it was thought by De Graf and others that the foetus existed in a miniature form in the ovum.

Later, in the 18th century Maupertuis propagated the theory of biparental inheritance. The alaqah is transformed into mudghah which means 'something that is chewed (having teeth marks)' and also something that is tacky and small which can be put in the mouth like gum. Both these explanations are scientifically correct. Prof. Keith Moore took a piece of plaster seal and made it into the size and shape of the early stage of foetus and chewed it between the teeth to make it into a 'Mudgha'. He compared this with the photographs of the early stage of foetus. The teeth marks resembled the 'somites' which is the early formation of the spinal column. This mudghah is transformed into bones (izâm). The bones are clothed with intact flesh or muscles (lahm). Then Allah makes it into another creature. Prof. Marshall Johnson is one of the leading scientists in US, and is the head of the Department of Anatomy and Director of the Daniel Institute at the Thomas Jefferson University in Philadelphia in US. He was asked to comment on the verses of the Qur'an dealing with embryology. He said that the verses of the Qur'an describing the embryological stages cannot be a coincidence. He said it was probable that Prophet Muhammad (pbuh) had a powerful microscope. On being reminded that the Qur'an was revealed

1400 years ago, and microscopes were invented centuries after the time of Prophet Muhammad (pbuh), Prof. Johnson laughed and admitted that the first microscope invented could not magnify more than 10 times and could not show a clear picture. Later he said: "I see nothing here in conflict with the concept that Divine intervention was involved when Prophet Muhammad (pbuh) recited the Qur'an."

According to Dr. Keith Moore, the modern classification of embryonic development stages which is adopted throughout the world, is not easily comprehensible, since it identifies stages on a numerical basis i.e. stage I, stage II, etc. The divisions revealed in the Qur'an are based on distinct and easily identifiable forms or shapes, which the embryo passes through. These are based on different phases of prenatal development and provide elegant scientific descriptions that are comprehensible and practical. Similar embryological stages of human development have been described in the following verses:

"Was he not a drop of sperm emitted (In lowly form)? Then did he become a clinging clot; Then did (Allah) make and fashion (him) in due proportion. And of him He made two sexes, male and female." [Al-Qur'an 75:37-39]

"Him Who created thee, fashioned thee in due proportion, And gave thee a just bias; In whatever Form He wills, Does He put thee together." [Al-Qur'an 82:7-8]

EMBRYO PARTLY FORMED AND PARTLY UNFORMED

At the mugdhah stage, if an incision is made in the embryo and the internal organ is dissected, it will be seen that most of them are formed while the others are not yet completely formed. According to Prof. Johnson, if we describe the embryo as a complete creation, then we are only describing that part which is already created. If we describe it as an incomplete creation, then we are only describing that part which is not yet created. So, is it a complete creation or an incomplete creation? There is no better description of this stage of embryo-genesis than the Quranic description, "partly formed and partly unformed", as in the following verse:

"We created you Out of dust, then out of Sperm, then out of a leech-like Clot, then out of a morsel of flesh, partly formed And partly unformed." [Al-Qur'an 22:5]

Scientifically we know that at this early stage of development there are some cells which are differentiated and there are some cells that are undifferentiated – some organs are formed and yet others unformed.

SENSE OF HEARING AND SIGHT

The first sense to develop in a developing human embryo is hearing. The foetus can hear sounds after the 24th week. Subsequently, the sense of sight is developed and by the 28th week, the retina becomes sensitive to light. Consider the following Quranic verses related to the development of the senses in the embryo:

"And He gave you (the faculties of) hearing and sight and feeling (And understanding)." [Al-Qur'an 32:9]

"Verily, We created Man from a drop Of mingled sperm, In order to try him: So We gave him (the gifts), Of Hearing and Sight." [Al-Qur'an 76:2]

"It is He Who has created for you (the faculties of) Hearing, sight, feeling And understanding: little thanks it is ye give!" [Al-Qur'an 23:78]

In all these verses the sense of hearing is mentioned before that of sight. Thus the Quranic description matches with the discoveries in modern embryology.

(Dr. Zakir Naik, "The Qur'an and Modern science, Compatible or Incompatible?")

HOW DID MAN MULTIPLY?

4.1 Pickthal's Translation:

MANKIND

O people! Be careful of (your duty to) your Lord, Who created you from a single being and created its mate of the same (kind) and spread from these two, many men and women; and be careful of (your duty to) Allah, by Whom you demand one of another (your rights), and (to) the ties of relationship; surely Allah ever watches over you

4:1 Shakir's Translation:

O mankind! Be careful of your duty to your Lord Who created you from a single soul and from it created its mate and from them twain hath spread abroad a multitude of men and women. Be careful of your duty toward Allah in Whom ye claim (your rights) of one another, and toward the wombs (that bare you). Lo! Allah hath been a watcher over you

Some people believe that at man's inception, it was necessary for him to procreate through incest. They assume this, from reading scriptures like the Bible. However, in the Qur'an, I see no mention of incest, but if you look closely you notice something to the contrary. It is not procreation, but God who expanded human population from two souls. I have read that even some scientists have incorporated incest in the origin of the first group of mankind. They deem this the only rational answer for how man could multiply. That is because, they subtract the God who "from the twain scattered COUNTLESS MEN and WOMEN"

Because incest is a grave sin in Judaism, Christianity and Islam, those who adhere to these faiths must not automatically jump to the conclusion that this sin was acceptable at one point, without proof of such an accusation. The Bible speaks of Adam and Eve and then it continues with the children that they begot and their children's child and so on. Therefore many Christians and Jews believe that their relationships must have been incestuous. That would mean that after the flood, Noah and his family again practiced incest. Fortunately, the Qur'an has the answer for this problem. Just as God expanded humanity in creation, he did it again with the people of lands in which his penalty rain down on (23:31, 42).

FOREHEAD FULL OF LIES

It has been recently discovered that the prefrontal lobe, the front of your brain, is the part of the brain responsible for our executive functions.

The term executive function describes a set of cognitive abilities that control and regulate other abilities and behaviors. Executive functions are necessary for goal-directed behavior. They include the ability to initiate and stop actions, to monitor and change behavior as needed, and to plan future behavior when faced with novel tasks and situations. Executive functions allow us to anticipate outcomes and adapt to changing situations. The ability to form concepts and think abstractly are often considered components of executive function. (www.minddisorders.com/Del-Fi/Executive-function.html)

There have been recent studies done which have determined heighten activity in the prefrontal lobe of a person when they are lying. Strangely enough, no studies were done in Arabia by Prophet Muhammad (pbuh), yet he said this:

96:15 Let him beware! If he desist not, We will drag him by the forelock,

96:16 A lying, sinful forelock!

WEIGHT OF CLOUDS

Did you know that clouds were heavy? Well I didn't, yet the author of the Qur'an did.

"The weight of clouds can reach quite astonishing proportions. For example, a cumulonimbus cloud, commonly known as the thunder cloud, can contain up to 300,000 tons of water. The fact that a mass of 300,000 tons of water can remain aloft is truly amazing. Attention is drawn to the weight of clouds in other verses of the Qur'an:

It is He Who sends out the winds, bringing advance news of His mercy, so that when they have lifted up the heavy clouds, We dispatch them to a dead land and send down water to it, by means of which We bring forth all kinds of fruit... (Al-Qur'an, 7:57)

It is He Who shows you the lightning, striking fear and bringing hope; it is He Who heaps up the heavy clouds. (Al-Qur'an, 13:12)

At the time when the Qur'an was revealed, of course, it was quite impossible to have any information about the weight of clouds. This information, revealed in the Qur'an, but discovered only recently, is yet another proof that the Qur'an is the Word of Allah."

(Harun Yahya, "Miracles of the Qur'an")

SENT DOWN IRON

57:25 We sent aforetime our messengers with Clear Signs and sent down with them the Book and the Balance (of Right and Wrong), that men may stand forth in justice; and We sent down Iron, in which is (material for) mighty war, as well as many benefits for mankind

In this verse, the Qur'an mentions itself, in that it was sent down. This means that its contents are not of this world. It did not originate on earth. The same is true for iron. Iron is not a metal which was formed on earth, but it descended onto the earth surface from out of space.

"Not only the iron on earth, but also the iron in the entire Solar System, comes from outer space, since the temperature in the Sun is inadequate for the formation of iron. The sun has a surface temperature of 6,000 degrees Celsius, and a core temperature of approximately 20 million degrees. Iron can only be produced in much larger stars than the Sun, where the temperature reaches a few hundred million degrees. When the amount of iron exceeds a certain level in a star, the star can no longer accommodate it, and it eventually explodes in what is called a "nova" or a "supernova." These explosions make it possible for iron to be given off into space"

There is also evidence for older supernova events: Enhanced levels of iron-60 in deep-sea sediments have been interpreted as indications that a supernova explosion occurred within 90 light-years of the sun about 5 million years ago. Iron-60 is a radioactive isotope of iron, formed in supernova explosions, which decays with a half life of 1.5 million years. An enhanced presence of this isotope in a geologic layer indicates the recent nucleosynthesis of elements nearby in space and their subsequent transport to the earth (perhaps as part of dust grains).

All this shows that iron did not form on the Earth, but was carried from Supernovas, and was "sent down," as stated in the verse. It is clear that this fact could not have been known in the 7th century, when the Qur'an was revealed. Nevertheless, this fact is related in the Qur'an, the Word of Allah, Who encompasses all things in His infinite knowledge.

(Harun Yahya, "Miracles of the Qur'an")

CITY OF IHRAM

89:6 Seest thou not how thy Lord dealt with the 'Ad (people),

89:7 Of the (city of) Iram, with lofty pillars,

89:8 The like of which were not produced in (all) the land?

Critics of the Qur'an ridiculed it for giving reference to a fictitious city because this place had long been a tale considered to be a myth. It was said to be a lost city in the Arabian Peninsula , but no one knew this to be true. With all the mythical stories going around, the Qur'an basically says, wait, this story is actually true. Some Muslims from the year 610 until 1978 probably felt ashamed of this mythical city mentioned in the Qur'an. The reason Muslims no longer feel ashamed was because archaeologists found proof of this city's existence and it was documented in National Geographic's in December 1978 edition volume 154 number 6. They found remnants of a city called Ebla and they had record of trade and business with "IRAM, an obscure city referred to in Surah 89 of the KORAN."

HAMAN AND THE PHARAOH

Modern archaeology has helped dispel another criticism of the Qur'an. The Qur'an says that in the time of Moses (pbuh), a man by the name of Haman oversaw the construction of a huge tower for which the Pharaoh said he would go up and meet with God (28:38). The criticism came from those who believe in the Torah or the Old Testament, which place Haman time on earth over 1,000 after the time of Moses (pbuh) and the Pharaoh. Yet recent discoveries in the Egyptian hieroglyphics have affirmed that, in fact, the Qur'an is correct in placing Haman at the Moses and the Pharoah and the Torah is inaccurate.

Through the decoding of hieroglyph, an important piece of knowledge was revealed: The name "Haman" was indeed mentioned in Egyptian inscriptions. This name was referred to in a monument in the Hof Museum in Vienna . This same inscription also indicated the close relationship between Haman and the Pharaoh.

In the dictionary of People in the New Kingdom, that was prepared based on the entire collection of inscriptions, Haman is said to be "the head of stone quarry workers." In the same vein, when speaking of different Egyptian rulers, the Qur'an makes a slight distinction between them. When speaking of the Egyptian ruler of Joseph's time, the Qur'an uses the word "malik" or king (12:43), but in the time of

Moses, the Qur'an uses the word "firawn" or pharaoh (10:75). This is because the rulers were not called Pharaoh at the time of Joseph, but they were in the time of Moses.

The use of the word "Pharaoh" in Egyptian history belongs only to the late period. This particular title began to be employed in the 14th century B.C., during the reign of Amenhotep IV. The Prophet Yusuf (pbuh) lived at least 200 years before that time.

The Encyclopedia Britannica says that the word "Pharaoh" was a title of respect used from the New Kingdom (beginning with the 18th dynasty; B.C. 1539-1292) until the 22nd dynasty (B.C. 945-730), after which this term of address became the title of the king. Further information on this subject comes from the Academic American Encyclopedia, which states that the title of Pharaoh began to be used in the New Kingdom.

(Harun Yahya, "Miracles of the Qur'an")

Decoding the hieroglyphic script is the means to verify that the Qur'an is accurate in its titles of the rulers. The other source which mentioned Joseph, Moses and the Egyptian rulers is the Bible. But it incorrectly calls both the rulers "Pharaoh." So from where did Prophet Muhammad (pbuh) get this information?

SOME SCIENTISTS' COMMENTS REGARDING THE QUR'AN

... There are too many accuracies [in the Qur'an] and, like Dr. Moore, I have no difficulty in my mind that this is a divine inspiration or revelation which led him to these statements. (Dr. T. V. N. Persaud, Professor of Anatomy, Pediatrics and Child Health, Obstetrics, Gynecology, Reproductive Sciences at the University of Manitoba)

... It follows, I think, that not only there is no conflict between genetics and religion but, in fact, religion can guide science by adding revelation to some of the traditional scientific approaches, that there exist statements in the Qur'an shown centuries later to be valid, which support knowledge in the Qur'an having been derived from God. (Dr. Joe Leigh Simpson, Professor of Obstetrics and Gynecology, Molecular and Human Genetics)

... As a scientist, I can only deal with things which I can specifically see. I can understand embryology and developmental biology. I can understand the words that are translated to me from the Qur'an. As I gave the example before, if I were to transpose myself into that era, knowing what I knew today and describing things, I could not describe the things which were described... So I see nothing here in conflict with the concept that divine intervention was involved in what he [Prophet Muhammad (pbuh)] was able to write. (Dr. E. Marshall Johnson, Professor Emeritus of Anatomy and Developmental Biology at Thomas Jefferson University)

... In a relatively few Aayahs [Quranic verses] is contained a rather comprehensive description of human development from the time of commingling of the gametes through organogenesis. No such distinct and complete record of human development, such as classification, terminology, and description, existed previously. In most, if not all, instances, this description antedates by many centuries the recording of the various stages of human embryonic and fetal development recorded in the traditional scientific literature. (Gerald C. Goeringer, Associate Professor of Medical Embryology at Georgetown University)

... It has been a great pleasure for me to help clarify statements in the Qur'an about human development. It is clear to me that these statements must have come to [Prophet] Muhammad (pbuh) from God, or Allah, because most of this knowledge was not discovered until many centuries later. This proves to me that [Prophet] Muhammad (pbuh) must have been a messenger of God, or Allah. (Dr. Keith L. Moore, Professor Emeritus, Department of Anatomy and Cell Biology, University of Toronto. Distinguished embryologist and the author of several medical textbooks)

... Because the staging of human embryos is complex, owing to the continuous process of change during development, it is proposed that a new system of classification could be developed using the terms mentioned in the Qur'an and Sunnah. The proposed system is simple, comprehensive, and conforms with present embryological knowledge. (Dr. Keith L. Moore, Professor Emeritus, Department of Anatomy and Cell Biology, University of Toronto)

... The intensive studies of the Qur'an and Hadith in the last four years have revealed a system of classifying human embryos that is amazing since it was recorded in the seventh century A.D... the descriptions in the Qur'an cannot be based on scientific knowledge in the seventh century... (Dr. Keith L. Moore, Professor Emeritus, Department of Anatomy and Cell Biology, University of Toronto)

... I think it is almost impossible that he [Prophet] Muhammad (pbuh) could have known about things like the common origin of the universe, because scientists have only found out within the last few years with very complicated and advanced technological methods that this is the case... Somebody who did not know something about nuclear physics 1400 years ago could not, I think, be in a position to find out from his own mind for instance that the earth and the heavens had the same origin, or many others of the questions that we have discussed here. (Alfred Kroner, Professor of the Department of Geosciences, University of Mainz, Germany. One of the world's most famous geologists)

... If you combine all these and you combine all these statements that are being made in the Qur'an in terms that relate to the earth and the formation of the earth and science in general, you can basically say that statements made there in many ways are true, they can now be confirmed by scientific methods... And that many of the statements made in there at that time could not be proven, but that modern scientific methods are now in a position to prove what [Prophet] Muhammad (pbuh) said 1400 years ago. (Alfred Kroner, Professor of the Department of Geosciences, University of Mainz, Germany)

... I say, I am very much impressed by finding true astronomical facts in Qur'an, and for us modern astronomers have been studying very small piece of the universe. We have concentrated our efforts for understanding of very small part. Because by using telescopes, we can see only very few parts of the sky without thinking about the whole universe. So by reading Qur'an and by answering to the questions, I think I can find my future way for investigation of the universe. (Professor Yushidi Kusan, Director of the Tokyo Observatory, Tokyo, Japan)

MANKIND

... Certainly, I would like to leave it at that, that what we have seen is remarkable, it may or may not admit of scientific explanation, there may well have to be something beyond what we understand as ordinary human experience to account for the writings that we have seen. (Professor Armstrong, Professor of Astronomy serving with NASA)

... It is difficult to imagine that this type of knowledge was existing at that time, around 1400 years back. May be some of the things they have simple idea about, but to describe those things in great detail is very difficult. So this is definitely not simple human knowledge. A normal human being cannot explain this phenomenon in that much detail. So, I thought the information must have come from a supernatural source. (Prof. Dorja Rao, Professor of Marine Geology at King Abdulaziz University, Jeddah, Saudi Arabia)

... I believe that everything mentioned in the Qur'an 1400 years ago is true and can be proven by scientific methods... This must be by inspiration from God, or Allah, Who knows all science. Thus, I believe that this is the time to say: "There is no god but Allah and Muhammad is the Messenger of Allah." (Prof. Tejatat Tejasen, Head of the Department of Anatomy and Embryology, University of Chiang Mai, Chiang Mai, Thailand)

... The Qur'an came several centuries ago, confirming what we discovered. This indicates that the Qur'an is the word of God. (Prof. Joly Sumson, Professor in Gynecology and Obstetrics)

... It [the Qur'an] discusses the past, the recent period, and the future. I do not know the cultural level of the people in the period of [Prophet] Muhammad (pbuh) and I do not know their scientific level. If it is as we know about the low scientific level in this ancient period, and the absence of technology, then there is no doubt that what we are reading nowadays in the Qur'an is a light from God. He inspired it in [Prophet] Muhammad (pbuh). I had made research into the early history of civilization in the Middle East in order to know if there was such perfect information as this. If there was no other information like the Qur'anic information in that ancient period, this strengthens the faith that God sent [Prophet] Muhammad (pbuh); He sent to him a little amount from His large science, which we have discovered only in recent time. We are hoping for continuous dialogue in the subject of science with the Qur'an in the field of geology. (Prof. Palmar, one of the major scientists in geology in the USA)

After a discussion about the function of mountains for the fixing of the earth: I believe that this [the Qur'an's information] is very, very strange, it is nearly impossible, I believe truly that if what you are saying is right, thus, this book [the Qur'an] is very valuable to be noticed, I agree with you. (Professor Syawda, a Japanese scientist famous in Japan and internationally in the field of oceanic geology.)

(Harun Yahya, "Miracles of the Qur'an")

When asked to perform a miracle, Prophet Muhammad (pbuh) said that the Qur'an is his miracle. Of all the miracles performed by prophets with God's permission, the Qur'an is the only miracle that can be examined and experienced today. It is a miracle of Arabic literature. Its usage of the Arabic language is so eloquent that it changed the language forever. It is the standard by which all Arabic literature is compared. And in this masterpiece of literature, it's amazing that its verses rhyme. When describing the perfect elements of science, when recalling the stories of the prophets, when giving man guidance in his law and his life, the Qur'an's verses maintain these rhythmic patterns in order to make them easier to remember and recite. This method should be appreciated by anyone who has ever written a paper, a novel or even a short story. Consider the difficulty of rhyming the entire work while conveying a concise message. Poets, songwriters, and rap artist rhymes words that are cohesive enough, if recited aloud, to fill the time of about three or four minutes. But imagine making a science book rhyme, the constitution rhyme, or the New Testament rhyme. This is another miracle in itself.

Now the fact that the Qur'an also coordinates certain related words within its message helps to illustrate that it is a miracle from God.

USAGE AND MENTIONING OF A WORD

Gary Miller, a mathematician, found another interesting aspect of the Qur'an. He found that the author of the Qur'an was aware of the different understand of words and whether the word is used for its meaning or it is simply mentioned. For instance, if I say "the Qur'an has 114 chapters," I am talking about the actual book, the Qur'an. But if I say "the Qur'an has 5 letters," I am talking about the word "Q-U-R-A-N." In the first instance, I used the word. In the second instance, I mentioned the word.

Well, in the Qur'an, it says that if the Qur'an was from other than ALLAH, you would find in it many "discrepancies." Of course, the meaning of this verse obviously means you won't find any mistakes, but if someone wanted to be clever, they could search for the use of the word "discrepancies." And if they found many times in which the actual word "discrepancies" was used in the Qur'an, they might say that this book is not from ALLAH. However, the Qur'an only uses this word one time, to avoid such things. Similarly, the Qur'an says "Jesus (pbuh) is like Adam." (3:59) The Qur'an explains the similitude between the two men and it also mentioned both men's name exactly 25 times. When the Qur'an says something is like something else, its uses the words for both the same amount of times, to outsmart would-be critics. The author of the Qur'an also makes a point to offset the amount of times words are mentioned which are said to be "unlike" each other in the Qur'an.

WORD REPETITIONS IN THE QUR'AN

-The statement of "seven heavens" is repeated seven times. "The creation of the heavens (khalq as-samawat)" is also repeated seven times.

-"Day (Yawm)" is repeated 365 times in singular form (another proof that the author is aware of the solar calendar), while its plural and dual forms "days (ayyam and yawmayn)" together are repeated 30 times. The number of repetitions of the word "month" (shahar) is 12.

-The number of repetitions of the words "plant" and "tree" is the same: 26

-The word "payment or reward" is repeated 117 times, while the expression "forgiveness" (mughfirah), which is one of the basic morals of the Qur'an, is repeated exactly twice that amount, 234 times.

-When we count the word "Say," we find it appears 332 times. We arrive at the same figure when we count the phrase "they said."

-The number of times the words, "world" (dunya) and "hereafter" (akhira) are repeated is also the same: 115

-The word "satan" (shaitan) is used in the Qur'an 88 times, as is the word "angels" (malaika).

-The word faith (iman) (without genitive) is repeated 25 times throughout the Qur'an as is also the word infidelity (kufr).

-The words "paradise" and "hell" are each repeated 77 times.

-The word "zakah" is repeated in the Qur'an 32 times and the number of repetitions of the word "blessing" (barakah) is also 32.

-The expression "the righteous" (al-abraar) is used 6 times but "the wicked" (al-fujjaar) is used half as much, i.e., 3 times.

-The number of times the words "Summer-hot" and "winter-cold" are repeated is the same: 5.

-The words "wine" (khamr) and "intoxication" (saqara) are repeated in the Qur'an the same number of times: 6

-The number of appearances of the words "mind" and "light" is the same: 49.

-The words "tongue" and "sermon" are both repeated 25 times.

-The words "benefit" and "corrupt" both appear 50 times. "Reward" (ajr) and "action" (fail) are both repeated 107 times.

MANKIND

-"Love" (al-mahabbah) and "obedience" (al-ta'ah) also appear the same number of times: 83

-The words "refuge" (maseer) and "forever" (abadan) appear the same number of times in the Qur'an: 28.

-The words "disaster" (al-musibah) and "thanks" (al-shukr) appear the same number of times in the Qur'an: 75.

-"Sun" (shams) and "light" (nur) both appear 33 times in the Qur'an. In counting the word "light" only the simple forms of the word were included.

-The number of appearances of "right guidance" (al-huda) and "mercy" (al-rahma) is the same: 79

-The words "trouble" and "peace" are both repeated 13 times in the Qur'an.

-The words "man" and "woman" are also employed equally: 23 times.

-The number of times the words "man" and "woman" are repeated in the Qur'an, 23, is at the same time that of the chromosomes from the egg and sperm in the formation of the human embryo. The total number of human chromosomes is 46; 23 each from the mother and father.

-"Treachery" (khiyanah) is repeated 16 times, while the number of repetitions of the word "foul" (khabith) is 16.

-"Human being" is used 65 times: the sum of the number of references to the stages of man's creation is the same: i.e.,

Human being 65

Soil (turab) 17

Drop of Sperm (nutfah) 12

Embryo ('alaq) 6

A half formed lump of flesh (mudghah) 3

Bone ('idham) 15

Flesh (lahm) 12

TOTAL 65

-The word "salawat" appear five times in the Qur'an, and Allah has commanded man to perform the prayer (salat) five times a day.

-The word "land" appears 13 times in the Qur'an and the word "sea" 32 times, giving a total of 45 references. If we divide that number by the of the number of references to the land we arrive at the figure 28.888888888889%. The number of total references to land and sea, 45, divided by the number of references to the sea in the Qur'an, 32, is 71.111111111111%. Extraordinarily, these figures represent the exact proportions of land and sea on the Earth today.

(Harun Yahya, "Miracles of the Qur'an")

CONCLUSION

If you are honest with yourself, could there be any other explanation of the Qur'an but that a supernatural being gave this revelation to the man, Prophet Muhammad (pbuh). The Qur'an's contents are proof of the divine. The understanding of the use and mentioning of a word is something used in logic today. Most people don't even think about something like this and it is far-fetched to believe Prophet Muhammad (pbuh) considered this development in logic and left this secret message to his future critics of 1400 years. What use is this for Prophet Muhammad (pbuh) if he is long gone from the earth? This is naught but the wisdom of ALLAH. This like the repetition of words is a tool used to demonstrate to critics and affirm the belief of Muslims that this Qur'an is preserved and guarded by ALLAH. Every word is intact. It is as it was 1400 years ago, which a Muslim can verify by comparing his Qur'an with that of the two existing Qur'ans in the city of Tashkent of Uzbekistan and Istanbul of Turkey. This preservation is also a fulfilled prophecy in the Qur'an.

15:9 We have, without doubt, sent down the Message; and We will assuredly guard it (from corruption).

What is the purpose of Prophet Muhammad (pbuh) telling the people of Arabia of all these scientific facts, in which they would never be able to confirm? To their credit, they believed them to be true without adequate proof, but on the strength of the validity of other evidence from the Qur'an. Today we have further proof that the Qur'an is as it says "the truth from ALLAH, with absolute certainty (69:51)." These things are not hypotheses. Prophet Muhammad (pbuh) is claiming that everything he uttered of the Qur'an is ABSOLUTE FACT. Where did this man get such confidence without any research? The answer is obvious. The probability that this man or any man or any committee of men 1400 years ago, or even today or 1,000 years from now, can GUESS with complete accuracy on all these issues without knowledge of these subjects is almost equivalent to the probability that this universe exists without a creator. When you are holding the Arabic Qur'an in your hands, you are reading the words GOD has put into order for you. When you read the Qur'an's translation, you are reading the meaning of the message that GOD has given to mankind, the instruction manual to success.

ALLEGATIONS OF PLAGIARISM

If it is agreed that the Qur'an is the words of God, this settles whether Prophet Muhammad (pbuh) was a liar or a lunatic as some suggests (23:70). If the Qur'an is true, then he is neither. But let's explore the allegations some have made against the Qur'an. They say the Qur'an was authored by Prophet Muhammad (pbuh) or the Qur'an was authored by a committee of people then attributed to Prophet

Muhammad (pbuh) and God. They also say that Prophet Muhammad (pbuh) forged or copied the Qur'an.

First of all, Prophet Muhammad (pbuh) was unable to read or write, as was over 90% of Arabia. This admittance is not the Muslim insulting his intelligence, as many critics suggest, but rather a statement of fact. The Qur'an specifically states that it is a book sent down as an Arabic RECITATION so Muhammad (pbuh) would be able to understand it (12:1-3). In those times, literacy was not as important as it is today. There were no typewriters, or computers. Books were handwritten, which means there were very few books available and very few people able to read them.

29:48 And thou (Muhammad) was not (able) to recite a Book before this (Book came), nor art thou (able) to transcribe it with thy right hand: In that case, indeed, would the talkers of vanities have doubted.

The choice of an illiterate prophet is again the wisdom of ALLAH. He knew that Prophet Muhammad (pbuh) would be accused of concocting the Qur'an on his own. In order to show the implausibility of such an argument, he chose an illiterate, yet highly revered and respected man. In addition to this, ALLAH litters the Qur'an with statements of science and history that no man of that time could have known was "the truth with absolute certainty."

25:4 But the disbelievers say: "Naught is this but a lie which he has forged, and others have helped him at it." In truth it is they who have put forward an iniquity and a falsehood.

25:5 And they say: "Tales of the ancients, which he has caused to be written: and they are dictated before him morning and evening."

MANKIND

25.6 Say: "The (Qur'an) was sent down by Him who knows the mystery (that is) in the heavens and the earth: verily He is Oft-Forgiving, Most Merciful."

It has been established that the author of the Qur'an knows the mysteries of the universe, thus it is futile to conclude that Muhammad (pbuh) wrote the Qur'an or any number of people wrote it in or before his time.

17.88 Say: "If the whole of mankind and Jinns were to gather together to produce the like of this Qur'an, they could not produce the like thereof, even if they backed up each other with help and support

The Qur'an is a miracle unachievable without God's assistance. So what about those who say that Prophet Muhammad (pbuh) copied from other religious scriptures? The Qur'an is very similar to the Jewish and Christian scripture in terms of some of its stories and characters. Critics suggest that this is due to the plagiarism of Prophet Muhammad (pbuh). The Qur'an calls the Turaat (Torah) of Moses, the Zabur (Psalms) of David, and the Injil (Gospel) of Jesus (pbut) the true words of God. However, none of these revelations exist today, nor did they exist in the time of Prophet Muhammad (pbuh).

The Torah and Psalms of the Bible are both books traditionally attributed to Moses and David (pbut), but Biblical scholars admit that it is very doubtful that these books are authored by Moses or David (pbut). And the gospels of the New Testament are all authored by someone other than Jesus (pbuh). Muslims believe the actual words God revealed to these Prophets are not in the Bible, but that the scriptures which the Jews and Christians possess contain some truth and some falsehood.

5:48 To thee We sent the Scripture in truth, confirming the scripture that came before it, and "muhaimin alayhi:" so judge between them by what Allah hath revealed.

The words "muhaimin alayhi" have been translated "guardian over it," "watcher over it" or "criterion over it" and all of these translations are accurate. But I suggest "criterion over it" is the best because it better correlates to the rest of the verse which says judge between these scriptures using the Qur'an. The Qur'an is actually called THE CRITERION (AL FURQAN), or the standard by which you determine right from wrong. The Qur'an is the scripture which corrects the mistakes of previous man-made scriptures. The Qur'an claims that the message of the Prophets was altered deliberately or forgotten (5:13). Muhammad (pbuh) is asked to speak to the people who have their own scriptures and he will be able to explain their book to them, using the Qur'an (16:43-44).

There is the Old Testament and the New Testament. The Qur'an says it is the Last Testament, the final message from God. In response to the allegations of forgery the Qur'an offers several challenges. In Surah or chapter 17:88, ALLAH asks mankind to produce something like the Qur'an. Because this feat is impossible to accomplish, the Qur'an lightens the challenge in chapter 11:13. The author asks those who believe the Qur'an to be a forgery to bring 10 chapters like it. Then the Gracious God makes the task even easier and asks the critics for 1 chapter like that of the Qur'an. Like the challenge to find a mistake in the Qur'an, this challenge is almost a taunting (10:38). Of course, the reason for this is to provoke man to not just make allegation but to substantiate them. The Qur'an repeatedly asks detractors to "bring your proof" (6:150, 14:10, 21:24, 37:157, 46:4). It demands proof of any accusation that you make, so it can be analyzed. This is because if what they bring is the truth, it will be in full agreement with the Qur'an and if it is false, the Qur'an will correct it. So correction should not be confused with plagiarism and forgery.

While in a debate with a Christian who insisted that the Qur'an was plagiarized, I asked "how do you correct something without mentioning it?" His argument was the Qur'an uses the same character and storyline as the Bible, so it's plagiarized. But the Qur'an says some things in their scripture are false and it corrects these falsehoods.

MANKIND

You must make reference to the story in order to correct it. So the Qur'an begs them to bring the story which is forged and EVERY SINGLE TIME two of the same stories or topics are mentioned in the Qur'an and the Bible, the Qur'an corrects the scripture in question. I will give you some examples.

CAMEL THROUGH THE EYE OF A NEEDLE

Matthew 19:24 It is easier for a camel to go through the eye of a needle, than for a rich man to enter into the kingdom of God.

Al-Qur'an 7:40 To those who reject Our signs and treat them with arrogance, no opening will there be of the gates of heaven, nor will they enter the garden, until the camel can pass through the eye of the needle: Such is Our reward for those in sin.

The gospel of Matthew insinuates that being rich is a sin. The rich man spoken of in this verse had kept all the laws of Moses (pbuh). But the gospels say Jesus (pbuh) said the man must be perfect and give away of his possessions. Perhaps this man loved his wealth more than he loved God, which seems to be unlikely if he kept all of God's laws. But the gospel suggests that Jesus (pbuh) felt that all rich people had a similar sickness because it generalizes them all in 19:24. The Qur'an, on the other hand, diagnoses the symptoms of those people who will find difficulty in getting into Paradise. Is it more accurate to say "It is hard for rich people to make it to heaven" or "it is hard for those who reject God's signs to make it to heaven?" To be more practical, is it more accurate to say "it's harder for boys to play basketball" or "it is harder for those who ignore the rules of basketball to be able to play?" The answer is obvious, so too is the CORRECTION.

WHO WILL INHERIT THE EARTH?

Psalms 37:11 But the meek shall inherit the earth.

Matthew 5:5 Blessed are the meek: for they shall inherit the earth.

The first quote is supposedly from the Psalms of David (pbuh). This verse from Psalms is said to be quoted by Jesus (pbuh) in the gospel of Matthew. The word "meek" is sometimes translated as humble or gentle. All these words denote a sense of submission not necessarily to God but to man. The Qur'an clears up this ambiguity.

Al-Qur'an 21:105 Before this We wrote in the Psalms, after the Message (given to Moses): My servants the righteous, shall inherit the earth."

It says that the true Psalms says the "righteous" instead of the "meek" will get the reward, which is more in tune with a just God who rewards you for your good and right actions and intentions which he prescribes, not simply because you are humble, gentle and meek.

A MUSTARD SEED

On two occasions, Jesus (pbuh) is said to have mentioned a mustard seed when he was teaching his disciples and others in the crowd, Matthew 17:20 and Matthew 13:31-32. In both instances, Jesus (pbuh) is said to use the size of mustard seed to magnify a particular point. In the first instance, he suggests that a small amount of faith can do wondrous things. In the second instance, it appears that Jesus (pbuh) is describing the establishment of righteousness in a person or an institution which if it were planted like a small seed would grow incredibly. Yet there are problems with both the stories.

Matthew 17:20 And Jesus (pbuh) said unto them, Because of your unbelief: for verily I say unto you, If ye have faith as a grain of mustard seed, ye shall say unto this mountain, Remove hence to yonder place; and it shall remove; and nothing shall be impossible unto you.

In the first instance, it appears that Jesus (pbuh) is merely exaggerating to get his point across. He does not literally mean that you can move mountains with faith. However, upon review of the context we find that Jesus (pbuh) meant this literally. There was a man whose son suffered from lunacy. He brought his son to the disciples to be healed, but they were unable to heal the man's son. Because of their inability to heal the boy, Jesus (pbuh) rebukes them as "faithless and perverse." At this point, Jesus (pbuh) heals the boy and says if they had a small amount of faith, they could move mountains. This point is again reiterated in Mark 16:17-18, where Jesus (pbuh) says his followers' belief will allow them to cast out demons, speak in tongues, handle snakes and drink poison without harm, and heal illnesses by laying hands the sick in his name. I doubt that he would say such a thing. Though millions of people have a mustard seeds worth of faith, I do not think it's enough to move mountains, drink poison or heal the sick.

Matthew 13:31 He proposed another parable to them. "The kingdom of heaven is like a mustard seed that a person took and sowed in a field.

Matthew 13:32 It is the smallest of all the seeds, yet when full-grown it is the largest of plants. It becomes a large bush, and the 'birds of the sky come and dwell in its branches.'"

In the Matthew 13, Jesus (pbuh) is giving the Sermon on the Mount where he is telling a parable about the Kingdom of God. Unfortunately, this passage suggests that the mustard seed is the smallest seed on earth, which is not the case. For instance, an orchid seed is smaller than a mustard seed. Though it is in a parable, the words "it is the smallest of all seeds" seems to be added as commentary and is meant to be taken literally. Mark and Luke tell the same parable, but Luke omits "the smallest of all seeds," whereas Mark retains these words. Perhaps as some apologists suggest, the use of a mustard seed is to demonstrate the smallest seed that the people around him could imagine. The Qur'an also uses the mustard seed to signify what seems to be the consensus view in that region, that the mustard seed is the smallest seed.

Al-Qur'an 21:47 We shall set up scales of justice for the Day of Judgment, so that not a soul will be dealt with unjustly in the least, and if there be (no more than) the weight of a mustard seed, We will bring it (to account): and enough are We to take account.

Those who believe the Qur'an to be the words of God are very fortunate for its usage of the mustard seed. In the first place, it can't be taken literally in the sense that it is not discussing the power of a small amount of faith, but rather it is speaking of an account of every great and small deed a person has done. Also, the Qur'an does not affirm the erroneous belief that the mustard seed is the smallest of all seeds.

Al-Qur'an 34:3 The Unbelievers say, "Never to us will come the Hour". Say, "Nay! But most surely, by my Lord, it will come upon you;- by Him Who knows the unseen,-from Whom is not hidden the least little atom in the heavens or on earth: Nor is there anything less than that, or greater, but is in the Record Perspicuous

And in case, one did not get the point, the Qur'an makes this matter very clear. Your every deed will be accounted for, down to the weight of a mustard seed and an atom, which were at that time what the people perceived to be the smallest seed and smallest element. But the Qur'an also adds the phrase "and ANYTHING LESS than" the mustard seed or the atom. By saying such, the Qur'an conveyed its message to the audience in terms that they understood and it eludes the criticism that the Bible faces today.

This is but a few items. The three books I have written, "There Is No Trinity," "Jesus (pbuh) Was Not Crucified," and "The Jewish Torah is Not the Words of God," are more thorough explanations of corrections made by the Qur'an on very crucial issues. They deal with the contrasting stories of Moses' (pbuh) request to see God, Noah (pbuh) and the flood, the story of Joseph (pbuh), Abraham (pbuh) and his visit with the angels, the Sacrificial Son, Moses' (pbuh) plague on the Egyptians, Aaron (pbuh) and the golden calf, the birth of Jesus (pbuh), the alleged crucifixion of Jesus (pbuh), the apotheosis of Jesus (pbuh), the vilification of the Prophets of God, the character of GOD and creation. In ever instances, the Qur'an corrects the Christian and Jewish scriptures. This is why the Qur'an asks them to bring what they claim to be the originals, because when it is compared to the Qur'an, the validity of the Qur'an is only strengthened.

THE ALLEGATIONS OF PLAGIARISM IN PERSPECTIVE

In respect to the allegation that Prophet Muhammad (pbuh) or his cohorts wrote the Qur'an by plagiarizing other texts, it should be laughable by now. Some critics maintain that Prophet Muhammad (pbuh) copied Greek philosophers who formulated hypotheses on the movement of the celestial bodies in the universe. This only compounds their problem.

The critics of the Qur'an wish to individualize each piece of evidence and marginalize the miracles of the Qur'an. It is possible to say that Prophet Muhammad (pbuh) guessed one or two things accurately. But when you view the Qur'an's miracles collectively, the critics have no leg to stand upon. Let's put their allegations in perspective.

1400 years ago, an illiterate man, in an illiterate society compiled a book, single-handedly or with a group, that has affected the lives of billions upon billions of people. He learned about all the guesses of Greek philosophers on science, and he, by chance, pick ALL THE RIGHT ANSWERS. He had one Bible translated into Arabic, where he had someone read the entire Bible to him. He selected sections of the Bible to discuss and CORRECTED EVERY SELECTION HE CHOSE, without any knowledge or schooling on any of the subjects he chose. Then he burned or buried the Bible to leave no trace of it. I say this because no Arabic Bible existed at the time of the Prophet. So he had to find a person who spoke Aramaic, Hebrew, Greek and Arabic and they read it to him. Remember, all of this took place in a time when literacy was abnormal. In this very day, there are but a handful of people who are qualified to do such a job, but Prophet Muhammad (pbuh) was extremely lucky. He also had these translators read him Jewish folklore, which he suggested were actual true stories made into folklore. Again an Aramaic, Greek and Hebrew speaking person was needed for the job. And this scenario continues.

Supposedly, Prophet Muhammad (pbuh) then excavated the caves and pyramids of Egypt, where he found hieroglyphic writings AND he conveniently found the Rosetta Stone used to translate them. He translated them all by himself. Then he closed the pyramids back up to be rediscovered in modern times. Prophet Muhammad (pbuh) also made grand predictions that could have stifled the religion in its infancy, but "LUCKILY" the prophecies were fulfilled. And we cannot forget that he stated facts of biology, oceanography, zoology, physiology, astronomy, physics, geology, geography, botany and embryology. So Prophet Muhammad (pbuh) made the first telescope, the first microscope and he was the first to travel into outer space in his self-made space shuttle. He made his own scuba gear and he was the first to split an atom. Amazingly, he kept all this equipment a secret, which he apparently buried or destroyed. The person who can do all these things is indeed a miracle man.

Consider the allegations of plagiarism again. What is so interesting about the claims that Prophet Muhammad (pbuh) copied the works of Greek scientists is that he omitted all of their errors. Every single verse dealing with science is fact, unlike the Greek scientists' proclamations. Even if Prophet Muhammad (pbuh) copied the Greeks and if he copied the Bible, he must have been divinely guided to leave out the hundreds of mistakes and only copy the truth. Oh yeah, Prophet Muhammad (pbuh) couldn't read or write, which makes this even more miraculous. Who would find the assertions of AN ILLITERATE man on the universe unremarkable, considering that he had to NO EQUIPMENT and in fact, he DID NO RESEARCH and ALL his assertions are TRUE? Where did he get the courage and audacity to say, this is absolutely true, when he had not researched a thing?

Realistically no man, no group of men could have known all these items of science and religion were completely and utterly true. It is impossible that someone 1400 years ago knew all these things. This is why the Qur'an is a miracle. It is a miracle that can be affirm today and every day we live.

7:204 When the Qur'an is read, listen to it with attention, and hold your peace: that ye may receive Mercy.

As there are numerous names to describe ALLAH, there are also a multitude of names used for the Qur'an. It is called noble, the word, light, guidance, wisdom, a blessing and so on. But I think the three which best define the Qur'an are "The Glad Tidings (Bashir, 41:4)," "The Warning (Nadhir, 41:1)" and "The Reminder (Dhikr, 21:50)." It gives man the path to righteousness and the good news of its rewards and it warns of the penalties of following the path of iniquity. Then the Qur'an reminds man repeatedly of his path to reward or punishment.

39:23 Allah has revealed (from time to time) the most beautiful Message in the form of a Book, consistent with itself, (yet) repeating (its teaching in various aspects).

A verse of the Qur'an is called an ayah. Ayah also means a sign. These signs, like the secrets of science in the Qur'an are, to gain acceptance from man of this "most beautiful message." Every story of history, every analogy, every parable, every word of every verse is for this purpose. Because these verses articulate this message through rhyme, the Qur'an is easy to understand and remember, as chapter 54 suggests. (The translations of the Qur'an are something a bit different. It was rather difficult for me to understand the messages of the Qur'an, when I first read it, because the translator used words that are not spoken in everyday language. So I bought audio CDs and different translations to better understand the Qur'an). But this message is not received by everyone. To those who are excited and ignited by truth, the Qur'an is of stupendous importance, but to others, the truth hurts. When the truth of the Qur'an is revealed to them, it strengthens their resistance to Islam. They do not wish to give up their bad deeds which bring them success in this life for the true success which lasts forever.

17:82 We send down (stage by stage) in the Qur'an that which is a healing and a mercy to those who believe: to the unjust it causes nothing but loss after loss.

22:72 When Our Clear Signs are rehearsed to them, thou wilt notice a denial on the faces of the Unbelievers! they nearly attack with violence those who rehearse Our Signs to them. Say, "Shall I tell you of something (far) worse than these Signs? It is the Fire (of Hell)! Allah has promised it to the Unbelievers! and evil is that destination!"

WHAT ABOUT DINOSAURS?

MANKIND

One time in discussions with a group of atheists, I mentioned some of the things that I have addressed in this book about the accuracy of the Qur'an in terms of science and one person responded, "Well, why does not the Qur'an mention dinosaurs?" My response was that the phone book is accurate, so too is a cookbook, yet neither of them describe dinosaurs. This is because they are very concentrated books specifically gear to inform on a certain topic. The Qur'an too is a very concentrated book. It's not a "once upon a time" type storybook, yet it has stories. It is not a history book, yet it has tells about phases of history. It is not a science book, yet it has aspects of science in it. It is not a book of poetry, yet its verses are poetic.

The Qur'an uses all these devises for an ultimate goal, which is to guide man on a straight path to GOD. Though dinosaurs may be important to you and somehow impact your life, their discovery is not what may guide man to GOD. I asked, "If you found that the Qur'an spoke of dinosaurs, would you believe in it? I doubt it, especially considering that Prophet Muhammad (pbuh) made countless assertions in the Qur'an that he couldn't possibly have known of, and in light of this you stand firmly opposed to him." (The Qur'an does hint at how God can end man's existence from a falling meteor, asteroid, or comet in 34:9, which is how the dinosaur is said to have been extinguished from the earth.)

Also, to include every element and animal that exists or existed on earth would be a pretty large volume and that would most certainly overshadow the intended message, which is to instruct mankind on the method to get to GOD. The Qur'an is best in this area, not documenting the history of earth, how the earth was formed, or how man was formed. If you read the Qur'an you will notice, that there is not one chapter solely dedicated to these subjects. These subjects are scattered throughout the Qur'an as road signs that lead to the path to God. As a phonebook gives you direction to further truth, so too does the Qur'an mention science and history or geography, then it asks you to research the topic. Ask someone who is an expert in the field and you will confirm what is in the Qur'an.

ABROGATION?

2:106 None of Our revelations do We abrogate or cause to be forgotten, but We substitute something better or similar. Knowest thou not that Allah Hath power over all things?

Unfortunately, many Muslims think that this verse indicates that the Qur'an has verses which correct other Quranic verses, when in fact the context is in reference to past revelations and the way they are handled or mishandled by some "People of the Book." So the Qur'an abrogates past revelations, not itself. "People of the Book" are generally viewed as Jews and Christians and perhaps any other group who uses scripture as their authority. The abrogation or replacement of revelation is in congruency with the situation of a people of a specific time. In the Bible, Jesus (pbuh) abrogated a few of the laws of Moses to correct the Jews' lost of compassion within their pursuit of justice and brotherhood. When circumstances change, rules are changed. They are loosen or stricken in order to correct a problem. However the Qur'an is not like that. It contains no inconsistencies (4:82), it verses are perfected (11:1).

An example of a verse cited by Muslims as a abrogated verse might be when the Qur'an first says don't come to pray while intoxicated (4:43) and it also says don't drink intoxicants (5:90). This is not an abrogation. An abrogation cancels or puts an end to something. If I said don't drive fast in a residential district and I also say don't speed, I am not putting an end to the rule against driving fast in the residential district. The latter statement included my former statement. This is a counter-distinction, not an abrogation. As Gary Miller said, if we chose not to use distinction in making laws, man could alleviate all his rules and replace them with the word "BEHAVE." Behave might includes all the rules, but specifications are necessary.

It is no coincidence that literacy is at an all time high in the history of man. Mass communication exists. Telephones, cell phones, text messages exist. The internet exists, where you can communicate with someone in China in a matter of seconds. The last revelation of God is given in this time, in order to reach the whole of mankind. Prophets were formerly sent to one group of people, but the last prophet and the last message is to the whole of mankind (7:158). How fitting for it to still exist in its original form in such a day and age. And in a language which makes its text and message practically impossible to be erased. It was revealed in a time when memorization was the prevailing method for preservation. In addition to Prophet Muhammad's (pbuh) continuous recitation to the angel to keep its preservation intact, was the innumerous Muslims who memorized the Qur'an as well. And God made it an obligation to remember and recite parts of the Qur'an five times a day. This book has to be the most guarded book in the history of mankind.

The success of the internet is largely based upon people's need to have others read their point of view. To have people to accept and adopt, consider, understand or at least respect their ideas is the goal. Thus discussion of religion is only natural.

A CLOSER LOOK AT ISLAM

It has been established that the unseen GOD has given revelation to man. The spiritual beings called angels are those who carry out God's will to mankind. Angels are spirits which appear to human beings in order to deliver God's message. The Qur'an describes another spiritual being along with angels called jinn. Neither jinns nor angels have a gender as drawings, paintings and other depictions suggests (43:19). And angels obey God totally and completely (2:30), but the jinn similar to man has free will. The Qur'an says men and jinn could both try to create a book like the Qur'an and they could not do it (17:88). Noticeably the angels are not mentioned in this conspiracy because of their nature, but it is obvious that the jinn has free will to sin. However, jinns' free will is very limited in relation to man. Where angels send revelation and invite man to righteousness, the jinn can invite man to sin. They are called whisperers (114:4). Whereas some religions depict satan as a fallen angel, Islam portrays satan as a jinn, who chose to disobey God and lure man away from the straight path of God. Perhaps it is no coincidence that the Qur'an verse 66:6 more adamantly asserts that angels CANNOT disobey God. This seems to be in responsible to the Christian understanding that satan was a rebellious angel. Also in Islam, no one and nothing has the capacity to compete with God. Satan is not God's enemy, but man's avowed enemy (12:5) and man is superior to the influence of satan. Of course, it is quite easy for man to conquer his foe, simply by employing his morals and overcoming his urge for indulgences in things immoral.

16:98 When thou dost read the Qur'an, seek Allah's protection from Satan the rejected one.

16:99 No authority has he over those who believe and put their trust in their Lord.

16:100 His authority is over those only, who take him as patron and who join partners with Allah.

The Qur'an says ALLAH created man by his act of will. This is precisely how God performed creation and all that he intends. He wills things into existence. He is not like a carpenter or sculptor who is in the midst of his creation hammering and nailing things together. He is not in the scheme of things. GOD merely says "BE" and His creation begins to take form. And man was created in the same manner (2:117).

The Qur'an says after the creation of the father of the human race, ADAM, God commanded the angels to bow before ADAM and all of them bowed except satan (shaitan in Arabic, meaning to separate) or iblis (meaning frustrated) (2:34). We find in another chapter that the reason that iblis did not bow was because he was not an angel, but a jinn who was of the ranks of the angels and he felt himself superior to man (18:50). So he was unwilling to humble himself towards a being he felt superior to. God put him out of the ranks of the angels and iblis vowed to sway man from the path of righteousness. For this reason, man is advised to seek refuge from satan (23:97-98). Yet satan seized an opportunity with Adam and his wife (The name, Eve, is not in the Qur'an).

Though they were given an abundance of food in Paradise , he persuaded them both to eat from a tree which God forbade them from approaching. Consequently, Adam and his wife felt the guilt of disobedience of God. They both repented and GOD forgave them. However, they and their descendants were to earn their place in paradise (2:35-39). Apparently God had already decreed that man was to be ruler representing God on earth (2:30) and their sin expedited the process.

WHY ISLAM?

One of the proofs of Islam validity to me was that Adam was a prophet of God. ALLAH "taught ADAM the names of all things" (2:31) and "Adam learned from his Lord words of inspiration" (2:37). Ranked amongst the Prophets of God (3:33), Adam (pbuh) was the first human being and the first Prophet, ever. How fitting is it that God would reveal his message to the first human being? He is vilified and fault is place upon him and his wife's shoulders for the fall of mankind in other religions, but in Islam they makes a great comeback from their error and Adam (pbuh) is the first representative of God to mankind. This highlights a fundamental difference between Islam and other religions.

Islam maintains that prophets were not sent to one specific group of people but that prophets were sent to every people on earth. This would explain the different religions with similar moral codes and standards. It would also explain the similar figures in different religions all over the world. The prophets came to a specific group and through time the message was altered into tribal, racial or ethnic religions. And some religions turned their attention away from God and focused on his representative as the one worthy of worship and praise. Though they are different, their similarities are due to a common source, GOD. If Adam (pbuh) was a prophet, what was the message that he preached? I would say that Adam preached the exact same message that every prophet taught, SUBMISSION TO THE WILL OF GOD. Is this not the message and goal of every person of faith? What person of any faith would shun submission to the will of God?

In my quest to find the true religion, I considered that there are 6.8 billion people on earth and an estimated 100 billion more who have lived on earth. Whatever the religion, it must be able to encompass the 6.8 billion of the present and the countless others that inhabited the earth. Christianity was founded 2000 years ago. Buddhism was founded 2600 years ago. Judaism is said to begin with the covenant between God and Abraham (pbuh) about 4000 years ago. Hinduism is believed to have begun around 3500 years ago. However Hindu and Hinduism originated as terms to describe people who lived in the Indian subcontinent near the Indus River, called Sindhu. Their belief systems is more accurately called "Sanatan Dharma" meaning eternal teaching. This suggests that it has always existed to be taught to man. Though its name may denote a universal religion, its practitioners are almost exclusively from the Indian continent from which the religion gets its name. And the religion is not a proselytizing religion, so the perpetual exclusivity of this faith seems inevitable. Though Islam is commonly believed to have come into existence 1400 years ago with the Prophet Muhammad (pbuh), it did not. As the name "Sanatan Dharma" express eternal teachings, so too does the name Islam. It means submission to the will of God.

42:13 The same religion has He established for you as that which He enjoined on Noah - the which We have sent by inspiration to thee - and that which We enjoined on Abraham, Moses, and Jesus (pbuh). Namely, that ye should remain steadfast in religion, and make no divisions therein: to those who worship other things than Allah, hard is the (way) to which thou callest them. Allah chooses to Himself those whom He pleases, and guides to Himself those who turn (to Him).

42:14 And they became divided only after Knowledge reached them,- through selfish envy as between themselves. Moses, Abraham, Noah and Jesus (pbut) have no record of an expressed religion, yet they all received revelation from God.

If you asked them, "what is the way to God?" they all would tell you to do what God has given you to do. Do not follow your own will, but the will of God. This is completely, ISLAM. If someone asked Jesus, Moses or Abraham (pbut) "what is your religion?" I doubt that they would say Judaism, but rather they would say a total submission to the will of God. Who would disagree with me? The Qur'an makes specific note of the religion of Abraham (pbuh).

3.65 Ye People of the Book! Why dispute ye about Abraham, when the Law and the Gospel Were not revealed till after him? Have ye no understanding?

3.66 Ah! Ye are those who fell to disputing (Even) in matters of which ye had some knowledge! but why dispute ye in matters of which ye have no knowledge? It is Allah Who knows, and ye who know not!

3.67 Abraham was not a Jew nor yet a Christian; but he was true in Faith, and bowed his will to Allah's (Which is Islam), and he joined not gods with Allah.

Abraham (pbuh) is the patriarch from whom all three great monotheistic religions are based, but the Qur'an asserts that he could only have been a practitioner of Islam, because the Torah and the Gospels were not written until after he was on this earth. Both Abraham (pbuh) and Moses (pbuh) were given laws and guidelines from God to follow and to have their people follow. When the people adhered to the laws, they became submitters to the will of God. Jesus (pbuh) also practiced and taught total submission to God's laws, i.e. submission to GOD's will, which in at least one instance was contrary to Jesus' (pbuh) will. As Jesus (pbuh) prayed to be spared from the crucifixion, he ended his pray with these words, "not as I will, but as thy (God) wills" (Matt. 26:39).

He says more specifically, "I have come down from heaven, not to do My own will, but the will of Him who sent Me" (John 6:38). Jesus (pbuh) is forsaking his own will and submitting to the will God. He is practicing ISLAM. Perhaps it is no coincidence that Jesus (pbuh) greeted and prayed as Muslims do today (John 20:2, Matt. 26:39). Peace be unto you or As Salamu Alaikum is the universal greeting for Muslims around the world. Also Jesus (pbuh) gave his prayer to God with his head touching the ground as Muslims do 5 times a day.

A CLOSER LOOK AT ISLAM

22:18 Seest thou not that to Allah bow down in worship all things that are in the heavens and on earth,- the sun, the moon, the stars; the hills, the trees, the animals; and a great number among mankind?

When pondering the meaning of the word "Islam," we find that submission to God is not simply a teaching or a religion. It is an action. An action that any and everything can do. It does not require Prophet Muhammad's (pbuh) presence or the presence of the Qur'an. So not only does Islam encompass ever person who lives or has ever lived, but it includes everything that every existed, as well. Everything besides ALLAH is his creation and every single one of God's creations does or will submit to the will of ALLAH. In other words, it does what God wants it to do. Without even delving into the particulars of Islam, I found this quality of uniqueness to be exclusively possessed and expressed in Islam. It encompasses every person ever born and everything that has ever existed. Can a tree be a Buddhist? Can the earth be Hindus? Yet, the entire galaxy is in submission to the will of God. A cow, a gnat, everything is in a state of Islam.

Judaism comes from the name Judah and it means "to praise God," so a Jew is one who praises God. A Muslim submits to God and by submitting to God, he is praising God. In like manner, the Qur'an says:

17:44 The seven heavens and the earth, and all beings therein, declare His glory: there is not a thing but celebrates His praise; And yet ye understand not how they declare His glory! Verily He is Oft-Forbear, Most Forgiving!

Everything in the universe praises and glorifies God. The skeptic might ask, how so? Their submission to the laws he has set is a declaration of the majesty of God. The definition of Islam encompasses the definition of Judaism. The same is true for Buddhism. Buddha literally means the enlightened or awakened one. You are enlightened, awakened and made whole when you realize that this world is a test and you must submit to God to pass this test. The Sanatan Dharma or eternal teaching in Islam is not eternal. Only God is eternal, having no beginning or ending. The religion of submission began not with God, but when God created something to submit. And it was not just for mankind but for everything God has created. Christianity is the teaching of Christ (pbuh). It has been shown that the true teaching of Christ (pbuh) is Islam, submission to God. He himself practiced Islam. But the concept of love in Christianity is defined in Islam as beneficence and mercy for all creation and a special love for those who are righteous. The Greek word for someone who is "born again" is gennatha anothen. It literally means generated from above. Jesus (pbuh) said you can't see the kingdom of God unless you are "generated from above" (John 3:3) meaning you have the understanding of righteousness given to you by God. When you understand that righteousness is ultimately from God, you submit to the will of God.

The Jews, before and during the life of Jesus (pbuh), thought the Messiah (translated Christ) would lead them to victory over the Roman Empire. Obviously their understanding of the prophecies of Messiah was inaccurate, because the Roman oppression ended without help from the Messiah. And the Jews are still waiting for this Messiah to come. But their Messiah has already come and most of them missed him. They reject Jesus (pbuh) as the Messiah, because he preached of a kingdom in heaven, not the Jewish kingdom of earth. If you read the Jewish Torah you will find a complete neglect of the subject of heaven and the afterlife. What you will find are books dedicated solely to the pursuit of material gain. To a people with such a mentality, God Almighty would most certainly send a prophet who focuses on the hereafter. As the Qur'an says Jesus (pbuh) was their Messiah, translated Christ.

3:45 Behold! the angels said: "O Mary! Allah giveth thee glad tidings of a Word from Him: his name will be Christ Jesus (pbuh), the son of Mary, held in honour in this world and the Hereafter and of (the company of) those nearest to Allah

If this is true, the next step in Judaism is Christianity, which is to follow the teaching of Jesus (pbuh). Of course, some Jews revile Jesus (pbuh) or at least discredit him as the Messiah, but many rabbis have admitted that his actual teachings, as reported in the gospels, are not grounds for blasphemy in Judaism. In fact, Christianity began as a sect of Judaism, which was really Jews who accepted Jesus (pbuh) as the Messiah. Jesus (pbuh) did not bring them a new religion, but reformation to what they already had. I believe if they look into the teachings of their own scripture as Jesus (pbuh) recommended, they would find that they should have been listening to him.

Christians are to follow the teachings of Jesus (pbuh). If they do so to the exclusion any other writer of the New Testament, they would find themselves in very close relations to ISLAM. Christianity's doctrines of the Original Sin, Atonement and Trinity have no basis in the words of the Old Testament or the words of Jesus (pbuh). In the gospels, Jesus preaches the adherence to the will of God, through the laws of Moses (pbut). However, his criticism of the Jews of his day provoked violence against him. In a situation where your audience becomes your enemy, it is quite difficult to fully convey your message. Jesus (pbuh), aware of the plots to kill him, warned of another who would come after him to lead mankind into all truth, the Comforter. This Comforter was the same prophet who Moses (pbuh) spoke of as a prophet like himself (Deut. 18:18).

At the time of John the Baptist (pbuh), the Jews were awaiting three prophets, Elijah (pbuh), the Messiah (pbuh) and "that prophet" (John 1:21). Jesus says John was Elijah (Matt. 11:12-14) and Jesus (pbut) was the Messiah (John 4:25-26), so "that prophet" had not come yet. That prophet is the Comforter. This is not the time to debate whether the Comforter was the Holy Spirit or not or whether Jesus (pbuh) was the prophet like Moses (pbuh). I have discussed these topics in my book entitled "Jesus (pbuh) Was Not Crucified." For now, I will say that if you insist that the Holy Spirit was the Comforter and Jesus (pbuh) was the prophet like Moses (pbuh), that does not account for "that prophet." That prophet was the last prophet, Muhammad (pbuh) . He guided man into all truth. The Qur'an confirms that Jesus (pbuh) prophesied about the coming of Muhammad (pbuh), calling him by a shorten version of his name, Ahmad (i.e. Robert and Bob).

61:6 And remember, Jesus (pbuh), the son of Mary, said: "O Children of Israel! I am the messenger of Allah (sent) to you, confirming the Law (which came) before me, and giving Glad Tidings of a Messenger to come after me, whose name shall be Ahmad."

The belief in karma is held by those of the Buddhist and Hindus faith. The general principal of karma, you reap what you sow, is also shared by Muslims. But the idea that your behavior in this world leads to a reincarnation in which you are prosperous or denigrated is what a Muslim would have problems with. This view of time is circular. It means that right now everyone is placed in a position in life which they have ordained for themselves by their previous life. One who believes in karma might say that those who live in poverty, those who are helpless, diseased, starving or oppressed deserve their fate. Buddhists and Hindus consider these conditions to be like a curse for your bad deeds. And those who would lead righteous lives will die and return even more prosperous than before. So people reincarnate with the same soul but different bodies. Those who are weak in this world can be virtuous and gain ground for their next life, but they can also fall deeper into despair and even be reborn as animals or insects.

When the general rule of karma is stretched in this way, one can view the weak, the disabled as someone who deserves his affliction. This kind of thinking is what fueled the caste system of Hinduism, from which Buddhism came. The caste system is a system enforced by law and its common practice is to discriminate between people based on race, class and economic status. It declares one group superior to another based upon these criteria and the notion that the law of karma has placed each person in their role of master or servant.

The Jewish Torah similarly ostracizes the disabled (Lev.21:16-23). It is no coincidence that both Hinduism and Judaism maintain that a person is born special or not special, chosen or not and neither faith is a proselytizing religion. The Qur'an however commands Muslims to help those who are in need. The Muslim does not see adversity as retribution, but as a test. Those who suffer from hunger, poverty or any other problem are presented with a trial from God for them and for every Muslim. The afflicted are to be patient. They are to persevere and strive to be the best and most righteous that they can be according to their circumstances. And the Muslim is obliged to help with his money, his time, his effort and all that he can share to aid those are unable to help themselves.

In Islam every soul will taste death once, and when it comes to death man always wants a second chance (23:99-100). The belief in karma and reincarnation is but a manifestation of man's fear of death. This doctrine eases the anxiety, but it won't cause man to drastically change and become moral, because he is always provided another chance. Everyday people procrastinate with respect to living healthy or living righteous because they think, "there is always tomorrow." When they become sick or they get older is when they come to the reality that there may not be a tomorrow. Belief in karma through reincarnation always provides that tomorrow, so there is no rush to live right, to eat right, and to drink right. The Qur'an warns against this kind of thinking. The Muslim realizes that everyday could be his last, so he should capitalize on every moment to be righteous. Thus Islam calls for an abrupt change in your morality, in your remembrance of God, and in your need to be righteous and your wish to teach others to be righteous.

Islam is the completion and conclusion of these faiths. For the Jew, it is Judaism made universal. For the Christian, Islam is the reintroduction of it Jewish roots and a correction to the misunderstanding of God's nature and man's atonement for sin. Even to the atheist, Islam finishes their claim "that there is no God" with the words "except ALLAH." Unlike other scriptures and other prophets, the Qur'an and Prophet Muhammad (pbuh) declare themselves to be the end of the link between God and man (33:40). If others do not proclaim to be the seal of the communication with God, then the door is always open for a prophet and or a scripture to follow. Many people of different faiths believe their scripture to be the final revelation, yet the book itself makes no such claim. Would you assume that this is my last book, if I don't say that it is?

THE PURPOSE OF LIFE

The Qur'an warns man not to waste his life in past times and amusement (53:61), when he knows full well that there is a reason and a purpose for his life. Man has been searching for the purpose of life since his inception. But if you ask someone what is the purpose of life, you will get a plethora of answers. I was in a forum full of non-Muslims and the topic came up, what is the purpose of life? I gave the response of the Qur'an, first without explanation.

51.56 I have only created Jinns and men, that they may serve (or worship) Me.

I knew that this Quranic verses would be provocative, because at first glance, it presents God as an egotistical being in need of gratification or it would seem to present him as a slave master. This is often the mistake made by those who read a portion of the Qur'an and make an assertion without reading further. Since the Qur'an was written in segments, the total message of a topic will be understood when you read all of the Qur'an. The Qur'an itself says there are ambiguous verses and unambiguous verses in it. If you read the unambiguous verses with those that are ambiguous, you will understand the point being made. So if you read this verse, you might assume that man's life is predestined, because God made men and jinn to worship and serve him. It should be first noted that God does know all things, but beforehand knowledge of an event does not mean you ordain the situation to happen that way. I know that I will die one day, but that does not mean that I will be responsible for my death. Nonetheless, we already know from the Qur'an that both, jinn and men have free will. So this clarifies one possible understanding of the verse. But what does it mean to worship Almighty God?

The people I was corresponding with said the purpose of life was, "To love one another, to live happily and in prosperity, to be moral, to distinguishing right from wrong and conveying this to others, to connect with other people in love and in friendship, and to leave a legacy." I told them that these are all forms of worship and service to ALLAH, though none of these things benefit God in the least. In Islam, everything that you do that is not a sin is a form of worship to God. Therefore being a good father, being a good husband or a good friend is a form of worshipping ALLAH. Your purpose in life to serve God is, in fact, a plan for you and everyone you encounter to live a better life in this world and ultimately the hereafter.

18:7 That which is on earth we have made but as a glittering show for the earth, in order that We may test them - as to which of them are best in conduct.

So every human being's purpose on earth is to serve God by being righteous in order to pass life's test. And ultimately to do good for the sake of good as God does. When your parents taught you to be well-mannered as a child, at first you do it because it was incumbent on you. As you get older, you realize that people warm to you because you are well-mannered. Soon after, you are well-mannered because it's the right thing to do. Think about someone who sins, they don't sin in order to be punished by God. But because they are accustomed to sinning, it is second nature. Muslims are trying to transcend the mode of righteousness for a reward and make good deeds their second nature. This would differentiate someone from being a good person and someone who is just well-behaved.

God creates every human being in a state of Islam, as a Muslim. Man may be taught and steered away from Islam, but every child born is a Muslim. This is why the Qur'an says that a sinner will taste a small sample of punishment in this world before the real punishment after death, in order for him to RETURN (32:21). This return is in respect to every person being a Muslim at birth. Often times, you will see a person who has converted to Islam as being a "revert." This is a reference to everyone being born in a state of submission to God. Muslims use the words "servant" and "submission" to describe their obedience to God, though these words sometimes garner some negative connotation when it is not appropriate.

"Slavery to God, then, is the exact opposite of enslavement in the human sense. In the latter it means that the master exploit's the slave's power. In the former, however, it is quite the contrary: it is the master who bestows endless gifts on his slave and invests him with infinite perfections." (Dr. Mostafa Mahmoud, "Dialogue with an Atheist")

A MUSLIM AND A MU'MIN

3:19 The Religion before Allah is Islam (submission to His Will). Nor did the People of the Book dissent therefrom except through envy of each other, after knowledge had come to them. But if any deny the Signs of Allah, Allah is swift in calling to account.

3:20 So if they dispute with thee, say: "I have submitted My whole self to Allah and so have those who follow me." And say to the People of the Book and to those who are unlearned: "Do ye (also) submit yourselves?" If they do, they are in right guidance, but if they turn back, Thy duty is to convey the Message; and in Allah's sight are (all) His servants.

These verses are dictated to Prophet Muhammad (pbuh) to exclaim that the only religion in the sight of God is submission to the will of God and if anyone seeks to submit to God they will be successful. The Qur'an says ALLAH perfected and chose submission to his will as the religion for man (5:3). Some might say that socialism, capitalism, or communism is the best system in the world, but the Qur'an says submission to God is the best system because it is submission to the being that made all the rules. This submission to God is superior to every other -ism (48:28, 9:33, 61:9). So someone who abides by the codes of God should be the best of people (3:110). People of every faith believe that God's code of law is best. The question is which is the right code of God? What is the "true" will of God? The true will of God is contained in the true word of God, the Qur'an. Yet the Qur'an says there were

Muslims around before the Qur'an was revealed (28:52-53). After hearing the Qur'an, these people realized that they were Muslims all along. Jews and Christians are among those who will enter Paradise, if their intentions were to submit to the will of God.

2:62 Those who believe (in the Qur'an), and those who follow the Jewish (scriptures), and the Christians and the Sabians, any who believe in Allah and the Last Day, and work righteousness, shall have their reward with their Lord; on them shall be no fear, nor shall they grieve.

This verse and 5:69, just like it, show another great aspect of Islam. The label you give yourself does not negate your actions and intentions. I was for a long time puzzled by these verses. I could not understand why those who did not believe in Islam were spoken of as going to Paradise, especially considering that some groups of Jews and Christians are admonished in the Qur'an for their beliefs and practices. I always knew that there was a distinction between a Muslim and a Mu'min, but as I was researching for this book, I finally understand what the difference is.

When you look at Surah 2:62 and 5:69, you see that the Qur'an is speaking of several different groups, those who believe, those who follow the Jewish scripture, the Christians, the Sabians and most importantly ANYONE ELSE who believes in God. Anyone else also means everyone else. This is to further emphasize that any person of any religion or non-religion is included in this verse. Anyone who believes in ALLAH, THE DAY Of JUDGEMENT AND DOES GOOD DEEDS IS PROMISED NO FEAR OR GRIEF. As mentioned earlier in this book, man is already wired for these particular things. He is geared to worship God. His moral conscience is implanted in him (30:30), which includes a sense of justice and the pursuit of justice. As the Qur'an is saying, the criterion for reward from God is given to man naturally. The Qur'an and Prophet Muhammad (pbuh) are not necessary for you to believe in God, do good things and believe in final justice from that God.

6:151 Say: "Come, I will rehearse what Allah hath (really) prohibited you from": Join not anything as equal with Him; be good to your parents; kill not your children on a plea of want;- We provide sustenance for you and for them;- come not nigh to shameful deeds. Whether open or secret; take not life, which Allah hath made sacred, except by way of justice and law: thus doth He command you, that ye may learn wisdom.

6:152 And come not nigh to the orphan's property, except to improve it, until he attain the age of full strength; give measure and weight with (full) justice;- no burden do We place on any soul, but that which it can bear;- whenever ye speak, speak justly, even if a near relative is concerned; and fulfill the covenant of Allah: thus doth He command you, that ye may remember.

6:153 Verily, this is My way, leading straight: follow it: follow not (other) paths: they will scatter you about from His (great) path: thus doth He command you, that ye may be righteous.

These verses above can be accepted by almost every person on the face of the earth. These rules, like the gist of the Ten Commandments, are all laws which all civilized people agree on. Most people believe in God. Even polytheists have a supreme God. It is universally agreed upon that it is unacceptable to steal, lie, murder, commit adultery, be jealous or envious of others, and it is best to honor your parents. And that violation of these rules bears consequences. Belief in these things makes you a person who submits to the will of God. But there are levels and degrees to which man is ranked.

3:110 Ye are the best of peoples, evolved for mankind, enjoining what is right, forbidding what is wrong, and believing in Allah. If only the People of the Book had faith, it were best for them.

And the Qur'an speaks of some wandering Arabs who say they are "believers." But Prophet Muhammad (pbuh) is made to correct them. He says no, you are not believers, YET.

49:14 The desert Arabs say, "We believe." Say, "Ye have no faith; but ye (only) say, 'We have submitted our wills to Allah,' For not yet has Faith entered your hearts. But if ye obey Allah and His Messenger, He will not belittle aught of your deeds: for Allah is Oft-Forgiving, Most Merciful."

It is apparent from this verse that there is a distinction between a Muslim, one who submits, and a Mu'min, one who believes. The annunciation that the people are "desert Arab" is to point out that they have not heard the truth from Prophet Muhammad (pbuh) until that point, so it is impossible for them to believe in him. And this is one of the criteria of being more than one who submits but one who believes. The Surah continues...

49:15 Only those are Believers who have believed in Allah and His Messenger, and have never since doubted, but have striven with their belongings and their persons in the Cause of Allah: Such are the sincere ones.

This and several other verses of the Qur'an lay out the definition of a believer.

Islam Is The Truth

1. Believe Muhammad (pbuh)

2. The strive with their possessions and their person

3. Sincere (49:15)

4. They feel a tremor when Qur'an is recited

5. Establish prayer (8:2-3)

6. Believe in the unseen

7. Believe in the Qur'an and previous scriptures (2:2-4)

8. Believe the last day

9. Believe in angels

10. Believe in pass messengers

11. Charity for poor, orphans, to free slaves, etc

12. Patient and persevering (2:177)

13. Stand firmly for justice, even if it's against your family or yourself (4:135)

None of these items are required to simply be one who submits to God. But the goal is for all to be a Mu'min. In the case of Dr. Gary Miller, when he read the Qur'an for the first time, he realized that he was a Muslim all along, now he is a believer.

28:53 And when it is recited to them, they say: "We believe therein, for it is the Truth from our Lord: indeed we have been Muslims (bowing to Allah's Will) from before this.

28:54 Twice will they be given their reward, for that they have persevered, that they avert Evil with Good, and that they spend (in charity) out of what We have given them.

The Muslim who becomes a Mu'min is granted twice the reward for his acceptance of the Qur'an and its contents. So for the Christians, the Jews, the Buddhists and everybody else, you are to now take the next step and become believers. The Qur'an says believers, Jews, Christians and Sabians who actually submit to God and do righteous deeds will go to Paradise . The point to be made is that ALLAH judges man by the scope of his knowledge. If a man be Christian, he is judged by the righteous standards of his faith. He does not judge him by the standards of Islam, if he has not been given the truth of Islam. If he is presented with the truth of Islam and he accepts it, he is a Mu'min, a believer and a Muslim. If he rejects the truth of Islam, he is a kafir or a disbeliever. That means that all non-Muslims are not kafir, only those who know Islam to be the truth and reject it are kafir.

Related to the word for believer, "Mu'min" is "iman." Iman is often translated as faith. Faith insinuates a belief in something without proof. This is not the definition of "iman." Iman means confirmation and acceptance of the truth. It is belief in something because you have proof. This is why the Mu'min does not doubt anymore (49:15). So a believer is not the best translation for Mu'min, but "someone with confirmation of the truth" may be more adequate. The Qur'an often speaks of "iman with certainty" (44:7, 45:4, 45:20), to illustrate that this is not faith but confirmation and understanding of the truth. All these verses cited speak of the Qur'an and its content as giving FURTHER proof to your belief in God. There is no such thing as certain faith. Certainty implies knowledge. And a person who is uncertain about God and their role in life, is not a disbeliever or kafir. The Qur'an makes a distinction between doing wrong out of ignorance (16:119, 27:84) and he who knowingly commits wrong deeds.

KAFIR

The Qur'an continuously speaks about making Islam clear to those listening to the message (9:115, 16:44, 16:64, 47:25). The people in error are not condemned in Islam until the matter is made clear to them. Only then are they responsible for adherence to the message. So, one is not a disbeliever until he knows the truth and rejects it.

Consider a man who lived his entire life in the jungle. If you ask him does he believe in democracy, he may answer you, but in reality he does not know whether he believes in it or not until you explain it to him and/or show it to him. When you explain democracy to him and expose him to democracy, then he can make a sound choice. If he accepts democracy as the best form of government, yet he does not wish to live by it, then he is someone who rejects the truth that he has recognized and acknowledged.

Kufr is the rejection or concealment of truth. It comes from the root KFR, meaning to cover up, or hide. That is to say that a kafir is a person who knows the truth as a Mu'min does, but they reject it anyway. They are the people who read up to this point and consider it to be sound, but go on rejecting Islam for whatever reason. I have been in debates with people who conclude the debate in full agreement with my stance and go on living life as if we had never spoken.

And because you know the truth and reject it, your acceptance of the truth at the time of your death is rejected. When you recognize the truth, you are to act on it immediately, not at your leisure or at a time of convenience for you. If you knew there was a treasure under your house, would you want until you are at the point of death to acquire it? Probably not.

4:18 Of no effect is the repentance of those who continue to do evil, until death faces one of them, and he says, "Now have I repented indeed," nor of those who die rejecting Faith: for them have We prepared a punishment most grievous.

A kafir might also include someone who has heard something of the truth, but refuse to investigate it. I am often puzzled by such people. In debate, I purposely make a provocative, but true remark to arouse their attention, yet they do not budge. (The Qur'an was revealed in a provocative manner. Prophet Muhammad (pbuh) is often instructed to say things like, "has the story of Moses reached you? Then he tells a bit of the life of Moses (pbuh). This is directed to an audience composed of Jews and Christians. It purposefully provokes their interest and the interest of onlookers. Those who believe Muhammad (pbuh) to be a prophet clamored at his every word, while those who do not believe or those who are doubtful, wait patiently to hear him "put his foot in his mouth" in front of the Jews and Christians.)

The titles of my books are made to be provocative. If you believe Jesus (pbuh) was God, how could you not skim through a book, which says the exact opposite? It was a practice of mine to pillage through books, articles, television shows, and web-sites looking for some allegations against Islam. If the allegations were true, then Islam is false. If I could find that the allegations were false, my iman would grow to more certainty. So the point is, even though you do not have full responsibility for knowing the truth and rejecting it, you are held responsible for neglecting to investigate whether something pertinent was true or false.

Also the Qur'an ridicules those who say that they follow a religion because they found their parents following that religion (2:170, 5:104). This doesn't prove anything, so this kind of justification of faith should be avoided by Muslims and non-Muslims. You are to search for truth or at least be able to explain the truthfulness of the beliefs that you have.

SIN

If a person living in a particular city or state does not accept the police department of that state as legitimate, he will eventually violate their laws. Even if he set his own system of law up, or followed someone else's system, he will inevitably come into conflict with laws of his state. The same is true with life. God sets the law. If you do not accept his authority, it is most likely that you will violate his rules. The Qur'an speaks of believers and disbelievers in general terms. If you believe in God and live righteously as he commands, you will be successful (2:3-5). If you do not believe in God and you live unrighteous, you will be amongst the loser (5:5). And everyone will bear the burden of their own sin, just as they reap the benefits of their own righteousness (6:164). Sin is the transgression of God's laws. Sin also includes persuading, enticing, assisting, allowing, or conforming to the transgression of God's law.

In Islam, sin is not human nature, but a part of human nature just as righteousness and morality is a part of human nature. Human nature is the free will to choose sin or righteousness. And each sin and righteous deed is rewarded in Islam. The righteous deed is rewarded several more times than the actual deed. But in Islam, the sin can either be forgiven or you are punished. Yet the punishment is not multiplied as is the reward for good deeds. Also the magnitude of your righteous action can negate some sins, but the reverse is not true. The acceptance of Islam and sincere repentance wipes your entire slate clean.

8:38 Say to the Unbelievers, if (now) they desist (from Unbelief), their past would be forgiven them; but if they persist, the punishment of those before them is already (a matter of warning for them).

This is truly a God of mercy. He gives you every opportunity to get in his good graces. All he wants from man is repentance (which only you and he know is sincere), a return to a path of righteousness and an amends for your sin, if it is possible. When man decides to repent, ALLAH aids him in his path to righteousness (8:53, 13:11).

In Islam, there are different degrees of sin (4:31). All sins are not equal. Assaulting someone and stealing someone's pencils are not treated the same. Also one sin does not make you a sinner, just as one righteous deed does not make you righteous. God is unlike man, in that he judges man as a whole for all his good and bad deeds. Man is apt to disregard all a person's good deeds, when he commits one sin. If a person lied to you once, he may be branded as a liar for the rest of his life. God, on the other hand, takes your every action and intention into account. Man also may absolve someone of all their bad deeds, if they do one good thing. Of course, this depends on the severity of the sin and the degree of benevolence in the righteous deed. But in general, if you continuously do bad things, a momentary lapse into the realm of righteousness does not erase you pass actions.

Islam also promotes archaeology and the investigation of history to sway man away from sin. The Qur'an on numerous occasions mentions mighty nations destroyed in the past because of their sins (30:42, 47:10). This is an appeal to man's sense of justice. He must know that his injustices will be punished in this world and/or the hereafter. Greater nations have crumbled before God because they were without GOD. God is asking man to learn from history and not repeat it. The Qur'an also differentiates natural phenomenon from punishment from God. When God destroys a town, he sends a DEFINITE ORDER, a warning from his prophets for the people to repent (17:16). Therefore calamities on earth are not punishment of God, unless they are specifically stated as such. It is no coincidence that man is more advanced than ever in terms of archaeology and technology. In this time, he is more equip to find the remnants of the past and learn from the sins of others.

LOVE OF ALLAH

The righteous and pious man is one who loves and fears ALLAH. The love and relationship that a Muslim has with ALLAH does not negate his duties to ALLAH, but they are personified by his fulfillment of these duties. The love of God is that of obedience to God. This is why the Qur'an says man should not love anything or anyone more than ALLAH and his messenger. This is obviously not the same love one has for his parents, his wife or his own child, but it is in reference to a man not allowing his parents, his wife, even his children to steer him away from his obedience to ALLAH.

9:24 Say: If it be that your fathers, your sons, your brothers, your mates, or your kindred; the wealth that ye have gained; the commerce in which ye fear a decline: or the dwellings in which ye delight - are dearer to you than Allah, or His Messenger, or the striving in His cause;- then wait until Allah brings about His decision: and Allah guides not the rebellious.

The word "rebellious" is indicative of a person who has strayed away from the straight path due to his loyalty to someone or something other than God. Though a person is not to ignore Allah's decree for his parent's sake, the Qur'an is very adamant about the love and respect that a person must given his parents (17:23-24), even if they wish to make him reject Islam.

31:14 And We have enjoined on man (to be good) to his parents: in travail upon travail did his mother bear him, and in years twain was his weaning. (hear the command), "Show gratitude to Me and to thy parents: to Me is (thy final) Goal.

31:15 "But if they strive to make thee join in worship with Me things of which thou hast no knowledge, obey them not; yet bear them company in this life with justice (and consideration), and follow the way of those who turn to me (in love): in the end the return of you all is to Me, and I will tell you the truth (and meaning) of all that ye did."

Christians are usually those who are most critical of Islam in terms of how Muslims relate to God. They might say that Islam is a religion, a list of rules to follow, whereas Christianity is a relationship with God. But in order to be a Christian or Christ-like one must follow a list of rules. You must do as Christ did and abstain from the things in which he abstained. Thus by definition, Christianity is a religion of do's and don'ts. Also, a relationship with God, however they might define it, does not negate a Christian's responsibility to God. The gospels of the Bible suggest that Jesus (pbuh)' definition of the love of God is in accordance with that of Islam.

Matthew 10:37 He that loveth his father or mother more than me is not worthy of me: and he that loveth son or daughter more than me is not worthy of me.

In this instance, Jesus (pbuh) is equating love with obedience. He wants his followers to put his authority above all others, because his authority is from God. The gospel of Luke obscures this meaning slightly, when it purports that Jesus (pbuh) commands his disciples to "hate" his family members (14:26). But Mark 3:33-35 connects the dots between Luke and Matthew.

When Jesus (pbuh) is beckoned to speak with his mother and brothers, he asks "who are my mother and my brothers?," yet he answers the question himself. He asserts that the crowd around him is actually his mother and brothers. He says that his family are those who "do the will of God." In Arabic, they would be called Muslims.

REMEMBER

How often do you remember God? You spend your day at work, at the computer, watching television, listening to the radio, playing sports, watching sports, reading the newspaper, reading books and exercising. But how much of your time is given to the one who made all those things possible? How often do you think about the one who has you in his knowledge at all times? Some people think of him in times of great pleasure and/or great pain. But perhaps we should think about God more often.

One manifestation of man's love and remembrance for ALLAH is prayer. Jews pray three times a day, four times on Sabbath and holidays and five times on Yom Kippur. In the Hebrew scripture, Daniel prayed three times a day (Daniel 6:11). So too did David (Psalms 55:18). Christianity is founded by and centered around a Jew, so Christianity is to be a continuous of its practices. Yet Christians have no set time to pray nor do they have a set amount of prayers to give God. In fact, they have no set words to say in prayer as there are two versions of how Jesus (pbuh) told them to pray (Matt. 6:9-13, Luke 11:2-4). If the Jews needed Jesus (pbuh) to come to them to make them more righteous, what might God prescribe them in terms of prayer? More prayers. And to those who have no uniformity in their prayer, what might be their prescription? A set time for prayer, a set number of prayers, set words of prayer and an epicenter for all participants to pray.

The Bible's depiction of the call to assemble prayer (Numbers 10:1-3), the removal of shoes before prayer (Exodus 3:5, Acts 7:33), the ablution before prayer (Exodus 40:31-32, Acts 21:26) and prayer in a singular direction (Daniel 6:10) are mirror images of the Muslim at prayer. And the prophets of the Bible prayed with their face to the ground, just as the Muslim is commanded to (7:206, 13:15, 17:107-109, 22:77, 38:24). The patriarch Abraham (pbuh) (Gen. 17:3), Abraham's servant (Gen. 24:52), Moses (pbuh) and Aaron (pbuh) (Numbers 16:22), Joshua (pbuh) (Joshua 5:14), Elijah (pbuh) (1Kings 18:42), and Jesus (pbuh) (Matthew 26:39), all prayed as Muslims do today.

The epicenter for Muslims' prayer is the Kaaba in Mecca . It is a small building built by the prophets of Islam, Abraham (Ibrahim) (pbuh) and Ishmael (Ismail) (pbuh). Around the world, Muslims face this Kaaba and bow their head to the ground in unison to the one true GOD, five times a day (17:107). This prayer is called Salat. It is a formal prayer which consists mainly of verses of the Qur'an, praises to ALLAH, requests for God to keep the person on the straight path, and blessing to the prophet and the Muslim community.

To inform everyone of the prayer, one Muslim calls the others to prayer with what is called the Adhan. This call is performed 5 times a day. The person who performs the Adhan is called a muezzin. The first person appointed to call the Adhan was a freed Ethiopian slave named Bilal. He was chosen because of his beautiful voice. A person's voice is something taken into consideration for them to become a muezzin because this person will be waking everyone up at dawn to chant the following:

Allah is the Greatest, Allah is the Greatest.

Allah is the Greatest, Allah is the Greatest.

I bear witness that there is no god but Allah.

I bear witness that there is no god but Allah.

I bear witness that Muhammad is the Messenger of Allah

I bear witness that Muhammad is the Messenger of Allah

Come to the Prayer, come to the Prayer.

Come to real success, come to real success

Allah is the Greatest, Allah is the Greatest.

There is no god but Allah.

In the dawn prayer, the muezzin gives the Muslims a little incentive by adding this:

"*Prayer is better than sleep, Prayer is better than sleep*"

Before the prayer, Muslim men and women cleanse themselves, by washing the exposed body parts or washing their entire body.

5:6 O ye who believe! When ye prepare for prayer, wash your faces, and your hands (and arms) to the elbows; Rub your heads (with water); and (wash) your feet to the ankles. If ye are in a state of ceremonial impurity, bathe your whole body. But if ye are ill, or on a journey, or one of you cometh from offices of nature, or ye have been in contact with women, and ye find no water, then take for yourselves clean sand or earth, and rub therewith your faces and hands, Allah doth not wish to place you in a difficulty, but to make you clean, and to complete his favour to you, that ye may be grateful.

The Muslim makes his intention to perform which ever prayer is due for that time.

1. The dawn prayer (Fajr)~24:58

2. The noon prayer (Dhur)~17:78

3. The afternoon prayer (Asr)~2:238

4. The sunset prayer (Maghrib)~11:114

5. The night prayer (Isha'a)-24:58

29:45 Recite what is sent of the Book by inspiration to thee, and establish regular Prayer: for Prayer restrains from shameful and unjust deeds; and remembrance of Allah is the greatest (thing in life) without doubt. And Allah knows the (deeds) that ye do.

All five prayers can be done at home, but it is more preferable that they are done in the Masjid, the place of worship, to establish the unity of the believers. On Friday, there is a special prayer called Jumu'ah. This is a congregational prayer were a sermon (Khutbah) is given. This prayer is of great importance and should be observed whenever possible.

62.9 O ye who believe! When the call is proclaimed to prayer on Friday (the Day of Assembly), hasten earnestly to the Remembrance of Allah, and leave off business (and traffic): That is best for you if ye but knew!

62:10 And when the Prayer is finished, then may ye disperse through the land, and seek of the Bounty of Allah: and celebrate the Praises of Allah often (and without stint): that ye may prosper.

In every prayer, as the Muslims stands, bows and prostrate with their head to the floor in glorification of the God Almighty, they are shoulder to shoulder and foot to foot. Every person, from the poor and homeless to the president of the country, are at that very moment as one in humility and in servitude to ALLAH. No matter race, color, nationality or ethnicity, you all are one. This is why the gathering at the Masjid is so important. At every prayer you are brushing shoulders with a fellow believer in the God that you hold dear. He or she has similar values as you, yet your personalities, your experiences, your upbringings, your cultures maybe worlds apart.

49:13 O mankind! We created you from a single (pair) of a male and a female, and made you into nations and tribes, that ye may know each other (not that ye may despise (each other). Verily the most honoured of you in the sight of Allah is (he who is) the most righteous of you. And Allah has full knowledge and is well acquainted (with all things).

This is not a message to believers but to mankind. We are to learn and appreciate the diversity of all human beings. The practice of Salat in the Masjid serves as a great means of destroying the cultivated bridges built upon the roots of prejudice, discrimination, bigotry and racism. How can you feel superior to your brother, when you both are infinitesimal beings standing before God? During your prayer, you offer your fellow Muslim brothers and sisters peace and blessings. On every occasion you are reprogramming yourself from the ill thoughts that you may have once harbored. This is exactly the intention of Salat. It is a programming or conditioning, into remember what is right and good. Praying 5 times a day is nothing but the power of suggestion at work. If a person prays every day as they should, it is almost impossible to sin.

After you make Salat, you know subconsciously that in a few hours, you will have to make Salat again. You would have to schedule your sin around Salat. It would be very difficult to make Salat, and then rob a bank. You have to sin and make time for your next prayer. All this without feeling any guilt as you stand before God. This brings up another benefit of Salat, punctuality. When you prayer five times a day, though prayer may take no more than 10 or 15 minutes, your body becomes your watch. If you pray 5 times a day, you have some general idea of the time at every minute of the day, so it helps you with your timeliness, as well.

Muslims also perform invocation using God's attributes or giving him praise called Dhikr (remembrance). These prayers, as well as any other informal prayers (Dua al mas'alah or prayer of asking) offered to God, are done at the discretion of each person. With Dhikr, a Muslim invokes the names or praise of God repetitively. It is similar to the rosary of the Catholics. Often Muslims use prayer beads to count the praise given to God. This remembrance is so greatly praised because it serves as a reminder to man that God is ever present and ever aware of all that we do. It is like having your parents with you wherever you go. People are much better behaved when there is authority around and since God is subtle, at times we take him for granted. The remembrance and awareness of the consequences of our actions, helps keep man of the right path. And the Qur'an recommends Muslims to remember God when they think of doing something evil (7:201).

Finally, the Muslim greeting As Salaamu Alaikum is actually an exchanging of prayers. The Muslims is saying to his brother "may peace be upon you" and his brother is obliged to give an equal greeting or a better greeting back (4:86). This brother might say Wa Alaikumu Salaam, "may peace be upon you also" or he might say Wa Alaikumu Salaamu wa Rahmatullahi wa Barakatu, which means "may the peace, mercy and blessings of Allah be upon you."

PILGRIMAGE

The prostrations of prayer are done according to the physical ability of a particular person. Muslims are commanded to perform a pilgrimage to Mecca and the Kaaba, if they are financially able to do so.

3:96 The first House (of worship) appointed for men was that at Bakka: Full of blessing and of guidance for all kinds of beings:

3:97 In it are Signs Manifest; (for example), the Station of Abraham; whoever enters it attains security; Pilgrimage thereto is a duty men owe to Allah,- those who can afford the journey; but if any deny faith, Allah stands not in need of any of His creatures.

The Kaaba is the centerpiece for the Muslim's prayer. And Muslims from all over the world make a pilgrimage to the city of Mecca to worship ALLAH at the House that Abraham (pbuh) and his son Ishmael (pbuh) built for that purpose. Muslim men and women dress in the same simple white garb, so as to have no distinction between the wealthy, the poor and those in between. You are but human beings submitting yourselves to God in a single brotherhood and sisterhood. This surreal experience is what drove Malcolm X from his racist views in the Nation of Islam to the true acceptance of Islam, shared by every race and nationality.

CHARITY

2:177 It is not righteousness that ye turn your faces Towards east or West; but it is righteousness- to believe in Allah and the Last Day, and the Angels, and the Book, and the Messengers; to spend of your substance, out of love for Him, for your kin, for orphans, for the needy, for the wayfarer, for those who ask, and for the ransom of slaves; to be steadfast in prayer, and practice regular charity; to fulfill the contracts which ye have made; and to be firm and patient, in pain (or suffering) and adversity, and throughout all periods of panic. Such are the people of truth, the Allah-fearing.

The word for charity or alms in Islam is Zakat. Zakat literally means to purify. It is a cleansing of your soul and a sign of selflessness when you give to those in need. The Buddhist asks for money, but the Muslims are to give of his wealth and possessions. The spare money that you would spend for your leisure or the money spent on alcohol or gambling could be put to better use. The Qur'an speaks against squandering your money away (17:26). For a small amount of your extra money, you can make a world of difference to a person or family in need. People often feel that the money they give to charity is used for other means. This should not stop you from giving. ALLAH judges by your intentions. If you intend to give you money or shelter or food to a needy person that is what you will be rewarded for. A few bad apples in the bunch should not halt your desire to help others, because it definitely does not halt the need for help. And if you are unable to provide charity, or if you are in need of charity yourself, a smile, a kind word and good manners can be your charity to others. Any righteous deed that benefits others is an act of charity.

ALLAH understands man's competitive nature, so he recommends that man compete in deeds of righteousness (5:48). Give your effort and time as well as a small portion of your wealth. Islam requires Muslims to pay 2.5% of their yearly income in charity. If everyone adhered to this amount, there would be no poverty, no problems of starvation, and no families without health care.

100:8 And violent is he (man) in his love of wealth.

There are multi-millionaires and multi-billionaires in a country where the minimum wage is $5.85. There are people who fly personal jets and helicopters in the same countries where families can't afford to buy a car or even pay for gas. People parade around in attire worth more than some families make in 10 years. If you give of the abundance that you have, the happiness that you have will be shared with others. There are those who have money that can't be spent in 5 lifetimes. Why not give to a good cause? Rick Warren, the author of "Purpose Driven Life" said it is not a sin to have money, but it is a sin to die with money." And this sentiment is echoed in the Qur'an.

63:9 O ye who believe! Let not your riches or your children divert you from the remembrance of Allah. If any act thus, the loss is their own.

63:10 and spend something (in charity) out of the substance which We have bestowed on you, before Death should come to any of you and he should say, "O my Lord! why didst Thou not give me respite for a little while? I should then have given (largely) in charity, and I should have been one of the doers of good."

FASTING

The Qur'an contains a code of ethics for mankind to follow. It instructs man on how to relate to other people, whether they are of the same faith or of a different faith. It is commanded that a Muslim should not insult other's faith or gods (6:108) and that he should not compromise his own religion (68:9). A Muslim is to be mindful of God at all times and in all things, for all his non-prohibited actions are a form of worship to ALLAH. And he is not to mention future events without being mindful of God.

18:23 Nor say of anything, "I shall be sure to do so and so tomorrow"

18:24 Without adding, "So please Allah!"

The Qur'an instructs Muslims to keep their promises (61:2-3), not to deal in fraud (83:1-5), to avoid envy of those with material wealth (28:79-80), to avoid calling people by offensive nicknames, to avoid mockery (49:11), and not to be arrogant (17:37). ALLAH wants Muslims to think good of other people. Assume that they are innocent until proven guilty (24:12, 16). The Qur'an says that some suspicion of others should be avoided, as it may be a sin. The Qur'an also eschews backbiting and spying on others (49:12). And when a Muslim is insulted, he is to reply with gentleness.

25:63 And the servants of (Allah) Most Gracious are those who walk on the earth in humility, and when the ignorant address them, they say, "Peace!"

Muslims are to forgive others for the wrongs that they have incurred. It is allowed for Muslims to defend themselves against attacks, be it verbally or physical. But it is recommended that the Muslim forgive the person. Even if it is his own family who is his enemy, if he overlooks and forgives them, then he gains forgiveness for his past sins from GOD (64:13-15).

In the ninth month of the lunar calendar, all these ethics and morals given to Muslims are to be reaffirmed or if necessary reestablished. The Muslims are to abstain from food and sexual relation (not including kissing and hugging your wife), from sunrise to sunset for the entire month. This observation by Muslims is called Ramadan. This is the month in which the Night of Power occurs. The night that the Qur'an was first revealed to Prophet Muhammad (pbuh), thus it is customary for Muslims to read the entire Qur'an within this month.

In observance of Ramadan, Muslims abstain from the usage of bad language, and they stop bad habits like smoking and gossiping. This is a time for reflection and revisiting the moral code given to man. If he may have drifted from the path, every year he can restart his engine.

By restricting the times that you can eat food and drink (even for Muslims who live in the desert), it is also a means by which a Muslim can momentarily feel the pain and hunger of those who do not know where there next meal is coming from. They can better understand the life of those in need. The restriction of sex is simply your mind over matter. You maintain control over your instincts and urges. I would recommend this fast be attempted by every non-Muslim at least once in their lifetime for at least one week. It will reveal so many things about you.

2:183 O ye who believe! Fasting is prescribed to you as it was prescribed to those before you, that ye may (learn) self-restraint,

2:184 (Fasting) for a fixed number of days; but if any of you is ill, or on a journey, the prescribed number (Should be made up) from days later. For those who can do it (With hardship), is a ransom, the feeding of one that is indigent. But he that will give more, of his own free will,- it is better for him. And it is better for you that ye fast, if ye only knew.

2:185 Ramadhan is the (month) in which was sent down the Qur'an, as a guide to mankind, also clear (Signs) for guidance and judgment (Between right and wrong). So every one of you who is present (at his home) during that month should spend it in fasting, but if any one is ill, or on a journey, the prescribed period (Should be made up) by days later. Allah intends every facility for you, He does not want to put to difficulties. (He wants you) to complete the prescribed period, and to glorify Him in that He has guided you; and perchance ye shall be grateful.

CONTROVERSIAL SUBJECTS

MISNOMERS

Continuous prayer, Charity, Hajj and Fasting are looked at by some people as hardship and heartache for Muslims. But the Muslim sees them as blessings from ALLAH. As they are commanded repeatedly in the 55th Surah, Muslims look inexhaustibly for blessings from God. [Knowing that man is fixated on the negative, ALLAH even challenges man to count all his blessings and favors from God (16:18)]. A Muslim will find in these practices remembrance of God, familiarity with the words of God, prevention from sin, a sense of unity and camaraderie, a system for the disassembling of racism, culturalism, classism and any other prejudice. It is a system which abolishes slavery and poverty simultaneously. It establishes and reinforces morals, ethics, self-restraint, and willpower. Not only do these practices build your self-esteem, but it promotes punctuality, health and hygiene, cleansing your body and mind. It is conducive to self-evaluation, altruism, empathy and sympathy. And most importantly these practices provide man favor with God and the map to a straight path to Paradise.

These practices along with the belief in ALLAH are the core, the soul of Islam. I would be surprised if anyone, whether a theist or an atheist, would have a problem with these methods and their goals. They are methods geared to solve the ills of society. Practitioners of Islam are to be philanthropist and humanitarians because adherence to these practices would cause great positive change for themselves and society at large. So what happens when you pursue philanthropy more fervently? Strict adherence would only increase and intensify its positive effect. For this reason, I object to misnomers like "Islamist," "fundamentalist," "radical Islam" and "extremist." These words are given meanings which do not fit. Every Muslim is an "Islamist." If a racist is someone who believes his race is superior to others, then an Islamist is one who believes submission to God is superior to any other way of life. A Muslim chose Islam because he believes that it is the best and correct religion, just as Christian view Christianity, Jews view Judaism and Buddhist view Buddhism.

Also, ever Muslim practices "radical" Islam. The definition of radical is something "proceeding directly from the root." Islam is rooted in the teachings of the Qur'an which was revealed 1400 years ago. Every Muslim and Mu'min believes that these roots are relevant to and compatible with the times of today. In fact, getting back to the roots planted by Prophet Muhammad (pbuh) is the ideal place for all Muslims, due to its outstanding results in terms of propagating Islam, freeing slaves, providing for the poor, giving women rights and abstinence from sin. Also every Muslim begins with the fundamentals of the teaching of Islam. That would make him a "fundamentalist." The common name given to Muslims who disassociate themselves with terrorists is "moderate" Muslim. Moderate meaning one who does only what is required. In other words, they are the mediocre or average Muslim. Maybe most people fall in the category of "average," but this is not a goal to reach for. After a fundamentalist has mastered the basics, his goal is to be a Muslim "extremist" or one who advocates or resorts to measures beyond the norm in his submission to ALLAH. He offers extra prayers to ALLAH, he gives more of his time and wealth to charity, he goes to Hajj twice, he sponsors others to go for Hajj, and he fasts more than the month of Ramadan. What is the problem with this? The Muslim should be correcting these misnomers. The words that they are looking for is fake Muslims, false Islam or Muslims in error. Radical, fundamental turned extreme Islamists would be nothing but a blessing to the world.

SUNNI OR SHIA

Muslims, too, are guilty of giving themselves inappropriate names. They called themselves Sunni or Shia. The Qur'an does not make such a distinction. You are a Muslim, a Mu'min or you are not. A Sunni Muslim is one who follows the Sunnah or way of Prophet Muhammad (pbuh). Well every Muslim on earth has this goal in mind when he practices his religion. Shia means party. It is short for the Party of Ali, the son-in-law and a successor of Prophet Muhammad (pbuh).

The name of these two groups are but a division to signify that one group, the Sunni, accept the four leaders after Muhammad, Abu Bakr, Uthman, Umar and Ali, (may ALLAH be pleased with them) whereas the Shia only accept one leader after Prophet Muhammad (pbuh), Ali. A dispute over the successors of Prophet Muhammad (pbuh)1400 years ago is the reason that there are attacks, slander and murder of thousands of people to this very day. There is little wonder why ALLAH forbade such divisiveness.

6:159 As for those who divide their religion and break up into sects, thou hast no part in them in the least: their affair is with Allah: He will in the end tell them the truth of all that they did.

If asked what kind of Muslim I am, I say that I am Muslim Muslim, a Mu'min Mu'min. The Qur'an asks Muslims to come to common ground with Christians and Jews. We must do the same with our brothers. There is so much that we agree on,

CONTROVERSIAL SUBJECTS

why does something not mentioned at all in the Qur'an cause such a rift? We all believe in ALLAH, in the Qur'an, in prayer, Hajj, fast and charity. We all are those who submit to God and believe. This is the ground we must stand upon. We can disagree on certain intricacies in a cordial manner. We all know that it is a grave sin to kill a fellow believer, so it is all Muslims obligation to mend this fence and unite as the Qur'an and ALLAH COMMANDS.

49:9 If two parties among the Believers fall into a quarrel, make ye peace between them: but if one of them transgresses beyond bounds against the other, then fight ye (all) against the one that transgresses until it complies with the command of Allah; but if it complies, then make peace between them with justice, and be fair: for Allah loves those who are fair (and just).

49:10 The Believers are but a single Brotherhood: So make peace and reconciliation between your two (contending) brothers; and fear Allah, that ye may receive Mercy.

WOMEN

Perhaps the most controversial and divisive topic of discussion in Islam is the role and treatment of women. It must first be stated that women have all the religious obligations that a man has, which means she also has the same reward and punishment for her good and bad deeds. In anticipation for the question of equality between men and women, ALLAH makes it abundantly clear that the pillars and moral conduct of Islam is for every adult, male and female.

33:35 For Muslim men and women,- for believing men and women, for devout men and women, for true men and women, for men and women who are patient and constant, for men and women who humble themselves, for men and women who give in Charity, for men and women who fast (and deny themselves), for men and women who guard their chastity, and for men and women who engage much in Allah's praise, for them has Allah prepared forgiveness and great reward.

Believing men and women are protecting friends of one another. They aid and guide each other into righteousness (9:71). So, women's religious duties are the same as men's duties, but what about their social life. When pondering this topic, it is best to strip away all preconceived ideas and get our guidance from the Qur'an. Taking this approach, it becomes impossible to justify the treatment of women in much of the Muslim world. There is a sharp contract between culture and religion. Yet these lines are blurred so often when discussing Islam that the distinction is rarely made between the two. Female circumcision/mutilation, women walking behind men, and women prevented from driving cars are all examples of culture being mistaken for Islam. None of these things are to be found in the pages of the Qur'an. So before an allegation is made, it must be shown to be a part of Islam and not simply a practice performed by Muslims.

In the times of Prophet Muhammad (pbuh), it was more preferable to have a son than a daughter. Parents were upset when the new addition to the family was female. Yet Prophet Muhammad (pbuh) denounced such behavior. He maintained that a female's birth is as equal a blessing as a male's birth. But this was not simply a problem of preference. The practice of female infanticide was implemented for those unsatisfied with their newborn baby girl. The Arabs used to bury their daughters alive. To extinguish this grave sin, Prophet Muhammad (pbuh) outlawed infanticide (16:58-59). The Qur'an also makes mention that those who practiced such brutality will have to face the consequences of their deeds in the hereafter (81:8-9). This is to show that Islam directly impacted the life of women in a dramatically positive way.

CONTROVERSIAL SUBJECTS

Before women could fight for their civil rights, Prophet Muhammad (pbuh) fought for their right to live. He fought for their right to be treated with fairness and with the love that a parent would have bestowed upon a male child. Not only did he fight for their rights, but when Islam became the religion of Arabia , he won them their rights and their right to live. He saved thousands, if not millions of women's lives. But instead of Prophet Muhammad (pbuh) being respected and praised for his efforts to emancipate women from this barbarism, he is most often vilified for propagating sexism. But what does the Qur'an say about men and women? The Qur'an testifies that man covets or he passionately wants things in this world, but he should want more passionately the rewards of the hereafter.

3:14 Fair in the eyes of men is the love of things they covet: Women and sons; Heaped-up hoards of gold and silver; horses branded (for blood and excellence); and (wealth of) cattle and well-tilled land. Such are the possessions of this world's life; but in nearness to Allah is the best of the goals (To return to).

3:15 Say: Shall I give you glad tidings of things Far better than those? For the righteous are Gardens in nearness to their Lord, with rivers flowing beneath; therein is their eternal home; with companions pure (and holy); and the good pleasure of Allah. For in Allah's sight are (all) His servants.

The number one thing that men so passionately want is WOMEN. Of course, this is not a new revelation, but merely a confirmation of the truth. Alongside, women are children, then wealth and possessions. The Qur'an instructs man on how to conduct himself in pursuit of his goals and how to conduct himself when he has a hold on these things. As it pertains to a family, the man must marry the woman that he wishes to have. But the woman must be a believing woman, or a woman from the People of the Book (2:221, 4:25, 5:5). Their mutual reverence for God and their commitment to keeping his commandments build an extremely important foundation for a lifelong marriage.

Though it is often assumed that marriage in Islam is an arrangement which is without the consent of the woman or the man or both, this is not what the Qur'an stipulates. This is again, culture and not the religion of Islam. The Qur'an says that a man cannot take a woman to be his wife against her will. ALLAH wishes a man and woman to live with tranquility between them, with love and mercy in their hearts.

The man is to treat his wife with kindness and respect. He is specifically told not to treat his wife harshly. And their marriage should he kept together honorably (4:19, 30:21). A man is command not to hurt or take advantage of women, even if the marriage ends in divorce (2:231). Your relationship with your spouse is reflective of the relationship you have with God. It should be comprised of love, fidelity, loyalty, honor, obedience and trust.

The reason that man is addressed so often, when it comes to the treatment of his wife is because the Qur'an says that a man is protector, maintainer or supporter of women. In other words, he is to be MAN OF THE HOUSEHOLD (4:34). Some may take offense to this notion, but these are the same people who would teach their sons how to be good, strong men who can provide for his family and they would teach their daughters how to be great mothers and caretakers for the family. But the attitude against a man being the head of his household is due to the failure of men. Because many men are not responsible, loyal, devoted and hardworking, it forces women to be more independent. This cultivates a mentality where women go into a marriage feeling that they may not be able to depend on their husband to keep up his end of the bargain, so they assume the role of father and mother. But it is the man's job to provide food and shelter for his family. It should be stated that women are not forbidden to work or provide for the family. A woman can work, but she does not have to provide food and shelter, if she does not wish to. It is the man's duty to provide these things for his family. It is the woman's duty to be the primary caretaker of their children.

"If God elected women for home and man for the street, he trusted the building and construction on earth to man and the greater mission of bringing up humanity to women."(Dr. Mostafa Mahmoud, "Dialogue with an Atheist")

CONTROVERSIAL SUBJECTS

Though this role's importance has been downplayed tremendously in today's society, the role of a mother is the most important job on earth. This is not an inferior role at all, despite popular opinion. Would a person prefer a pay check or the admiration and love that a child garners for his mother? Would a woman rather build a bridge than build a child? Children today are being raised by their aunts, their uncles, their cousins, their elderly grandparents, their babysitter, their friends, their television, their radio and their video games. This is primarily because of the collapse of families. Think of how much mischief you would have avoided if your mother was there to keep you on the right track. How many times would you skip school, if your mother was home? How many reporter cards would you throw away, if your mother was their active in your school and your schoolwork? If both a child's parents are at work, the child is being cheated. Of course, the goal of the father working, while the mother takes care of the family is not always possible, but when it is possible, it should be practiced.

Also, both men and women are to "lower their gaze and guard their modesty" to avoid sin and avoid enticing others to sin (24:30-31). They are both encouraged to dress with modesty, so as not to attract the attention of the opposite sex. In addition, they are not to look upon the opposite sex in any lustful manner, unless the two are married. The phrase "lower their gaze" is to avoid lust and even its possibility if someone of the opposite sex is not dressing modestly. Men should not be bare chest or showing their body to draw any attention to themselves. Of course, women have a little more to conceal than men do, so they are not to "display their beauty and ornaments except what (must ordinarily) appear thereof; that they should draw their veils over their bosoms and not display their beauty except to their husbands" and family (24:31).

This veil is not the covering of a woman's face, which "ordinarily appears." The veil over women's face is not a commandment given in the Qur'an, thus it is an individual or a collective group's choice to cover a woman's face. The Qur'an says that Muslim women "should cast their outer garments over their persons" so to avoid accentuating their body parts (33:59). This is to distinguish chaste Muslim women from any other women on the street and to avoid harassment from other men. The veil or modest dress is not oppression of women. It is incorporated for the exact same reason that nuns are dressed the way that they are. It is a testament to their belief and devotion to God. And in the case of the Muslim woman, it is also a testament of devotion to her husband. It is also a sign of dignity and respect for themselves that they do not wish for or need the adulation of anyone other than their husbands. All the great women of faith dressed in this manner, yet it is eschewed in today's society as oppressive (though women CHOOSE to be Muslims) while skimpy dress is encouraged.

Women today go to work or the marketplace, with a bit of cleavage showing and tight fitting jeans to display their figure. Then they come home to their husband and get comfortable. They take off all the clothing that restricts their blood circulation and put on a huge t-shirt and jogging pants. They are doing the exact opposite of what the Qur'an says and what the sensible thing to do is. They are showing the world their goods and covering up for their husband. These are the same women who are offended when random men are disrespectful to them on the street and whose husband pay them little attention. You can take the advice of society at large or you can take the advice of Him who created the society at large. It is your choice.

Jews and Christians would do well to see what the Bible says about the relationship between men and women and the appropriate dress code and conduct for both of them, because their scriptures are in full agreement with the Qur'an's position in this matter. In fact, the Bible is a bit more harsh and crass in its views and its tone about women in general and wives specifically.

MARRIAGE

24:32 Marry those among you who are single, or the virtuous ones among yourselves, male or female: if they are in poverty, Allah will give them means out of His grace: for Allah encompasseth all, and he knoweth all things.

CONTROVERSIAL SUBJECTS

24:33 Let those who find not the wherewithal for marriage keep themselves chaste, until Allah gives them means out of His grace.

The Qur'an adamantly promotes marriage and monogamy between a man and a woman. However, the Qur'an does allow for polygamy in special circumstances.

4:2 To orphans restore their property (When they reach their age), nor substitute (your) worthless things for (their) good ones; and devour not their substance (by mixing it up) with your own. For this is indeed a great sin.

4:3 If ye fear that ye shall not be able to deal justly with the orphans, Marry women of your choice, Two or three or four; but if ye fear that ye shall not be able to deal justly (with them), then only one, or (a captive) that your right hands possess, that will be more suitable, to prevent you from doing injustice.

4:4 And give the women (on marriage) their dower as a free gift; but if they, of their own good pleasure, remit any part of it to you, Take it and enjoy it with right good cheer.

Though it is presented by Muslims and non-Muslims oftentimes as a very important part of Islam, it is clear that polygamy is not a widely practiced part of the religion. In fact, it is not prescribed but permitted in circumstances like the aftermath of a war where men are scarce. Today a very small percentage of Muslims practice polygamy. This is a testament to how prevalent the circumstances arise which allow for polygamy. Of course, the women involved decide whether this is suitable for them and some women have as a stipulation in their marriage dower that they will not be a part of any polygamous relationship.

The Qur'an also says in the same chapter that a man will not be able to deal justly between his wives, even if his intentions are sincere (4:129). The Qur'an is permitting, yet discouraging the practice of polygamy. In light of this, I do not deem it imperative to be overly apologetic for polygamy in Islam. If those who hold some contempt against Islam on this position are Jews and Christians, I would ask them to research the Bible before denouncing Islam. In there they will never find a passage which says "then (marry) only one" as the Qur'an does.

There is a verse in the New Testament which says that a bishop can only have one wife, but this only proves that polygamy is permissible to the general public in the New Testament (1Timothy 3:2). The Jewish Torah or the Old Testament, which the Israelites and Jesus (pbuh) is thought to have followed to the smallest letter, also condones polygamy (Exodus 21:10, Deut. 21:15-17, Deut. 17:17, Deut. 25:5-10). They may find verses which suggest that it is best to marry one person, but this is only agreeing with the Quranic viewpoint. And it is quite hypocritical for Westerner society to have contempt against the Islamic view, when it is not a punishable offense in any court to commit adultery, and it is praiseworthy to have as many partners as you would like as long as you DO NOT make a commitment and oath to be with them forever in marriage.

SEPARATION AND DIVORCE

Another practice which is permissible but discouraged is divorce. ALLAH wants divorce to be the last resort. The Qur'an recommends that the troubled couple reflect on the conflict to determine if their spouse is at fault or if it is they who are being unreasonable (4:19). If they find their spouse is guilty of disloyalty or ill-conduct, they are to correct them. If this does not resolve the conflict, then they are to sleep in separate beds. If sleeping in separate beds is ineffective, then the Qur'an prescribes another alterative. The problem is that Muslims disagree on what this alternative is.

CONTROVERSIAL SUBJECTS

In most Qur'ans, verse 4:34 says "(And last) beat them (lightly)" or something to that effect. The Arabic words used here is "adribu" (root: daraba) and it means to beat, to strike, to hit, to separate, to part. The word is used in all these different forms in the Qur'an. The translators of the Qur'an have deemed "to beat" to be the best fit for the verse in question. This is probably due to Hadiths which are used to explain the Qur'an, even though they have vastly different answers for this one question (one of which says do not beat women). But since the Qur'an is fully detailed, it explains itself (6:114). In another chapter, the Qur'an again speaks about this troubled marriage and it says that the couple is to separate for four months and after this separation, they can decide to return or to divorce.

2:226 For those who take an oath for abstention from their wives, a waiting for four months is ordained; if then they return, Allah is Oft-forgiving, Most Merciful.

2:227 But if their intention is firm for divorce, Allah heareth and knoweth all things.

Notice here that no beating is involved in this process. One does not abstain from being with his wife then come back to beat her, and then decide if he wants to reconcile or divorce. The four months is clearly a time to reflect on the marriage and to come to a rational decision. And if we look at the steps logically, it is clear that the word "adribu" should be translated as "separate from her" and not as "beat her."

Step 1. Admonish them- the couple is still together

Step 2. Refuse to sleep together- the couple is still together

Step 3. Beat her- the couple is still together.

The problem with this translation is the verse that succeeds this one.

4:35 If ye fear a breach between them twain, appoint (two) arbiters, one from his family, and the other from hers; if they wish for peace, Allah will cause their reconciliation. For Allah hath full knowledge, and is acquainted with all things.

This verse is directed towards a concerned person on the outside of the relationship. It is apparent that this person fears that the couple will divorce, so this third party is to try and reconcile the couple. This would only make sense if the third step was that the couple separated (for four months) and the third party felt that divorce was the inevitable result of this separation. If the man beats his wife, then there is no mention of separation. So how can they get BACK TOGETHER?

The Qur'an says that husband and wife are to live on equitable terms (4:19). This means if the translator was to assume that a husband can beat his wife, then a wife can beat her husband, which I am sure he will not agree with because later on in this chapter, the wife of a husband who commits disloyalty and ill-conduct, has the permission that a husband has in the same situation (4:128). Also the Qur'an says that a man is to treat his wife with kindness and not to treat her harshly or keep her against her will (4:19). Beating your wife to get her to do as you wish is contrary to all these principle of the Qur'an. Hopefully, Muslims will unite and change this translation and put an end to the idea that wife-beating is acceptable in Islam.

NO COMPULSION

2:256 Let there be no compulsion in religion: Truth stands out clear from Error: whoever rejects evil and believes in Allah hath grasped the most trustworthy hand-hold, that never breaks. And Allah heareth and knoweth all things.

CONTROVERSIAL SUBJECTS

Let me repeat that "THERE IS NO COMPULSION IN RELIGION". Let that resonate. Compulsion means an uncontrollable, repetitive, and unwanted urge to perform an act, to compel or to force. God continuously tells Prophet Muhammad (pbuh), "you are not the people's guardian." "You only convey the message" (3:20, 64:12, 50:45). It seems that Prophet Muhammad (pbuh) is distressed about people's unwillingness to accept his message. ALLAH continuously counsels him on how to cope with those who are disbeliever and those who say they believe but they really do not. Time and time again, ALLAH says a person's conversion is in no one's hands but ALLAH'S (10:99-100) and that person must be receptive to change.

30:52 So verily thou canst not make the dead to hear, nor canst thou make the deaf to hear the call, when they show their backs and turn away.

30:53 Nor canst thou lead back the blind from their straying: only those wilt thou make to hear, who believe in Our signs and submit (their wills in Islam).

This is again repeated in 27:80-81. The truth is a gift from God. If you turn you back on the gift that is your fault. Forcing something to take the gift makes the gift and the gesture meaningless. If they are not receptive, they will also be unappreciative of the value of the gift that they possess, just as the Qur'an says of a person who held the Torah and did not understand its value (62:5). The second sentence is the crowning jewel of 2:256. "Truth stands out clear from falsehood." This means that the truth is so apparent and recognizable that compulsion is unnecessary.

Perhaps the greatest myth of Islam is that it was spread by the sword. This is a lie which was formulated centuries ago and still exists today, despite the evidence to the contrary, such as the Arab Coptic Christians of Prophet Muhammad's (pbuh) time, who had successive generations of Christians until today in Arabia. If the Muslims forced conversions, they would not exist. Another misconception with the issue of spreading Islam by the sword is with the people who accept Islam to avoid punishment. Many times, history records this as forced conversions, when this is completely untrue.

When a person decides to be a Muslim, he must declare to another Muslim that he has converted by repeating the oath or "Shahadah" as follows:

"I bear witness that there is no God but ALLAH"

"I bear witness that Muhammad is His messenger."

When he says this, he must be immediately embraced as a Muslim, by the Muslim community, whether you suspect him to be truthful or not. It is not up to Muslims to decipher the intent of another person. His intention is in his and ALLAH'S knowledge. This understanding has helped save the lives of many people who were being held captive by groups of terrorists. Though this practice can be used to emancipate the innocent, in many cases it is used as a tool of manipulation. Many criminals and enemies of Islam have used this as a means of escaping death. They profess to be a Muslim in an effort to avoid the death penalty for whatever crime they have committed. Many times these cases are recorded as Muslims spreading their religion by the sword, when this is furthest from the truth.

A famous case is that of Sabbetai Tzvi in the year 1666. He was a Jew who was thought by about one third of the Jewish population to be the long awaited Messiah. This nefarious character used his persuasive nature, bribery and trickery to make many believe he was the Messiah and to acquire leniency for his many terms of imprisonment. He had aspirations of overturning the kingdom of Turkey and becoming its king as a sign that he was the Messiah. However one of his opponents, Nehemiah ha-Kohen, pretended to embrace Islam in order to inform the Sultan of Turkey, Mehmen VI, of Sabbetai's treasonous plot. When Sabbetai was captured, he was advised by Mehmen VI's physician, a former Jew, to embrace Islam in order to nullify his crimes of treason. Treason was, as it is today in many countries, punishable by death. He did as he was advised and it worked in his favor. He was spared from execution and pardoned for treason because he made the "Shahadah."

CONTROVERSIAL SUBJECTS

But Islam is charged with forcing him to embrace Islam with the sword. To this day, I still see documentaries on prominent television broadcast and "scholars" of the Middle East saying that Muslims forced him into Islam. Muslims did not force him to accept Islam. He forced Muslims to accept him.

And what about the countries overwhelmingly inhabited by Muslims? None of these Muslims countries of the world were forced to embrace Islam. No army went to Malaysia, Indonesia, or the countries of Africa with a sword demanded their conversion. The Muslims did not force their religion on others. On the contrary, the conquests, which detractors of Islam speak of, were Muslims using force to control land. They did not even propagate their religion. They felt that the religion of Islam made them superior to those who they conquered and they did not wish to close this gap. These wars were for money and power, which is just as sinful as forcing someone to convert to your religion by force, but completely dissimilar.

The Muslims ruled Spain for 800 years and they converted almost no one, by propagation or by the sword. They were also deeply involved in the slave trade, in direct conflict with the Islamic efforts to abolish slavery, but their involvement in the slave trade had nothing to do with conversion and everything to do with greed, corruption and cruelty. Their unfortunate actions have stamped Islam with the stain of being spread by the sword. But of course, ALLAH is the best of planners. In order to help Muslims defend their faith, he gives the Muslim modern examples to illustrate that Islam is not spread by the sword. In Europe, Islam is the fastest growing religion. In America , Islam is the fastest growing religion. In the entire world, Islam is the fastest growing religion. And this is without propagation, by in large and most importantly without a sword. This accomplishment is in the face of the continuous vilification of Islam throughout the world and the misrepresentation of Islam by terrorists. The only explanation for this phenomenon is that ISLAM IS THE TRUTH. When Islam is mentioned so often, even in a negative light, it arouses people's curiosity. They want to know about this religion with nearly 2 billion followers. They want to know what the Muslims believe and from where do they draw their inspiration. They are at first inquisitive, then intrigued and finally convinced of the truth.

Islam Is The Truth

21.18 Nay, We hurl the Truth against falsehood, and it knocks out its brain, and behold, falsehood doth perish! Ah! Woe be to you for the (false) things ye ascribe (to Us).

WHAT NON-MUSLIMS HAVE TO SAY ABOUT THE ALLEGATION THAT ISLAM WAS SPREAD BY THE SWORD

1. M.K.GANDHI: "I became more than ever convinced that it was not the sword that won a place for Islam in those days in the scheme of life. It was the rigid simplicity, the utter self-effacement of the prophet, the scrupulous regard for his pledges, his intense devotion to his friends and followers, his intrepidity, his fearlessness, his absolute trust in God and in his own mission. These, and not the sword carried everything before them and surmounted every trouble." YOUNG INDIA, 1924.

2. EDWARD GIBBON: "The greatest success of Mohammad's life was affected by sheer moral force without the stroke of a sword." HISTORY OF THE SARACEN EMPIRE, London, 1870.

3. A.S. TRITTON: "The picture of the Muslim soldier advancing with a sword in one hand and the Qur'an in the other is quite false." ISLAM, London, 1951, page 21.

4. DE LACY O'LEARY: "History makes it clear however, that the legend of fanatical Muslims, sweeping through the world and forcing Islam at the point of sword upon conquered races is one of the most fantastically absurd myths that historians have ever repeated." ISLAM AT CROSSROADS, London, 1923, page 8.

5. K.S. RAMAKRISHNA RAO: "My problem to write this monograph is easier because we are not generally fed now on that (distorted) kind of history and much time need not be spent on pointing out our misrepresentations of Islam. The theory of Islam and sword, for instance, is not heard now in any quarter worth the name.

CONTROVERSIAL SUBJECTS

The principle of Islam, there is no compulsion in religion, is well-known." MOHAMMED THE PROPHET OF ISLAM, Riyadh 1989, page 4.

6. JAMES A. MICHENER. "No other religion in history spread so rapidly as Islam .... The West has widely believed that this surge of religion was made possible by the sword. But no modern scholar accepts that idea, and the Qur'an is explicit in support of the freedom of conscience." ISLAM THE MISUNDERSTOOD RELIGION, READERS DIGEST (American Edition) May 1955.

7. LAWRENCE E. BROWNE: "Incidentally these well-established facts dispose of the idea so widely fostered in Christian writings that the Muslims, wherever they went, forced people to accept Islam at the point of the sword." THE PROSPECTS OR ISLAM, London 1944.

No compulsion in religion includes the religion of ISLAM, meaning that Muslims are not to force other Muslims to be better Muslim. This is not in terms of preventing, stopping or punishing a crime, but in terms of a Muslims following the pillars of Islam. If fasting and prayer are only to benefit the person performing this act, then the negligence of these duties only affects him. In fact, he is harming himself. Negligence of a religious duty is not a punishable offense. And forcing someone to perform such acts doesn't increase his sincerity. A Muslim should suggest that his brother practice his faith, but he must not force him to. Force only causes resentment and loathing or it causes a person to be brainwashed into acceptance, when Islam is to convince one of the truth.

Many people see fit to shelter their family from other religions and ideologies, as a means of keeping them on the right path. Islam doesn't adhere to such monasticism. In fact, you are more pious if you accept and practice Islam in an unfavorable environment. A Muslim's practices and his character should illuminate through the darkness of those who are not Muslims. The truth is Islam is a beacon of light that shines through the darkness. Its truthfulness should contrast that which is false, so any investigation and comparison of something to Islam should convince one that Islam is what should be embraced. Many people feel it is their obligation to shield their family from something like atheism. A Muslim and any theist should welcome the comparison. It is "prayer, charity, forgiveness, empathy" versus "do as you please." A pursuit of truth that leads to certainty or the pursuit to establish uncertainty. The list of solutions opposed to a perpetual list of problems. If what you believe is the truth, it will be accepted because it is the best system, with the best methods to solve problems.

17:81 And say: "Truth has (now) arrived, and Falsehood perished: for Falsehood is (by its nature) bound to perish."

PROPAGATION

16:125 Invite (all) to the Way of thy Lord with wisdom and beautiful preaching; and argue with them in ways that are best and most gracious: for thy Lord knoweth best, who have strayed from His Path, and who receive guidance.

This verse should be on the tip of every Muslims tongue, for it instructs them on this important duty and it is a great defense to use against those who insist that Islam is a religion forced on others. ALLAH knows that man holds his beliefs dear to his heart and this vulnerability demands sensitivity from those who do not share his views. ALLAH also knows man's inclination to rub his knowledge in the face of others.

Often times, the first thing one does when he learns something new and contrary to the view of the majority is to belittle a person for his implausible belief. I have firsthand knowledge of this, for as a young man, I ridiculed people for what they believed in. Yet, even when I was absolutely correct, I was astounded that no one took heed. This is when I realized that my approach was wrong to begin with. As I grew older, I began to understand the impact that religion has on people and as I read the Qur'an more, my approach became more in accordance with 16:125.

CONTROVERSIAL SUBJECTS

People are more receptive to advice than to ridicule. They are more receptive to the beauty of Islam, than to the error of their religion. They are more receptive to the solution than to a list of problems.

ALLAH says the best people in speech are those who invite others to him, work righteousness and submits to him (41:33). And offering this invitation is not a recommendation but a duty of all Muslims. Propagation was the first and second commandment given to Prophet Muhammad (pbuh) (96:1-5, 74:1-3). Not fasting, not Salat, not charity, but evangelism was the task to be addressed first and foremost. This came at a time when Prophet Muhammad (pbuh) had very little information or knowledge to give. But he was to give WHATEVER that he knew of the truth. Knowledge is to be shared, not hoarded. It is to be shared even with those whom you think are doomed to failure.

7:164 When some of them said: "Why do ye preach to a people whom Allah will destroy or visit with a terrible punishment?"- said the preachers." To discharge our duty to your Lord, and perchance they may fear Him."

Whether a person will believe in Islam or not, it is up to the Muslim to deliver the message (17:107). But the invitation is not the only duty spoken of. The Qur'an also asks Muslims to argue with others. It encourages debate and it requires that you have some knowledge of the subject that you are debating. The Muslim is supposed to confront others with the truth (103:3). Of course, honesty is the most important aspect to any debate. In chapter 3, the Qur'an is dealing with the topic of Jesus' (pbuh) death and his alleged divinity. It states that Jesus (pbuh) is not divine and that he did not die. And it also gives, in this chapter and others, its argument as to why Jesus (pbuh) can't be divine and how it is that he was not killed. Obviously this is in direct contradiction to the popular Christian belief, thus the explanations are for Muslims to debate with the Christian audience. And the Qur'an offers an interesting request for the debate.

3:61 If any one disputes in this matter with thee, now after (full) knowledge Hath come to thee, say: "Come! let us gather together,- our sons and your sons, our women and your women, ourselves and yourselves: Then let us earnestly pray, and invoke the curse of Allah on those who lie!"

The wisdom in this verse is profound. The request for families to meet is one which sets a stage for honesty and integrity in the debate. No one wants to humiliate or embarrass another in the presence of that person's family and no one wants to be embarrassed. Also people are more receptive to their family members giving them advice and telling them the truth on the outcome of the debate. Finally, ALLAH suggests that both parties pray for the truth to manifest and to ask God to curse anyone who lies in the debate. If both sincerely believe in God, it is rather unlikely that one would be less than truthful after asking God to curse the liar. With these stipulations, it builds a better environment for both parties to arrive at the truth.

The Qur'an, in a short chapter dedicated to those who reject Islam, tells the Muslims what he must say to those who wish for no further debate or those who wish for no debate at all.

109.1 Say: O ye that reject Faith!

109.2 I worship not that which ye worship,

109.3 Nor will ye worship that which I worship.

109.4 And I will not worship that which ye have been wont to worship,

109.5 Nor will ye worship that which I worship.

109.6 To you be your Way, and to me mine.

CONTROVERSIAL SUBJECTS

This is the entirety of the chapter. There is no subsequent verse which commands Muslims to kill those who reject Islam. There is no call for Muslims to kill those who wish to convert Muslims to some other faith. Muslims are to engage non-Muslims in dialogue, to come to the truth. If they are in a position of authority over you, like a parent, Muslims are to reject their belief and bear with them with kindness and justice (31:14-15). There is no justification of a conflict or war on those who wish to convert you to their set of beliefs, except a cordial war of words.

WAR

9:5 But when the forbidden months are past, then fight and slay the Pagans wherever ye find them, and seize them, beleaguer them, and lie in wait for them in every stratagem (of war).

In this book, I have never made such a blasphemous claim that Prophet Muhammad (pbuh) is ALLAH, but I have those exact words in that exact order in this book. If someone quoted me saying Ishmael said "Muhammad is ALLAH" (in the section: Monotheism vs. Polytheism), technically they are telling the truth, but actually they are not. It is to divorce this phrase from its context, to declare that I intended to convey the message that Prophet Muhammad (pbuh) is the Supreme Being. What would you call a person who would do such a thing? If it is a mistake, it is somewhat understandable and forgivable, but if it's intentional, it's almost a crime. This mistake or lie is being perpetuated on Islam every single day. You see, someone can make a verse seem to say anything if you don't use its context.

At the time of the American Revolution, it is without doubt that American generals told their troops to go and kill the British. At the time of the World War II, there were generals who told the American troops to kill Germans. At the time of the Civil War, there were generals who told their troops to kill other Americans. Can I use their quotes to say that Americans are allowed to kill Britons, Germans and even other Americans, today? No. We must also realize that these generals were not pronouncing death on their adversaries, simply because they were British, German or American, but because they were deemed criminals.

The Qur'an's verse mentioned above is actually about the Arab pagans who broke a peace treaty with the Muslims, thus it is legally self-defense. If the context of Chapter 9 is explained, the claim that Islam promotes unwarranted violence becomes a joke. In fact, the entire verse 5 is generally not quoted. It is given in the manner that I have it above. This is because it is abundantly clear that this is a war (this is why "of war" is in parenthesis), not a random attack on non-believers. And more importantly, the Qur'an says that the Muslim's enemy can repent and be Muslim IN THE MIDDLE OF WAR. And if they seek shelter, the Muslim is to give it to them and take him to safety.

9.5 But when the forbidden months are past, then fight and slay the Pagans wherever ye find them, an seize them, beleaguer them, and lie in wait for them in every stratagem (of war); but if they repent, and establish regular prayers and practice regular charity, then open the way for them: for Allah is Oft-forgiving, Most Merciful.

9.6 If one amongst the Pagans ask thee for asylum, grant it to him, so that he may hear the word of Allah; and then escort him to where he can be secure. That is because they are men without knowledge.

Does the American military offer combatants shelter and the opportunity to enjoy democracy on the battlefield? Probably not. The Muslim is not to be a cold-blooded killer, but to be a fierce soldier as well as one who invites others to Islam even in the middle of war. In fact, religious obligations are still observed on the battlefield.

CONTROVERSIAL SUBJECTS

4:102 When thou (O Messenger) art with them, and standest to lead them in prayer, Let one party of them stand up (in prayer) with thee, Taking their arms with them. When they finish their prostrations, let them Take their position in the rear. And let the other party come up which hath not yet prayed -and let them pray with thee, Taking all precaution, and bearing arms: the Unbelievers wish, if ye were negligent of your arms and your baggage, to assault you in a single rush. But there is no blame on you if ye put away your arms because of the inconvenience of rain or because ye are ill; but take (every) precaution for yourselves. For the Unbelievers Allah hath prepared a humiliating punishment.

That the Muslim is to pray and invite other to Islam, even in the times of war, is a testament to the importance of these pillars of Islam and a testament to the true goal of a Muslim, to remember God and invite others to him. Interestingly, Jesus (pbuh) too prayed before battle (Luke 22:36-41).

I have seen the Qur'an's verses printed many times to substantiate the claim that Muslims are to kill non-believers, with the implication that it is simply because they are non-believers. I have even been at an interfaith dialogue where a non-Muslim "scholar" quoted these popular verses. Of course, I immediately raised my hand for questioning. My objective was to determine which category did this person fit, was he a person who made a mistake or a person who intentional smears Islam? So I was going to ask him to read the 2 verses before his quote and after his quote, because he had a Qur'an right in front of him. If he quickly saw his error and apologized, I would consider it a mistake. Any other action might render him something less respectable in this forum where he was being respected for his knowledge and honesty. Unfortunately for me and my test, but fortunately for the sake of truth, another Muslim brother quickly opened the Qur'an and read the verses aloud to prove that the verses this man had quoted were actually actions of self-defense.

Chapters 8 and 9 of the Qur'an deal specifically with the principles of war. And it is touched upon in various other chapters, as well. Because Islam is guidance for a complete way of life, it informs its followers on how and when to conduct war. As with most people who present the truth to those profiting off of falsehood, Prophet Muhammad (pbuh) and his followers' lives were endangered for their denouncement of the idolatry, alcoholism, slavery, harsh treatment of women, and the murder of female babies, etc. And the Qur'an advises its followers not to attack others on false pretenses, but they are to verify any accusations made before taking action (49:6). At the grassroots level of Islam in Arabia, the Muslims were an overwhelming minority. There would be little need to verify that the majority were non-Muslims, if Muslims killed non-Muslims simply because they were non-Muslims. It's apparent that the Muslim was to verify that those who have been accused of being his enemies are in fact his enemies. And they were. In these times, ALLAH sent revelation as an inspiration for these early Muslims to stand firm and fight, despite the tremendous odds, against corruption and oppression, until these things no longer existed.

2:190 Fight in the cause of Allah those who fight you, but do not transgress limits; for Allah loveth not transgressors.

2:191 And slay them wherever ye catch them, and turn them out from where they have Turned you out; for tumult and oppression are worse than slaughter; but fight them not at the Sacred Mosque, unless they (first) fight you there; but if they fight you, slay them. Such is the reward of those who suppress faith.

2:192 But if they cease, Allah is Oft-forgiving, Most Merciful.

2:193 And fight them on until there is no more Tumult or oppression, and there prevail justice and faith in Allah; but if they cease, Let there be no hostility except to those who practise oppression.

THE LEGAL DEFINITION OF SELF-DEFENSE

CONTROVERSIAL SUBJECTS

Defense, Self-Defense:

-A defense to certain criminal charges involving force (e.g. murder)

-Use of force is justified when a person reasonably believes that it is necessary for the defense of oneself or another against the immediate use of unlawful force. However, a person must use no more force than appears reasonably necessary in the circumstances.

-Force likely to cause death or great bodily harm is justified in self-defense only if a person reasonably believes that such force is necessary to prevent death or great bodily harm.

(http://www.lectlaw.com/def/d030.htm)

The legal definition of self-defense is nothing but a paraphrasing of verses in the Qur'an which stipulate the circumstances in which to wage a just war in self-defense. The Qur'an encourages Muslims to try to avoid war. First Muslims are commanded to live justly and kindly with non-Muslims who are in turn just and kind to them. But we are not to befriend those who drive us from our homes, who try to force us to change our beliefs or those who support others who do these things (60:8-9). We are to ignore the annoyances of those against us (33:48). And Muslims are told to bolster their army and their armor to try and deter the enemy from attacking them.

8:60 Against them make ready your strength to the utmost of your power, including steeds of war, to strike terror into (the hearts of) the enemies, of Allah and your enemies, and others besides, whom ye may not know, but whom Allah doth know. Whatever ye shall spend in the cause of Allah, shall be repaid unto you, and ye shall not be treated unjustly.

8.61 But if the enemy inclines towards peace, do thou (also) incline towards peace, and trust in Allah: for He is One that heareth and knoweth (all things).

If these things are not effective, then the Muslim is commanded to "FIGHT IN THE CAUSE OF ALLAH." This phrase is often mistaken to mean kill to spread the religion, but this is the furthest from the truth. Fight in the cause of ALLAH is explicitly self-defense. It is fighting against tumult and oppression (2:191), fighting those who fight you (2:190), fighting those who try to force Muslims to change their religion (60:9), and fighting those who drive Muslims from their homes simply because they are Muslims (22:39-40). Every time the Qur'an is quoted about "fighting in the cause of Allah" it is for these reasons. Therefore from now on, if you see this quoted whether from a Muslim or non-Muslim, and he is quoting out of context, ask him to read or explain the context of the verse.

4:75 And why should ye not fight in the cause of Allah and of those who, being weak, are ill-treated (and oppressed)?- Men, women, and children, whose cry is: "Our Lord! Rescue us from this town, whose people are oppressors; and raise for us from thee one who will protect; and raise for us from thee one who will help!"

4:76 Those who believe fight in the cause of Allah, and those who reject Faith fight in the cause of Evil. So fight ye against the friends of Satan: feeble indeed is the cunning of Satan.

Self-defense also includes defending the livelihood of those unable to defend themselves in the legal definition as well as the Qur'an. A Muslim's duty is to fight tyranny and oppression against himself and anyone else. Notice 4:75 says men, women and children, not Muslim men, women and children. In some translations this verse begins "what is wrong with you that you do not fight in the cause of ALLAH?" and indeed when the cause is clearly defined, it does beg this question.

4:77 Hast thou not turned Thy vision to those who were told to hold back their hands (from fight) but establish regular prayers and spend in regular charity? When (at length) the order for fighting was issued to them, behold! a section of them feared men as - or even more than - they should have feared Allah. They said: "Our Lord! Why hast Thou ordered us to fight? Wouldst Thou not Grant us respite to our (natural) term, near (enough)?" Say: "Short is the enjoyment of this world: the Hereafter is the best for those who do right: Never will ye be dealt with unjustly in the very least!

4:78 "Wherever ye are, death will find you out, even if ye are in towers built up strong and high!" If some good befalls them, they say, "This is from Allah"; but if evil, they say, "This is from thee" (O Prophet). Say: "All things are from Allah." But what hath come to these people, that they fail to understand a single fact?

4:79 Whatever good, (O man!) happens to thee, is from Allah; but whatever evil happens to thee, is from thy (own) soul. and We have sent thee as a messenger to (instruct) mankind. And enough is Allah for a witness.

The Qur'an insists that the cause for fighting is so justified that it is worth dying for and one should not fear death while he is defending himself or others. Death will come to you wherever you are. Running from death is futile (33:16). In the face of oppression, it can be a slow lingering death or a swift blow on a whim by a tyrant. Tyranny has no conscience, no ethics. It becomes a game of survival for you, your family and friends and anyone subject to this oppression.

2:216 Fighting is prescribed for you, and ye dislike it. But it is possible that ye dislike a thing which is good for you, and that ye love a thing which is bad for you. But Allah knoweth, and ye know not.

No one wants war, but it comes a time when it is absolutely necessary for your survival. The Qur'an says in this instance, war is good for you. But the things people love to do is procrastination and sit idly while things fall apart around them. The Qur'an speaks disparagingly of rich people who use their privilege for exemption from war or those who make excuses as to why they cannot fight in the cause of ALLAH (9:86-93). Allah requires that injustice be extinguished.

MARTYR (SHAHEED)

Those who do not fear war and death, but give of their wealth, their person and their life in defense of themselves and those unable to fight are called martyrs. In Islam, as in every society on earth, a martyr is celebrated and praised for his conviction and bravery in the face of tyranny. Death is the ultimate sacrifice. There is no more a person can give than his life, so they deserve all the praise that they get. And whether you face death and survive or you succumb, you will be greatly rewarded for your effort.

4:74 Let those fight in the cause of Allah Who sell the life of this world for the hereafter. To him who fighteth in the cause of Allah,- whether he is slain or gets victory - Soon shall We give him a reward of great (value).

CONTROVERSIAL SUBJECTS

These sentiments are echoed numerous times in the Qur'an (9:111, 3:169-172). And the Qur'an tells Muslims not to call a martyr dead, but say that he is alive with ALLAH (2:154, 3:169).

2:154 And say not of those who are slain in the way of Allah: "They are dead." Nay, they are living, though ye perceive not.

We cannot perceive it because the presence of ALLAH is far from the realm of our five senses. And the Qur'an does not say that a martyr will receive 72 virgins, thus this is not the reason that one becomes a martyr (the reward of paradise will be discussed later). In fact, you do not become a martyr on purpose. You are martyred by your enemy. Suicide is forbidden in Islam (2:195, 4:29). Murder is strictly forbidden in Islam. It is only permissible to kill someone in self-defense or in the requirements of justice and law for punishment (6:151). The Qur'an emphasizes the importance of human life by reiterating the impact that one act of murder has on humanity.

5:32 On that account: We ordained for the Children of Israel that if any one slew a person - unless it be for murder or for spreading mischief in the land -it would be as if he slew the whole people: and if any one saved a life, it would be as if he saved the life of the whole people. Then although there came to them Our messengers with clear signs, yet, even after that, many of them continued to commit excesses in the land.

5:33 The punishment of those who wage war against Allah and His Messenger, and strive with might and main for mischief through the land is: execution, or crucifixion, or the cutting off of hands and feet from opposite sides, or exile from the land: that is their disgrace in this world, and a heavy punishment is theirs in the Hereafter;

5:34 Except for those who repent before they fall into your power: in that case, know that Allah is Oft-forgiving, Most Merciful.

The Qur'an says killing one person unjustly is like killing everyone. Because the death of one person is so impactful, those who engage in mass murder are to be dealt with very harshly. Their punishment is dependent upon the severity of their atrocities. And these punishments are used as deterrents for others from committing these crimes. Their punishment can be reduced if they cease their evil ways and repent before the tyranny is put to a halt. Though the punishments seem harsh, they are effective. There is less crime in the country of Saudi Arabia than in the city of Washington, D.C.

PEACE

Muslims fight oppression until it ceases. He is not to live in a state of oppression without challenging it. But when the enemy wishes to surrender he immediately halts the fighting.

8:61 But if the enemy incline towards peace, do thou (also) incline towards peace, and trust in Allah: for He is One that heareth and knoweth (all things).

But this cease-fire comes with stipulations. Peace treaties are drawn up and those who fought against the Muslims are to pay a Jizya tax. This tax often causes quite a stir of emotions, maybe because it is reminiscent of the British tax on the 13 colonies (though I find little fault with a tax which subsidized the cost of war for the establishment of the colonies' existence in the first place). I suppose that those who are repelled by this tax never consider that the people who caused the war should also compensate for it. Neither do they consider that every Muslim pays Zakat as it is a tenet of Islam, and non-Muslim should also pay a tax. Also the Jizya tax is less than the Zakat that the Muslim pays. The Jizya tax's purpose is the exact same purpose that the American government has for the taxes that it TAKES from its citizens. Americans are not given the option to pay or not. Taxes are extracted before the worker receives his or her pay. These taxes provide health, safety and security benefits. The argument against such a tax in Islam is actually an argument against taxes in general.

JIHAD

The battles in Islam are not always physical. The word jihad means struggle. This struggle can be an inner struggle or an external struggle. The external struggle can be the fighting in the cause of Allah or simply the struggle to propagate Islam to others.

2:207 And there is the type of man who gives his life to earn the pleasure of Allah: And Allah is full of kindness to (His) devotees.

Malcolm X was a Muslim man who gave his life for the spread of the truth of Islam and though he never fought in war, he is a Muslim martyr. Ahmed Deedat, though he was not killed, he gave his life in another way to the spread of Islam. Both these men's lives were in a state of jihad. They were mujahideen or those who practice Jihad. Jihad can be applied by force in terms of self-defense, or by your words and deeds to spread Islam. If a Muslim is incapable of speaking out or defending himself against injustice, the lowest form of Jihad is to hate sin in his heart.

But the most important Jihad is the one which the Muslim has with himself. In fact, he cannot struggle with the world, until he has first grappled with the instinct and urges inside of himself. Though the internal struggle is ever present, it is controllable by man. He struggles daily to be righteous and to do what is best and resist what it wrong. In all, jihad is not a holy war, but an internal and external struggle to do what is right. In this sense, everyone is a mujahideen.

RIGHT HAND POSSESS

When slaves are spoken of in the Qur'an they are called "those who your right hand possesses." This is not the traditional definition of slavery in which a person is kidnapped and forced to work for free under harsh treatment. Of course, this form of slavery is denounced in Islam, as Prophet Muhammad (pbuh) freed Bilal, the first muezzin, from his cruel slave master. "Those who your right hands possess" are prisoners of war. It is recommended for Muslims to teach these prisoners Islam and if they believe, then they are permissible to marry (4:25). Yet the Qur'an never encourages, establishes or endorses slavery in any form. In fact, the Qur'an encourages, establishes and endorses the abolition of slavery. The Qur'an systematically prepared an end to slavery.

4:36 ...do good to what your right hands possess

9:60 Alms are ...for those in bondage

4:92 Never should a believer kill a believer, but by mistake. If one (so) kills a believer, it is ordained that he should free a believing slave

CONTROVERSIAL SUBJECTS

5:89 He will call you to account for your deliberate oaths: for expiation give a slave his freedom.

3:79 It is not (possible) for any human being unto whom Allah had given the Scripture and wisdom and the prophethood that he should afterwards have said unto mankind: Be slaves of me instead of Allah's.

47:4 So when you meet in battle those who disbelieve, then smite the necks until when you have overcome them, then make (them) prisoners, and afterwards either set them free as a favor or let them ransom (themselves) until the war terminates.

2:177 ... it is righteousness... to spend of your substance... for the ransom of slaves

24:33 Let those who find not the wherewithal for marriage keep themselves chaste, until Allah gives them means out of His grace. And if any of your slaves ask for a deed in writing (to enable them to earn their freedom for a certain sum), give them such a deed if ye know any good in them: yea, give them something yourselves out of the means which Allah has given to you.

Speaking of slavery, when my father was about seven years old, he was told by his grandmother about her childhood. She recalled when her great grandmother, who as a slave, told her how they would pray in a barn and put a huge kennel in front of the door to drown out the sound, so the slave master would not hear them praying.

If he heard them praying, he would kill the leader of the prayer. This story always stuck with my father. He thought white people to be so hateful, that they would teach the slave Christianity, and then beat or kill him for practicing it. Later in life, my father became interested in the Nation of Islam (A sect of Islam). He began telling his family about the religion. And every family member had some disparaging remarks about his newfound faith (One friend of the family said he had never heard of Islam or a Muslim, but he knew if they don't believe in Jesus (pbuh), they were going to hell). My father decided to ask his grandmother about her opinion of the religion. He brought a couple of books. One of them was entitled something like "The Black Man at Prayer." In the book was a picture of a man (the Imam) standing and people lined up behind him performing Salat as Muslims do 5 times a day. His grandmother immediately recognized the posture as the same one her great grandmother described doing. My father's grandmother had solidified the truth of Islam to him. The slave master was not beating them for practicing Christianity, but for practicing Islam.

My father told this story to another Muslim, whose grandparents told him the same story. My father said as a child, he always loved movies like "Ali Baba and the 40 thieves" and "The Arabian Knights." He said though they had bad pronunciation of Arabic, he always felt chills when they uttered "ALLAHU AKBAR." He recalled a conversation he had with yet another Muslim brother, who told him how he was immediately drawn to Islam, as soon as he heard its message. Both became convinced that many of the African American Muslims of today were first attracted to Islam because they were descendants of Muslim slaves from Africa.

FORGIVENESS

Some will be surprised, if they have never read the Qur'an, as to the continuous command to believers to show mercy for those you cause them harm. It is often said that the God of Islam and the Hebrew scripture is so cruel, but Jesus (pbuh) is so forgiving. But it has been seen that God is full of forgiveness and he does so inexhaustibly. The source of Jesus (pbuh)' compassionate and forgiving teachings is ALLAH.

42:39 And those who, when an oppressive wrong is inflicted on them, (are not cowed but) help and defend themselves.

42:40 The recompense for an injury is an injury equal thereto (in degree): but if a person forgives and makes reconciliation, his reward is due from Allah: for (Allah) loveth not those who do wrong.

42:41 But indeed if any do help and defend themselves after a wrong (done) to them, against such there is no cause of blame.

42:42 The blame is only against those who oppress men and wrong-doing and insolently transgress beyond bounds through the land, defying right and justice: for such there will be a penalty grievous.

42:43 But indeed if any show patience and forgive, that would truly be an exercise of courageous will and resolution in the conduct of affairs.

If anyone is familiar with the Bible, they knows that Moses (pbuh) gave the punishment "an eye for an eye" (Leviticus 24:19-20). Jesus (pbuh) later suggests that one should turn the other cheek and forgive, instead of using the "eye for an eye" method (Matthew 5:38-39). Later Jesus (pbuh) uses a whip to clear out the temple and asks his disciples to buy swords to defend against those opposing him (John 2:14-15, Luke 22:36). Prophet Muhammad (pbuh) reconciles these two images of Jesus (pbuh) depicted in the Bible, as well as the Law of Moses (pbuh). It is permissible and acceptable to harm someone as they have harmed you in self-defense, as long as you do not transgress bounds (2:190), meaning commit a sin in doing so (a Muslim cannot kill an innocent family member of one who kills his family member because this is a sin), but it is more beneficial to you if you forgive them for their transgressions and reconcile your differences with words. This type of Muslim forgives even when they are angry (42:37), because Allah recommends forgiveness.

Muslims are to forgive the non-Muslims for all the problems that they caused (45:14). This includes those who try to turn him away from Islam (2:108-109). The Qur'an accuses the people of previous scriptures of changing, forgetting or distorting the message of God on several occasions (2:59, 2:27, 3:78), but the Muslim is told to forgive and overlook their deceit (5:13). Those who wage war on ALLAH and the Prophet (pbuh) and cause mischief in the land can repent for their sins (5:33-34, 9:74). How can this be a violent religion, a religion spread by the sword when apostates can try to kill the Prophet (pbuh) and they are still eligible for forgiveness?

PROPHETS (pbut)

40:78 We did aforetime send messengers before thee: of them there are some whose story We have related to thee, and some whose story We have not related to thee.

God has sent a messenger to ALL the people of the world (4:41, 10:47, 35:24). Many are mentioned the Qur'an and many more are not. The Qur'an lists as prophets:

Adam (2:31, 3:33)

Hud (7:65)

Salih (7:73)

Shuaib (7:85)

Idris [Enoch] (19:56-57)

Dhul Kifl [Ezekiel] (21:85-86)

CONTROVERSIAL SUBJECTS

Ibrahim [Abraham]

Ishaq [Isaac]

Yaqub [Jacob]

Nuh [Noah]

Dawud [David]

Suleiman [Solomon]

Ayyub [Job]

Yusuf [Joseph]

Musa [Moses]

Harun [Aaron]

Zakariyya [Zachariah]

Yahya [John the Baptist]

Isa [Jesus (pbuh)]

Ilyas [Elias]

Ismail [Ishmael]

Al Yasaa [Elisha]

Yunus [Jonah]

Lut [Lot] (6:83-86)

and Luqman (31:12-13) (pbut) may also be a prophet of ALLAH. Muhammad (pbuh) is the prophet sent to the whole world (21:107, 34:28) and the last of the prophets.

33:40 Muhammad is not the father of any of your men, but (he is) the Messenger of Allah, and the Seal of the Prophets: and Allah has full knowledge of all things.

Though Prophet Muhammad (pbuh) is to guide the whole of humanity and he is the last prophet, the Qur'an is adamant that Muslims are to make no distinction between the prophets of Islam (2:136, 285, 3:84, 4:152). Despite an effort to combat the reverence other religious people have for their prophets, it seems Muslims often fall victim to exalting Prophet Muhammad (pbuh) above other prophets. Though ALLAH gives different prophets different gifts and honors (2:253), it is ALLAH who may distinguish between the honor due a particular prophet over another. Because one prophet is more successful than another is no ground to exalt one over the other. All their messages come from the same source, but it is the people who decide whether to believe or not. And the miracles one works does not determine the status in Islam, either. Different circumstances call for different means to convey and convince. In the end, the words and deeds done by a prophet is from ALLAH, thus the distinction is impossible, because you are comparing ALLAH'S gift with ALLAH'S gift.

The Qur'an is not a story book, so you will not find "once upon a time" tales of the prophets, but rather aspects of their lives and mission highlighted in order to convey the message of Islam to mankind. It speaks of Noah's (pbuh) ark, Abraham's (pbuh) sacrifice and how he used his own reasoning to find God, David's and Solomon's (pbut) rule as king and messengers of God, as well as the plight of the other prophets. The Prophets, Moses and Jesus (pbut), are said to have prophesied about the coming of the Prophet Muhammad (pbuh) (7:157, 61:6), so perhaps it is no coincidence that these two figures are spoken of on numerous occasions in the Qur'an. Moses is spoken of so often because of his leadership through the children of Israel's emancipation and his role as king and lawgiver. Jesus (pbuh), on the other hand, is seen by the Qur'an to be a highly misrepresented figure. Thus the Qur'an is intent on setting the record straight on this great prophet. It explains his miraculous birth, his first miracle and subsequent miracles thereafter. The Qur'an says he was a prophet sent to the Jews, but he is not God, he was not a sacrifice for mankind and he was not crucified.

[An interesting side note is that the Qur'an calls Jesus (pbuh), "Isa" in Arabic instead of Yasoa (the Arabic rendering of the Hebrew name, Yeshua). This point is harped on by some Christians, who assume that the Qur'an has made a tremendous blunder. Fortunately for Muslims, "Isa" is identical in sound to "Eesho" the name Jesus (pbuh) would be called by in Aramaic, the language which Jesus (pbuh) spoke. And the Qur'an also calls Jesus' (pbuh) followers "Nasara" which means Nazarenes, not Christians or "Masihi," a nickname given to his followers long after his time on earth. The Qur'an seems to differentiate between the followers of Jesus (pbuh) during his lifetime and those who followed him later. As Gary Miller pointed out, the Qur'an is carefully not to put the word "Christian" on the lips of Jesus (pbuh), because it would be an anachronism. These are more proofs that Prophet Muhammad (pbuh) did not copy his information from the Gospels or from Christian sources, but he got his information from the supreme source of truth and knowledge.]

THE PROPHETS' (pbut) ENEMIES

Because of the stature and honor of messengers and prophets in Islam, it is often the custom of Muslims to name their child after one of these great men. This custom not only serves as a means of respect and honor given to these prophets, but as a lesson for children to discover the history of their names. It is also a standard to reach for a child. All of these men are examples by which every person should follow, but the problem is sometimes they are said to have done things which are not very admirable. Prophets are often attributed some very sinful and disgusting acts.

In the Bible, seemingly ever prophet is guilty of some major offense to the laws of God and the laws of decency. We must realize that the Bible is someone's account of the lives of the prophets of that time. It is the Hadiths or traditions of the prophets.

And it is history and HIS story, the author's view of the events. It is not the actual words of God, nor the autobiography of the prophets. When writing about your heroes, the author has the opportunity to embellish or alter aspects of their lives, as he sees fit. In a society which is largely illiterate, it is quite easy to write whatever you would like. But the danger is the diversion from the main focus of the "message" of the prophet, to the "life" of the prophet himself. The Qur'an warns the Muslim that for EVERY prophet there are enemies which mesmerize men with words to lure him from the message of Islam.

6:112 Likewise did We make for every Messenger an enemy, evil ones among men and jinns, inspiring each other with flowery discourses by way of deception. If thy Lord had so planned, they would not have done it: so leave them and their inventions alone.

6:113 To such (deceit) let the hearts of those incline, who have no faith in the hereafter: let them delight in it, and let them earn from it what they may.

6:114 Say: "Shall I seek for judge other than Allah? - when He it is Who hath sent unto you the Book, explained in detail." They know full well, to whom We have given the Book, that it hath been sent down from thy Lord in truth. Never be then of those who doubt.

6:115 The word of thy Lord doth find its fulfilment in truth and in justice: None can change His words: for He is the one who heareth and knoweth all.

6:116 Wert thou to follow the common run of those on earth, they will lead thee away from the way of Allah. They follow nothing but conjecture: they do nothing but lie.

CONTROVERSIAL SUBJECTS

6:117 Thy Lord knoweth best who strayeth from His way. He knoweth best who they are that receive His guidance.

These enemies of the prophets make up fancy stories about them in order for their own agenda to be met. If they wish to outlaw marriage, for example, they simply say that the prophet said "marriage is a sin." Though it is not from God at all, if a rule is said to be from the prophet, it may soon become a part of the religion. Some authors wishing to make their prophets more down to earth might write that the prophets were sinful or mischievous. But the Muslim is equip with the tool to decipher the true from the false.

25:30 Then the Messenger will say: "O my Lord! Truly my people took this Qur'an for just foolish nonsense."

25:31 Thus have We made for every prophet an enemy among the sinners: but enough is thy Lord to guide and to help.

25:32 Those who reject Faith say: "Why is not the Qur'an revealed to him all at once? Thus (is it revealed), that We may strengthen thy heart thereby, and We have rehearsed it to thee in slow, well-arranged stages, gradually.

25:33 And no question do they bring to thee but We reveal to thee the truth and the best explanation (thereof).

The Muslim is told in the Qur'an, that prophets are men of exemplary behavior. They are pious and devout and fearful of ALLAH, more so than anyone of their nation. This is why they were chosen by ALLAH. Armed with the CRITERION, Muslims can easily sift through the Bible and find the story of the drunkenness of Noah, the curse of Noah, the incest of Abraham, Jacob wrestling God, Moses' blasphemy, Aaron's idolatry, Elisha causing two bears to kill 42 children for teasing his bald-head, Ezekiel eating human feces, David's murder and adultery, Solomon's harem and Jesus (pbut) calling a sick child a dog as innovations used by the enemies of these prophets. The Bible even contains such Hadiths for God, where he is unable to see behind a tree, he is regretful, he needs advise, he eats food and he rests.

The Muslim can identify these things for what they are. When he sees that Abraham, Moses and Jesus (pbut) prayed like a Muslim, he understands this to be the truth confirmed in the Qur'an. But when he reads that Jesus (pbuh) says you will not reunite with your wife in Paradise, he must assume that this is not from Jesus (pbuh), but they are words falsely attributed to Jesus (pbuh). Unfortunately many Muslims do not use the Criterion as a measure of truth all the time.

HADITH

The criterion for judging other scriptures is most abandoned by Muslims with respect to the Hadiths of Prophet Muhammad (pbuh). The Muslim must be reminded that the Qur'an says for "every" prophet there are enemies who wish to divert attention from the message of that prophet to stories about the prophet, this includes Prophet Muhammad (pbuh). And the Qur'an is the Criterion for "every" scripture, that includes the Hadiths, which like the Bible contain numerous errors. But despite these errors, much of the things said to have been uttered by the Prophet, the things done by the Prophet and things which he condoned are believed to be the gospel truth. Muslims use the Hadiths to understand the Qur'an, when it should be the other way around. They denounce music, paintings, pictures, cameras and even the game of chess because there are traditions which states that Prophet Muhammad (pbuh) did not approve of these things. In fact, one Hadith says any game of chance is forbidden, which would include all games. Some Muslims do not eat with their left hand for fear that they are feeding satan and they do not urinate with their right hand, because this is the supposed custom of the Prophet (pbuh). Of course, none of these things are in the Qur'an. The justification for such strict

CONTROVERSIAL SUBJECTS

adherence to the Sunnah, or way of Prophet Muhammad (pbuh) is that he was the living Qur'an or the Qur'an in action and he is an example for all of mankind forever (33:21). Taking advantage of this fact, the authors of some Hadiths incorporated their own ways of Prophet Muhammad (pbuh).

Since Prophet Muhammad (pbuh) is the Qur'an in action, Muslims must first master the Qur'an, right? Instead, the Hadiths are advertised as inseparable from the Qur'an, even though they are admittedly transmitted through a number of people before being recorded and there are different versions to the same story. Due to its well known and numerous imperfections, it is even more important to be well acquainted with the Qur'an before accepting it. The Talmud, is supposed to explain the Jewish Torah, but it is filled with laws and rules which are in direct violation of the Jewish Torah. But the Jewish Torah is not the actual revelation sent to Moses by God and the gospels of the Bible are not the revelations sent to Jesus (pbut).

The Jewish Torah and the Gospels of the Bible are Hadiths or traditions of Moses and Jesus (pbut). The Bible is the Hadiths of the prophets of old. And the method that the Muslims use to distinguish the truth in the Bible must be implemented when reading the Hadiths of Prophet Muhammad (pbuh). Imagine if the Hadiths of Prophet Muhammad (pbuh) were the only source to formulate the religion of Islam. Imagine if Muslims had the same dilemma as Jews and Christians, that they have only the traditions of their prophet. If Muslims only had Hadiths, Islam would be quite different. This is why the Qur'an says that the majority of the most pious Muslims will come from the early generations of Islam. As time passes, Muslims are drifting further away from the Qur'an and closer to the traditions. But the Qur'an is actually what the Hadiths claim to be. The Qur'an is the narration of what Prophet Muhammad (pbuh) did and said in respond to others and what he taught to his followers pertaining to the religion of Islam.

When one is involved in comparative religion, it becomes easy to see how many Hadiths are complete fabrications. In debate, I have surmised on many occasions that the Jewish Torah is not the words of God because of its depiction of God. One example is how God is given advice or counsel by human beings. On several occasions, Moses (pbuh) advised God and God is said to have taken Moses' (pbuh) advice and changed his mind. GOD CHANGED HIS MIND according to the

Jewish Torah because of the words of his own creation. I concluded that a human being cannot be more reasonable or rational than God, so these stories in the Jewish Torah are not true. The Prophet Abraham (pbuh) is also said to converse with God and negotiate God's punishment on the people of Sodom and Gomorrah in the Jewish Torah. Once again, I scoffed at the idea that God can be bargained with. His knowledge, wisdom, compassion and justice cannot be trumped by that of his creation. When I mention these things to those who have faith in the Bible, there is very little offered in terms of a rebuttal. It is relatively clear that these things did not take place. What is astounding about this is that there are Muslims who see no correlation between these stories of the Bible and those of the Hadiths.

Prophet Muhammad (pbuh) is said to have NEGOTIATED with THE ALL-WISE AND ALL-KNOWING ALLAH on the amount of prayers that Muslims must perform daily. According to the Hadiths, ALLAH had insisted that Muslims prayer 50 times a day. And like Abraham and Moses (pbut) in the Jewish Torah, Prophet Muhammad, at the behest of Moses (pbut), is said to have talked God into accepting five prayers a day. This story is totally unacceptable. It is in fact blasphemous. When the angels questioned God about giving man the ability to do right and to do wrong, ALLAH said "I KNOW WHAT YOU KNOW NOT" and the angels conceded to this point (2:30). This is like a child asking their parent, "Why do I have to go to bed at nine o'clock?" Does the parent negotiate with their child? No, the parent says "Do not worry about it. I know what is best for you." If the Biblical stories are incorrect then this story in the Hadiths is incorrect, as well.

The Qur'an says that man with bear his own burden and no one else's burden (17:15). This is reasonable, rational and justifiable. I have pointed out to Jews and Christians that their scriptures sometimes have people punished for the crimes of their parents or even their great grandparents. I suggest that these punishments are unjust, thus impossible to be from God. Yet the traditions of Prophet Muhammad (pbuh) have people getting punished for the crimes of others, something totally contrary to the Qur'an. The Muslim is to judge the tradition by the Qur'an. If a report agrees with the Qur'an accept it, otherwise reject it. I believe in the Hadiths which are substantiated by the Qur'an and do not contradict the Qur'an in anyway.

CONTROVERSIAL SUBJECTS

While some Muslims might believe that I am less of a Muslim for not adhering to many of the Hadiths, belief in some of these Hadiths makes them more of a candidate to be a disbeliever, because some of these traditions are against the teaching of the Qur'an. If Muslims only used the Hadiths which are substantiate by the Qur'an, 9/10ths of their problems and question from non-Muslims would immediately disappear. The other 1/10 is from misunderstandings. I have found that most of the Muslims' problems do not come from the Quranic message, but from details of Prophet Muhammad's (pbuh) life, which are in the Hadiths. As they are words of man and fallible, many of these Hadiths make a rational religion seem irrational. There are perhaps thousands, maybe millions of people who have rejected Islam because of the content of Hadiths which are not supported by the Qur'an. And the Qur'an warns Muslims about following great leaders instead of ALLAH (33:67), following the masses instead of ALLAH (6:116), or following your our desires instead of ALLAH (6:56). The way to avoid being misled is to familiarize yourself with the words of ALLAH. Then you are able to discern the truth in everything and everyone on earth.

PROPHET MUHAMMAD (pbuh)

Prophet Muhammad (pbuh) was a man of such exalted character (68:4), that he was chosen by the God of the universe to deliver the last message of Islam to the mankind (33:40). He is described as a mercy to the world (21:107). He withstood mockery, scrutiny, ridicule, threats, bribery and attempts on his life to convey the message of Islam. This is why he is called a great example for mankind to follow (33:21). The Qur'an says that he was no more than a messenger (3:144), but this is in respect to God. In respect to man, a messenger of God is the highest position any human being can have. As a messenger, Muhammad (pbuh) is a witness, a bearer of glad tidings (for believers) and a warner (for disbelievers) (48:8). He was a kind and gentle man (3:159) and a man worthy of praise (33:56) and respect (2:104). And he was extremely devoted to the remembrance of ALLAH (73:20). Prophet Muhammad (pbuh) took his duty very seriously, perhaps too seriously. Many times in the Qur'an,

ALLAH comforts him and reminds him that his job is not to convert the people, but to convey the message. At one point, ALLAH tells Prophet Muhammad (pbuh) not to take the people's disbelief personally.

6.33 We know indeed the grief which their words do cause thee: It is not thee they reject: it is the signs of Allah, which the wicked contemn.

Prophet Muhammad (pbuh) was known for his honesty and truthfulness. His integrity was so well-known that many people who rejected Islam thought that he must have been insane (81:22), because they could not fathom him telling them a lie. He was also called a poet or soothsayer who simply mesmerized people with falsehoods (69:41-42) and they even called him a forger (11:13). The consensus amongst the disbelievers was that he was insane or a liar. The problem is that Prophet Muhammad (pbuh) could not be both at the same time. As Gary Miller suggested, if these two groups got together, they would have realized that their arguments cancel each other out. If he was lying, then he knew that what he said was untruth. If he was insane then he believed what he said was the truth. Today, we know that what Prophet Muhammad (pbuh) said that is preserved in the Qur'an is true, thus he was not a liar. And it is highly unlikely that an insane man told astounding truths in the Qur'an and founded the greatest religion known to man. Even in the time of Prophet Muhammad (pbuh), there were people who wanted him to manufacture a religion which conformed to their interests.

10.15 But when Our Clear Signs are rehearsed unto them, those who rest not their hope on their meeting with Us, Say: "Bring us a reading other than this, or change this," Say: "It is not for me, of my own accord, to change it: I follow naught but what is revealed unto me: if I were to disobey my Lord, I should myself fear the penalty of a Great Day (to come)."

CONTROVERSIAL SUBJECTS

If there were people who sought to change the message of Islam during Prophet Muhammad's (pbuh) life, we can be sure that they sought to change his message after his death. They found their opportunity in the Hadiths.

PROPHET MUHAMMAD'S WIVES (may Allah bless them all)

The traditions are where we find one of the most disturbing aspects of Prophet Muhammad's (pbuh) life, his marriage to Aisha. He was married to his first wife, Khadijah, until her death after 25 years. After her death, Prophet Muhammad (pbuh) is authorized in the Qur'an to remarry.

33:50 O Prophet! We have made lawful to thee thy wives to whom thou hast paid their dowers; and those whom thy right hand possesses out of the prisoners of war whom Allah has assigned to thee; and daughters of thy paternal uncles and aunts, and daughters of thy maternal uncles and aunts, who migrated (from Makka) with thee; and any believing woman who dedicates her soul to the Prophet if the Prophet wishes to wed her,- this only for thee, and not for the Believers (at large); We know what We have appointed for them as to their wives and the captives whom their right hands possess,- in order that there should be no difficulty for thee. And Allah is Oft-Forgiving, Most Merciful.

It is clear here that Prophet Muhammad (pbuh) was afforded a privilege exclusive to him, but what was that privilege? I was discussing the Prophet and his wives with a man who was well-acquainted with Islam though not a Muslim and I said that Prophet Muhammad (pbuh) had nine wives. To this the man responded, "Why do you believe such a thing, when the Qur'an does not say this?" I had no answer. It was the Hadiths that were stuck in my head that made me said he had 9 wives and this was the privilege afforded to him. But when I re-examined the Qur'an, I noticed something. 33:50 does not actually say who he married, but it listed who is eligible for him to marry. And one of those eligible was "any believing woman," which means that the other women on the list could be non-believers. Muslims are only allowed to marry Muslim women or women of the People of the Book, so it may be that Prophet Muhammad (pbuh) was not allowed to marry more than four women, but that he was allowed to marry non-Muslims. Of course, the reason behind this privilege would be for Prophet Muhammad (pbuh) to convert his wife to Islam. He would be better equipped to do so as a messenger of God and he would be less likely to succumb to a compromise of his religion for the religion of his wife. The point is that it is not incumbent on a Muslims to believe Prophet Muhammad (pbuh) had nine wives or twelve wives as the Hadiths suggested. And his marriages were not for carnal desires. Polygamy in the Qur'an, whether for him or the Muslims at large, was not a rule but an exception to the rule. It was used for extenuating circumstances.

His marriages after his beloved Khadijah were a means to combine the warring tribes of Arabia or to provide security and protect in marriage to these women who were widows and/or his elder. His marriages served as an example of how Muslims are to treat women and what women were lawful to marry. Opponents of Islam try to draw a disparaging picture of Prophet Muhammad (pbuh) for his marriages. But when the picture is put into focus of a 53 year old man, who stayed monogamous for 25 years to a former widow 15 years his senior, who spent two years in mourning and unmarried after his wife's death, and married women who some might consider undesirable, their accusations bear little fruit. This is a man who could have married any woman and as many women as he wanted.

One of Prophet Muhammad's (pbuh) wives which raise eyebrows was said to be a child by the name of Aisha. Wherever you find an avid anti-Islamist, you will find this issue rose. I do not fault them for bringing up this issue, because upon hearing this claim, I was in awe that anyone would believe it. I did not recall this being in the Qur'an, but I told myself that if it is in there then I do not believe or accept it. Fortunately, I found that it was, like all the other accusations, nowhere to be found

CONTROVERSIAL SUBJECTS

in the Qur'an, but in the Hadiths. In the Hadiths, it says that Prophet Muhammad (pbuh) married Aisha when she was six years old and he consummated the marriage when she was nine years old. I have heard and read every kind of explanation for this marriage, but there is absolutely no explanation that will suit me. The Hadiths are supposed to be the explanation of the Qur'an, but there is no mention of marriage and sex with children in it.

When I see the explanations for marrying a child, I immediately think of the Talmud were marriage and sex with children is spoken of favorably. The Talmud is supposed to explain the Jewish Torah, yet the Jewish Torah does not make such a

a girl becomes a woman at age 12 and both are now eligible for marriage. The Talmud, like many of the Hadiths, is someone's way of altering the message of God, just as they smeared the name of the Prophet Solomon (pbuh), the Prophet David (pbuh) and others with tales of sexual immorality.

I would go so far as to say, maybe the Hindus god, Krishna was a great and pious man, whose skin color was probably not blue and who probably didn't have 16,000 wives, but tradition records him as such. A man who lived only 43 years ago, Malcolm X, has outlandish and unsubstantiated stories circulating about him, in order to divert attention from his ultimate message, which is still highly misunderstood by both black and white people despite an autobiography, movies and plays to inform the masses. The smear campaign is very effective because it always draws attention and it will always have believers, no matter how outlandish and unsubstantiated the accusation is. But let's explore this supposed marriage a bit deeper.

One problem is that there are different accounts of how old Aisha was in the Hadiths, so it is inaccurate or deceitful to assert definitively that she was six. In debate with a Christian on this matter, I gave him an example of how it is impossible for him to say that she was six years old without good reasoning. In the four gospels of the Bible, there are four different versions of the sign over Jesus' (pbuh) head on the cross. For me to declare that the sign said "This is Jesus, King of the Jews" is not being honest, because there are three other possibilities, which I have not mentioned or disqualified.

THIS IS JESUS (pbuh) THE KING OF THE JEWS.

Matt. 27:37

THE KING OF THE JEWS

Mark 15:26

THIS IS THE KING OF THE JEWS

Luke 23:38

JESUS (pbuh) OF NAZARETH THE KING OF THE JEWS

John 19:19

In the same vein, there are Hadiths presenting Aisha's age at the time of marriage to be from 6 to 21 years old. To say definitive that she was 6 years old is a deception, when she was 6, 7, 8, 9, 10, 11, 12, 13, 14, 15, 16, 17, 18, 19, 20 or 21. And I would like to know how non-Muslims discern which Hadiths to believe in. Do they accept the remaining Hadiths as truthful as well which say that Muhammad (pbuh) was a prophet of God and the Qur'an is the words of God?

The honest answer about her age is that a reliable source for her age does not exist. And the Qur'an makes no mention of it. My belief is that Prophet Muhammad (pbuh) didn't marry a child because the Qur'an says a man can't marry a woman against her will (4:19), and a child has no will worth mentioning in this matter. The Qur'an also says that Prophet Muhammad (pbuh) had to choose between certain "women" (33:50, 33:52) as to who he would marry. And the Qur'an says that his wives were not like any other "women" (33:32). They were to be like Prophet

Muhammad (pbuh), exemplary figures for the Muslim women. Prophet Muhammad (pbuh), as the ruler of Arabia at this time, offered them the option of living a lavish life of wealth, possessions and independence or the duty of following the path of Islam. He informed them that their every action would be, as his was, a personification of Islam. They were to be role models and with this responsibility came an abundance of reward or an abundance of punishment from God (33:27-3). And his wives accepted the hard road of Islam over the easy path of riches. I ask, would this decision be given to a six or nine year old girl? And would a child not take money over prayer and fasting?

This allegation against Prophet Muhammad (pbuh), just simply makes no sense. The Qur'an says that in Paradise, the believers will be given companions of equal age to them (78:33). Thus the ideal marriage in Islam is couples whose ages are in close proximity to each other. Again the marriage between Prophet Muhammad (pbuh) and a child is not exemplary to God's message. And the nail in the coffin is that Muhammad's (pbuh) wives were the "MOTHERS OF THE MUSLIMS" (33:6). How exactly does a grown man seek any kind of advice and comfort from his 9 year old mother?

With this, I conclude that the Qur'an is declaring that all of Prophet Muhammad's (pbuh) wives were adults capable of making sound decisions and giving sound advice. Thus Prophet Muhammad's (pbuh) marriage to a child would be against the teaching of the Qur'an. And for Prophet Muhammad (pbuh) to perform such a blatant and egregious act contradictory to his own doctrine would have been a deathblow for Islam in the midst of those who hated it. He provoked every single group of people in Arabia with his preaching. In the middle of such a hostile environment, such an action would have been capitalized upon.

WHAT DO NON-MUSLIMS HAVE TO SAY ABOUT PROPHET MUHAMMAD (PBUH)?

Islam Is The Truth

"The lies (Western slander) which well-meaning zeal has heaped round this man (Prophet Muhammad (pbuh) are disgraceful to ourselves only." (Thomas Carlyle in 'Heroes and Hero Worship and the Heroic in History,' 1840)

"The good sense of Muhammad (pbuh) despised the pomp of royalty. The Apostle of God submitted to the menial offices of family; he kindled the fire; swept floors; milked ewes; and mended with his own hands his shoes and garments. Disdaining the penance and merit of a hermit, he observed without effort of vanity the abstemious diet of an Arab." (Gibbon in 'The Decline and Fall of the Roman Empire' 1823)

"Head of the State as well as the Church, he was Caesar and Pope in one; but he was Pope without the Pope's pretensions, and Caesar without the legions of Caesar, without a standing army, without a bodyguard, without a police force, without a fixed revenue. If ever a man ruled by a right divine, it was [Prophet] Muhammad (pbuh), for he had all the powers without their supports. He cared not for the dressings of power. The simplicity of his private life was in keeping with his public life." (Reverend Bosworth Smith in 'Muhammad and Muhammadanism,' London, 1874)

"If greatness of purpose, smallness of means, and astonishing results are the three criteria of a human genius, who could dare compare any great man in history with [Prophet] Muhammad (pbuh)?" (Alphonse de LaMartaine in 'Historie de la Turquie,' Paris, 1854.)

"I have always held the religion of Muhammad (pbuh) in high estimation because of its wonderful vitality. It is the only religion which appears to me to possess that assimilating capacity to the changing phase of existence which can make itself appeal to every age. I have studied him - the wonderful man and in my opinion for from being an anti-Christ, he must be called the Savior of Humanity...I believe that if a man like him were to assume the dictatorship of the modern world he would succeed in solving its problems in a way that would bring it the much needed peace and happiness: I have prophesied about the faith of [Prophet] Muhammad (pbuh) that it would be acceptable to the Europe of tomorrow as it is beginning to be acceptable to the Europe of today." (Sir George Bernard Shaw in 'The Genuine Islam,' Vol. 1, No. 8, 1936.)

"My choice of [Prophet] Muhammad (pbuh) to lead the list of the world's most influential persons may surprise some readers and may be questioned by others, but he was the only man in history who was supremely successful on both the secular and religious level. ...It is probable that the relative influence of [Prophet] Muhammad (pbuh) on Islam has been larger than the combined influence of Jesus (pbuh) Christ and St. Paul on Christianity. ...It is this unparalleled combination of secular and religious influence which I feel entitles Muhammad to be considered the most influential single figure in human history." (Michael Hart in 'The 100, A Ranking of the Most Influential Persons In History,' New York, 1978.)

"Four years after the death of Justinian, A.D. 569, was born in Mecca, in Arabia, the man who, of all men, has exercised the greatest influence upon the human race... To be the religious head of many empires, to guide the daily life of one-third of the human race, may perhaps justify the title of a Messenger of God." (Dr. William Draper in 'History of Intellectual Development of Europe')

"His readiness to undergo persecution for his beliefs, the high moral character of the men who believed in him and looked up to him as a leader, and the greatness of his ultimate achievement -all argue his fundamental integrity. To suppose [Prophet] Muhammad (pbuh) was an impostor raises more problems than it solves. Moreover, none of the great figures of history is so poorly appreciated in the West as [Prophet] Muhammad (pbuh).... Thus, not merely must we credit [Prophet] Muhammad (pbuh) with essential honesty and integrity of purpose, if we are to understand him at all; if we are to correct the errors we have inherited from the past, we must not forget the conclusive proof is a much stricter requirement than a show of plausibility, and in a matter such as this only to be attained with difficulty." (W. Montgomery Watt in 'Muhammad at Mecca,' Oxford, 1953.)

"He was sober and abstemious in his diet and a rigorous observer of fasts. He indulged in no magnificence of apparel, the ostentation of a petty mind; neither was his simplicity in dress affected but a result of real disregard for distinction from so trivial a source. In his private dealings he was just. He treated friends and strangers, the rich and poor, the powerful and weak, with equity, and was beloved by the common people for the affability with which he received them, and listened to their complaints.

His military triumphs awakened no pride nor vain glory, as they would have done had they been effected for selfish purposes. In the time of his greatest power he maintained the same simplicity of manners and appearance as in the days of his adversity. So far from affecting a regal state, he was displeased if, on entering a room, any unusual testimonials of respect were shown to him. If he aimed at a universal dominion, it was the dominion of faith; as to the temporal rule which grew up in his hands, as he used it without ostentation, so he took no step to perpetuate it in his family." (Washington Irving, 'Mahomet and His Successors')

"In all things [Prophet] Muhammad (pbuh) was profoundly practical. When his beloved son Ibrahim died, an eclipse occurred and rumors of God's personal condolence quickly arose. Whereupon [Prophet] Muhammad (pbuh) is said to have announced, 'An eclipse is a phenomenon of nature. It is foolish to attribute such things to the death or birth of a human being.' (James Michener in 'Islam: The Misunderstood Religion,' Reader's Digest, May 1955, pp. 68-70.)

[All these quotes courtesy of Dr. A. Zahoor and Dr. Haq, "Quotations from Famous People"]

CONTROVERSIAL SUBJECTS

APOSTASY

The penalty of death for apostasy is false and unQur'anic. To pronounce the death of someone based solely off of the report of people who said Prophet Muhammad (pbuh) said one should die for changing his mind about Islam is outlandish. The Qur'an prescribes the punishment of death for those who wage war against Allah and Prophet Muhammad (pbuh) and cause mischief in the land. It also gives the alternative punishment of maiming the culprit or exiling him from the land. So how is it that apostasy alone is grounds for death, when someone can wage war against Islam and can be eligible for exile? Some say apostasy is treason. You can leave a country to live somewhere else, but if you give away secrets to cause harm to your former country that is treason. And in that case, you wage war against Islam and death is still optional based upon the severity of your offense.

Belief is something inside of you. It is how you are convinced of a certain thing. It is different for everybody. Your iman or confirmation grows as you live and study Islam. This cannot be measured by man, which is why the Qur'an leaves it to God to regulate apostasy, unless your disbelief causes you to harm others. The verses dealing with one who changes his mind about his faith in Islam, all speak of ALLAH punishing him, not man because only ALLAH knows man's heart and intentions.

If I was taught about Islam by someone of little knowledge in Islam and I became a Muslim, then I was confronted by someone of another faith or no faith and he asks me a riddle that neither I nor my teacher or anyone I know could solve to my or the questioner's satisfaction, this may decrease my faith. I may even cease to believe in Islam, if the question is of great importance. Why should I be put to death because of this? Even if there is no good reason at all, except that I changed my mind, if there is no compulsion in religion, then I can change my mind whenever the wind blows. The matter is to be settled between me and ALLAH and no Muslim is supposed to expedite my meeting with my maker. It is more likely that the adherence to a law of death for apostasy would be a deterrent from Islam rather than a deterrent from leaving Islam. There are perhaps individuals now who believe in

Islam, but are afraid to tell another Muslim, for fear of changing his mind one day and facing death.

3:86 How shall Allah Guide those who reject Faith after they accepted it and bore witness that the Messenger was true and that Clear Signs had come unto them? but Allah guides not a people unjust.

3:87 Of such the reward is that on them (rests) the curse of Allah, of His angels, and of all mankind;

3:88 In that will they dwell; nor will their penalty be lightened, nor respite be (their lot);

3:89 Except for those that repent (Even) after that, and make amends; for verily Allah is Oft-Forgiving, Most Merciful.

3:90 But those who reject Faith after they accepted it, and then go on adding to their defiance of Faith,- never will their repentance be accepted; for they are those who have (of set purpose) gone astray.

3:91 As to those who reject Faith, and die rejecting,- never would be accepted from any such as much gold as the earth contains, though they should offer it for ransom. For such is (in store) a penalty grievous, and they will find no helpers.

4:137 Those who believe, then reject faith, then believe (again) and (again) reject faith, and go on increasing in unbelief,- Allah will not forgive them nor guide them nor guide them on the way.

CONTROVERSIAL SUBJECTS

5:54 O ye who believe! if any from among you turn back from his Faith, soon will Allah produce a people whom He will love as they will love Him, - lowly with the believers, mighty against the rejecters, fighting in the way of Allah, and never afraid of the reproaches of such as find fault. That is the grace of Allah, which He will bestow on whom He pleaseth. And Allah encompasseth all, and He knoweth all things.

9:66 Make ye no excuses: ye have rejected Faith after ye had accepted it. If We pardon some of you, We will punish others amongst you, for that they are in sin.

47:34. Those who reject Allah, and hinder (men) from the Path of Allah, then die rejecting Allah, - Allah will not forgive them.

In none of these verses is a call for man to punish an apostate. In fact, he is punishing himself by rejecting Islam. These verses speak of people who believe, then disbelieve over and over again, but every time they can be forgiven if they sincerely repent before they die. ALLAH is not harmed in the less bit. He will simply substitute them for those who are firm in their belief. So it is not necessary to kill someone for changing their mind.

The Qur'an also speaks of those who, under compulsion, denounce Islam. It stipulates that a Muslim, if threaten, has an option to proclaim his belief or claim unbelief (16:106). Of course, this is an example of why man must not persecute others for their decision to accept or reject Islam, because they have no idea what is in the heart of another man.

The penalty of death for apostasy is something the writers of the Hadiths have taken from the Jewish Torah. It is in this book, not the Qur'an that you find legitimacy in killing people for apostasy (Deuteronomy 17:2-7). If the Qur'an is a correction of the Torah that the Jews have, then in every instance that they differ, or when the Qur'an excludes man punishing apostasy and maintains that God will judge them, then the Qur'an is correcting this false punishment. By ignoring the Qur'an and adhering to supposed sayings of Prophet Muhammad (pbuh), Muslims are guilty of the same thing they accuse Christians of doing. They are overriding the words of God, with the words of man. When a Muslim debates a Christian and the Muslim uses Jesus' (pbuh) words to prove his case and the Christian uses Paul's words to prove his case, the Muslim points out that Jesus (pbuh) is the master. His words are the criteria to determine the truthfulness of his followers. Of the greatest authority is the words of God, yet Muslims use supposed words of Prophet Muhammad (pbuh) to prove their case. If I am quoting correctly from the Qur'an, then I automatically win the argument. Every Muslim on earth knows that the Hadiths have discrepancies. With this fact in mind, the Hadiths should be approached with caution, not with your complete confidence. Because it has discrepancies, it is of great importance to demonstrate the Hadith's validity through the Qur'an, especially in life or death matters.

DEATH FOR ADULTERY?

Western society does not view adultery as a crime. Though there may be laws prohibiting adultery in select city or states of America , these laws are not enforced. This is quite strange when we consider that having more than one wife is illegal, but having one wife and three mistresses is perfecting fine in the eyes of the law. Yet in the Qur'an, sex without marriage is a sin and a crime. Some Muslims are at odds, when it comes to the punishment for adultery in Islam. They argue whether the punishment is 100 lashes or stoning the adulterer and adulteress to death. These

CONTROVERSIAL SUBJECTS

two punishments are extremely different. But the Muslim's dilemma is self-inflicted. This is obvious when you ask them what does the Qur'an says on this matter.

The Qur'an says of those who have indulged in such unlawful sex that they are to be indefinitely confined to their homes until ALLAH ordains another way to punish them. But if they repent and turn from this sin, then they are to be left alone. It says ALLAH accepts the repentance of a sincere person, but he does not accept the repentance of one who repents only because he or she is facing death (4:15-18). The point to be made here is that stoning to death is nowhere to be found and if death were the prescribed punishment, then there would be no need for the sinner to repent because on every occasion, his repentance would be due to his impending death. This is not all that the Qur'an says on the issue. ALLAH did ordain a precise penalty for adultery.

24:2 The woman and the man guilty of adultery or fornication,- flog each of them with a hundred stripes: Let not compassion move you in their case, in a matter prescribed by Allah, if ye believe in Allah and the Last Day: and let a party of the Believers witness their punishment.

24:3 Let no man guilty of adultery or fornication marry and but a woman similarly guilty, or an Unbeliever: nor let any but such a man or an Unbeliever marry such a woman: to the Believers such a thing is forbidden.

This verse should settle the matter. It explicitly states the punishment for adultery. 100 lashes is the penalty. The Qur'an says that the adulterer can only marry one who is an adulterer as well or an unbeliever. How can one adulterer marry another, when both are to be stoned to death? The Qur'an also mentions that the Prophet's (pbuh) wives who commit such sins would receive double the penalty (33:30) and prisoners of war are to receive half the penalty (4:25). The prisoner of war has already undergone great pain and anguish as a result of defeat in war. This contributes to the disparity in the punishments they receive. Their level of knowledge and practice of Islam is also a major factor. As indicated in Surah 4:17, ALLAH considers the person's predisposition and knowledge of what is moral and immoral. And it should be obvious that the wives of the Prophet (pbuh) are more in tune with the laws of ALLAH than someone foreign to the religion. In any case, you cannot split or double the punishment of stoning to death. However you can do this with regard to the lashes given to an adulterer or adulteress.

The punishment of stoning the adulterer to death is actually from the traditions of Prophet Muhammad (pbuh) and not the Qur'an. This punishment is obviously inspired by the Jewish Torah, which enlists this exact punishment for adultery (Deut. 22:22-24). The problem that Muslims who believe in this punishment have is that it contradicts the Qur'an. And because the Qur'an is the ultimate source of authority and the criteria to determine the authenticity of the scriptures from anyone and from anywhere, it should be concluded that this tradition attributed to Prophet Muhammad (pbuh) is a forgery. It makes no difference who said that this is true, if it contradicts ALLAH, then it is false.

Some Muslims say that the Qur'an is only giving the punishment for the adulterer who is not married, whereas the traditions give the punishment for the marry party involved. This makes no sense. Why would ALLAH leave the most important punishment out of his word, thus leaving it to speculation? ALLAH says one life is equivalent to the whole of humanity. To kill a Muslim is to guarantee yourself hellfire (4:93). Is it not impractical to leave the punishment of death to be communicated in any book other than the word of God? The Hadiths are littered with imperfections, so how could any decent Muslim kill another human being based on this faulty information. It would be more logical for ALLAH to ordain death for adultery in the Qur'an and leave the lashes to be transmitted through word of mouth. In fact, there is a Hadith in Sahih Muslim which says that this punishment was a part of the Qur'an, but it was omitted somehow. This is a crystal clear CONTRADICTIONARY STATEMENT TO THE Qur'an, which says that the entire Qur'an was guarded and preserved by ALLAH. This just shows to what extent people will go to manufacture tenants of a religion and pass it off as authoritative. In all, it is clear that stoning people to death is nowhere to be found in the Qur'an and it should not be included in Islam.

One other point to be is that the Qur'an recommends that adulterers marry another person guilty of the same offense or an idolater. The marriage to an idolater struck me as odd. I wondered why ALLAH would want a Muslim to marry an idolater. But upon reading the verses again, I realized that the adulterers in this instance are not believers at all. It is clear when it says "let a party of the believers witness" and "it is for a believer forbidden to marry an adulterer." So these verses are in reference to someone who is already a disbeliever and now he has become an adulterer. This kind of person is forbidden for a believer to marry. In the case of a believer who commits adultery, he has further stipulations. He can only marry another adulterer or a disbeliever, but he must "not marry unbelieving women (idolaters), until they believe" (2:221).

ANSWERS TO COMMON MISCONCEPTIONS ABOUT ISLAM

61:8 Their intention is to extinguish Allah's Light with their mouths: But Allah will complete (the revelation of) His Light, even though the Unbelievers may detest (it).

NATION OF ISLAM

Islam Is The Truth

The name "Nation of Islam" is very deceptive. It conjures up a picture of a huge group or a country of Muslims in your mind. The name "Black Muslims" also conjures up a mental picture but this is a picture in which people are excluded who are not black. These titles are used in America to describe a sect of Islam which is a total pollution of the truth of the ALLAH, the Qur'an and Islam. Made popular by Elijah Muhammad, Malcolm X and presently Louis Farrakhan, this brand of Islam has left a impression in people's minds that is difficult to erase.

The members of the Nation of Islam wear suits and a bow tie and they are often seen on street corners selling their newspaper entitled "Final Call." Their doctrine includes the blasphemous, Un-Islamic notion that their founder, Fard Muhammad was ALLAH in the flesh. ALLAH came as Fard Muhammad to America to make Elijah Muhammad, formerly Elijah Poole, his messenger. Elijah was to spread this new version of Islam to the black people all over America. The message was that the black man should be proud of himself because he was a god on earth.

A scientist, by the name of Yacub, performed some experiments which resulted in the lightening of the skin color of blacks. And as their skin pigment lightened, they became more prone to evil. Ultimately the experiment ended with the formation of white people, who are deemed devils. White people are thought to be a perverted, diluted and corrupted version of the black man. I cannot stress enough that none of this doctrine is substantiated in the Qur'an. This is made up totally from the imagination of Fard Muhammad. The Nation maintains that the Qur'an is the word of God, but they ignore the Qur'an to teach as they see fit. Their intentions were to embolden Black people to fight against racism.

In true Islam, ALLAH judges on your actions and intentions and never ever on your skin color. The Black Muslims point to the color of earth or mud from which man was created to signify that the first man had to be a man of color, when his color is absolutely irrelevant, because ALLAH, not Yacub, split man into many nations so we can learn from each other. We are supposed to respect each other. Racism is not resolved by more racism. Its root cause is IGNORANCE, so the Qur'an tells Muslims to gain knowledge of and respect for one another (49:13)

CONTROVERSIAL SUBJECTS

The Nation of Islam's leading minister, Malcolm X, was excommunicated after he made some disparaging remarks about the demise of President Kennedy shortly after his assassination. Malcolm X had also found out the Elijah Muhammad had some extramarital affairs, which grieved him tremendously. This new discovery and his excommunication pushed him away from the Nation. He decided to take the Hajj or pilgrimage to Mecca, where he encountered true Islam, which was shared by every race and ethnicity on the planet. He shared food and shelter with those whom he had previously dismissed as white devils. His conversion to true Islam, his newfound willingness to build alliances with those of different faiths to combat the oppressive racism of America, along with his great influence drew great animosity from the members of the Nation of Islam. The Nation of Islam's membership began to decline as some of their followers split from the group to follow Malcolm. He was considered a trader, a Benedict Arnold for denouncing the Nation and Elijah Muhammad. This brought about a climate of hatred towards Malcolm by the Black Muslims, which resulted in his death.

Whether it was a direct order by the leaders of the Nation of Islam to have him killed is not pertinent to this book. The important point to be made is the distinction between the religion and way of life of Islam, which Malcolm X experienced and converted to and the beliefs of the "Nation of Islam" or the Black Muslims. The most important thing to address is the allegation that ALLAH came in the person of Fard Muhammad. This man cannot be God, for the same reason that Jesus (pbuh) or Krishna or anyone else can not be God. At some point, all these individuals, ate food, drank water, breathed their first and breathed their last and none of these things does God partakes in. He is self-sufficient at all times. He needs absolutely nothing, ever. He was never born and he will never die. No one gives him birth or gives him life. No one can take his life. And nothing and no one is even comparable to God (42:11), which refutes the idea that all black people are gods or godlike. Human beings can be godly, showing great reverence for God, but they cannot be godlike according to the Qur'an.

It is also interesting to note that Fard Muhammad was half black and half white, which should cause some kind of conflict within himself as partially god and partially the devil.

5 PERCENTERS

There is a splinter group popularly known as 5 Percenters, who share similar views with those of the Black Muslims. Elijah Muhammad said that 85% of the people on earth are ignorant. 10% have some knowledge, but they use it to take advantage of the 85% and 5% of the people have all the knowledge and they are the gods of the earth. A former Black Muslim named Clarence 13X built his following on Elijah Muhammad's doctrine and his followers where the 5% of the population. They view black and white people in the same manner as the Nation of Islam, and they are privy to calling themselves names which include ALLAH, as they see themselves as gods and call each other such. They, like the members of The Nation, view the idea of a God which cannot be understood through our five senses as illogical. They call such being a "mystery god," and they believe God to be a man. They believe Clarence 13X is ALLAH in the flesh. They use ALLAH as an acronym for a man to substantiate their claim that God is a man and that the black man is god.

Arm

Leg

Leg

Arm

Head

Unfortunately for them, this trick only works in English and ALLAH is an ARABIC word. Also, the first person on earth, if he was black, probably did not speak English. And the description given could also be that of anything from an ape to a kangaroo. Not to mention, that neither Clarence 13X, Elijah Muhammad nor Fard Muhammad were a picture of perfection as a Muslims or as a human being in general. I have great doubt that God was a criminal at some point in his life or that he was imprisoned by his own creatures. Yet all of these men have very checkered pasts. The Qur'an speaks of an altercation Abraham (pbuh) had with a man who believed himself to be God. The Muslim would do well to incorporate Abraham's (pbuh) logic when they are in a similar dispute.

2:258 Hast thou not Turned thy vision to one who disputed with Abraham About his Lord, because Allah had granted him power? Abraham said: "My Lord is He Who Giveth life and death." He said: "I give life and death." Said Abraham: "But it is Allah that causeth the sun to rise from the east. Do thou then cause him to rise from the West." Thus was he confounded who (in arrogance) rejected faith. Nor doth Allah Give guidance to a people unjust.

It is very important that the Muslim communicate the difference between these sects of Islam and true Islam.

ALLAH LEADS PEOPLE ASTRAY

One of the most misunderstood things about the Qur'an is when it says that ALLAH leads people astray or ALLAH seals their senses so they cannot understand. It also says that ALLAH guides whom he wills. This language causes some to think that Islam is a religion preordained to be accepted or reject by people. And that people actually have no control over their destiny according to Islam. To understand what is meant by these statements, let us look at the context in the Qur'an.

First, we must point out that ALLAH does not want man to be a disbeliever. He is pleased with man when man is mindful of him (39:7). And he extends his mercy to all mankind (7:156). ALLAH also makes the path easy for the righteous and for the wicked (92:7-10). It is your decision to follow either path. And the Qur'an says ALLAH ONLY misleads THE REBELLIOUS (2:26), which means they have already chosen this path. The rebellious are those who reject faith after it has been clearly shown to them (47:25, 32), they knowingly use falsehoods to try to weaken the truth, they view the signs of God in jest (18:55-57), they lend more weight to the words of their leader than to the words of God (33:67), they follow the crowd over following ALLAH (6:116) or they follow their own desires (6:56). These are the people who are said to be lead astray, misguided or sealed from the truth by ALLAH. And because they are rebellious to the path of ALLAH, they are transgressors of the laws of God, slanderers, hinderers from the path, they are cruel and deep in sin (68:10-14), they dishonor orphans, and ignore the poor (89:17-20). They don't reciprocate the love that Muslims have for them (3:119-120). The rebellious act as if they do not hear the truth (45:8-9) or they don't listen, at all. They don't use their intelligence and reasoning abilities (67:10, 25:44), thus leaving them in a state of confusion (50:5). You see they are given tools for investigation and understanding, but they don't use them.

46:26 And We had firmly established them in a (prosperity and) power which We have not given to you and We had endowed them with (faculties of) hearing, seeing, heart and intellect: but of no profit to them were their (faculties of) hearing, sight, and heart and intellect, when they went on rejecting the Signs of Allah; and they were (completely) encircled by that which they used to mock at!

If I give you food, a place to store it and a place to cook it and you starve, whose fault is it? So when the Qur'an says that ALLAH seals their understanding, it is in fact a result of their doing. Their immunity to the truth is something which they have earned for their disbelief and sins (7:30, 7:146, 83:14). The Qur'an gives an illustration of one's stubbornness in disbelief.

CONTROVERSIAL SUBJECTS

7:175 Relate to them the story of the man to whom We sent Our signs, but he passed them by: so Satan followed him up, and he went astray.

7:176 If it had been Our will, We should have elevated him with Our signs; but he inclined to the earth, and followed his own vain desires. His similitude is that of a dog: if you attack him, he lolls out his tongue, or if you leave him alone, he (still) lolls out his tongue. That is the similitude of those who reject Our signs; So relate the story; perchance they may reflect.

The sequence of events here is that ALLAH gives man his signs first, and then the person passes them by. After forsaking the strength given to him by God, he is susceptible to the whispers of satan. Subsequently, he follows satan and he has gone astray. This kind of person will not heed warning regardless of the truth of your message. When the Qur'an says they are lead astray, this is a cue to the propagating Muslim that there are people who will not accept Islam, even if you went over ever word in the Qur'an and every doubt in their minds with them. This is an assurance to the Muslim that his job is only to convey the message. If you refuse to accept Islam, then he is told to tell the disbelievers, "to you be your Way, and to me mine (109:6)."

Some Muslims are confused as to why some people do not believe, even after the truth is clearly manifested. But when you read the Qur'an you realize that the signs of ALLAH mean different things to different people. God sent plagues on the people of Egypt, but because of their imperial and sinful nature, this increased their disbelief, when it should increase one's belief in God (7:130-132). And when most of the children of Israel were finally convinced that Moses (pbuh) was sent by God, some of them continued to disobey GOD out of their iniquity and arrogance (27:14). A stop sign means stop to most people, but to a criminal it means go.

This is like me giving two people $1000.00 and telling them to do something positive with it. The bad spirited person will do what he thinks to be good, like using it to commit crimes or bribe someone, whereas the righteous person might give the money to charity or help a friend in need. So in actuality it is they who are at fault for going astray and they who deserve credit for following the straight path, because it was their intentions and decisions. But I gave them the opportunity to follow their path. In like manner, ALLAH gives man life and free will, thus he provides the opportunity for man to stray or stay on course. And his signs, which are meant to keep men straight, can be seen in different ways according to the mindset of the individual. The same thing that leads some people can be looked at by others and make them disbelieve (2:26-28). ALLAH uses the examples of things small or great to show the validity of Islam and the same item will be interpreted differently according to one's mindset. The Qur'an is accepted by some as proof of God and the hereafter while another can read the Qur'an and it pushes him further from its truth (25:30). Satan does the same. His deceit weakens some into disbelief and strengthens the faith of others.

AULIYA

5.51 O ye who believe! Take not the Jews and the Christians for your friends and protectors. They are but friends and protectors to each other. And he amongst you that turns to them (for friendship) is of them. Verily Allah guideth not a people unjust.

This verse has been misused and misunderstood to suggest that Muslims are not to befriend non-Muslims, especially Jews and Christians. This is really no fault of the reader, but the fault of the translator. The word the translator refers to as friend and protector is AULIYA. It is clear that this is but one word, but the word has more meaning than just a friend so the translator uses another word "protector" to help clarify the meaning. The word "auliya" is used numerous times in the Qur'an and with each reference is becomes more apparent what is meant by this word.

CONTROVERSIAL SUBJECTS

18:102 Do the Unbelievers think that they can take My servants as Auliya besides Me (Allah)?

46:32 "If any does not hearken to the one who invites (us) to Allah, he cannot frustrate (Allah's Plan) on earth, and no Auliya can he have besides Allah: such men (wander) in manifest error."

7:27 O ye Children of Adam! Let not Satan seduce you, in the same manner as He got your parents out of the Garden, stripping them of their raiment, to expose their shame: for he and his tribe watch you from a position where ye cannot see them. We made the evil ones Auliya (only) to those without faith.

9:23 O ye who believe! take not for Auliya your fathers and your brothers if they love infidelity above Faith: if any of you do so, they do wrong.

9:71 The Believers, men and women, are Auliya one of another: they enjoin what is just, and forbid what is evil: they observe regular prayers, practise regular charity, and obey Allah and His Messenger. On them will Allah pour His mercy: for Allah is Exalted in power, Wise.

13.16 Say: "Who is the Lord and Sustainer of the heavens and the earth?" Say: "(It is) Allah." Say: "Do ye then take (for worship) Auliya other than Him, such as have no power either for good or for harm to themselves?"

42.6 And those who take as Auliya others besides Him, Allah doth watch over them; and thou art not the disposer of their affairs.

42.9 What! Have they taken (for worship) Auliya besides Him? But it is Allah,-He is the Protector, and it is He Who gives life to the dead: It is He Who has power over all things.

If you can have ALLAH, or satan as your "auliya" it is obvious that this is more than a friend and even more than a protector. The best definition for this word is a person from whom you get your religious and moral guidance to live by. This is why the Qur'an says believing men and women are each other's AULIYA because they will ensure that each other are following the path set by God. A Jew or a Christian, because of his sincerity to his faith will lead you to the path of Judaism or Christianity. Just as a Muslims would advise a Jew or a Christian on the topic of religion in accordance to Islam. This is not to say that Muslims are not to associate with or befriend those who are not Muslims, but when in search of guidance, he is told to seek it from a Muslim, seek it from Prophet Muhammad (pbuh), seek it from the Qur'an and seek it from ALLAH because they all should be the same.

MURKY WATER

CONTROVERSIAL SUBJECTS

18:86 Until, when he reached the setting of the sun, he found it set in a spring of murky water. Near it he found a People. We said: "O Zul-Qarnain! (thou hast authority) either to punish them, or to treat them with kindness."

Some people allege that the Qur'an is unscientific because it says the sun set in the murky water. This is perhaps the most popular and the most foolish allegation against the Qur'an. If you ask the person who made this allegation, "what time does the sunset or rise?," they will give you a time according to their location. They, like everyone on earth, refer to the rise and set of the sun, knowing full well that the sun neither rises nor sets. These are only terms to describe our perception of the sun. Do these people also attack the weatherman for saying the sunsets at 6 o'clock? Probably not.

What these hypocritical literalist which to convey is that Prophet Muhammad (pbuh) actually thought that the sun went into the murky water, despite the fact that the Qur'an specifically says that the sun is in its own orbit in space (21:33). Why would he say the sun is in space and say it's in some spring? I believe that no one believes this claim to be true, not even the person saying or writing this allegation. It is but another attempt to discredit Islam at any expense, even at the expense of the truth. To suggest that Prophet Muhammad (pbuh) actually thought the sun was in the water is to call Prophet Muhammad (pbuh) stupid. Everyone knows that the sun is extremely hot, yet these detractors want us to believe that Prophet Muhammad (pbuh) thought people could live by the sun.

If we read further, it is obvious that this is but a figure of speech to describe Zul-Qarnain's point of view, because it says that he went to a place where the sun was rising. If we are to take the literalist route, we must continue down this path of absurdity and conclude that the sun was actually rising ON the people he saw.

18:90 Until, when he came to the rising of the sun, he found it rising on a people for whom We had provided no covering protection against the sun.

Are we also to believe that Prophet Muhammad (pbuh) thought the sun set by a certain people and rose on a certain people? The words "he found" are clear indicates that this is from the point of view of Zul-Qarnain, not the author. So, if Zul-Qarnain actually believed these unscientific observations, this does not implicate the author in anyway. When discussing the topic of those parents who are distraught when they have a female child, because they prefer a male child, the Qur'an again uses the involved party's perspective when it says that they receive "the bad news" of the birth of a daughter. The Qur'an goes on to condemn such behavior, but one could erroneously say that the Qur'an says the birth of a daughter is "bad news."

In an effort to explain this to someone using this argument once, I used this example: "You have found Islam to be false." I asked, "With this declaration, am I declaring Islam to be false? The answer is no because I believe it is true. I am simply articulating your observation and conclusion. Yet you say that ALLAH says the sun sets in the water because Zul "FOUND" the sun setting."

ISLAM AND IDOLATRY

Let's go back to the very first person on earth and the first person's first word used for the Supreme Being. Let us suppose that it was "GOD." Now let's say that it was thought that a certain man was "GOD." But when the man died, people realized that he does not meet the criteria to be GOD and they named something else like the sun and moon "God." Later, it was realized that none of the things which they imagined was actually "God" either. Then the people finally understood who and what "God" is and they start calling God, "God." Are these people worshipping the certain man that they assumed to be God at first, or the sun or the moon or anything that they had mistakenly took for God? No, especially if you specifically say that none of these things are or could have been "God" ever.

There was a man who led the children of Israel into the land of Canaan after Moses' (pbuh) death. His name was Joshua. In Hebrew it is Yahushua. It is the identical

CONTROVERSIAL SUBJECTS

name of the person believed to have died for the sins of man on the cross 2000 years ago. When Christians pray to Jesus (pbuh), are they actually worshiping the Joshua of the Old Testament or Jesus (pbuh) of 2000 years ago?

There were a number of people who were called the Messiah before Jesus (pbuh) came to this earth. When Christians worship Jesus (pbuh), are they worshiping all the false Messiahs of old? The Jews are still waiting for the Messiah. When a man comes and they pay respect to him as the Messiah, are they paying respect and honor to any of the false messiahs, at all? The answer to these questions is, absolutely not. Because you have the same name or because someone mistakenly named someone or something the name that is rightfully due to someone else in no way, shape or form affects the actual person or being who the name describes. Any rational person will acknowledge this fact, but there are those who go out of their way to discredit Islam, with pitiful arguments like Arabs use to call the moon-god ALLAH, thus Muslims today are worshiping the moon-god.

Their argument includes the notion that Muslims worship the Kaaba. Because people do not know that it was the first mosque, they are easily convinced that this is a huge idol which the Muslims worship five times a day. I have read great rebuttals to this argument which prove that this entire argument is nonsensical, but I felt it should be said that the argument is inconsequential, if you ask the person posing the question, how can you say that a Muslim worships the moon when no Muslim on earth makes reference to the moon or the Kaaba in worship or in any way of reverence? When the Buddhist prays to a statue of Buddha, they specifically speak to Buddha. When a Muslim prays towards the Kaaba, no one utters words in reference to the sacred mosque. Muslims give their worship to ALLAH. The only purpose that the Kaaba has is as a centerpiece for the worship of God. The Kaaba is like a king's ring. If his subjects kiss the ring, he is not paying respect to the ring, but to the king. Does anyone accuse the Christian of worshiping a cross or the Jews for worshiping the Wailing Wall?

The direction of prayer, or Qibla was at one time for the Muslims towards Jerusalem. But ALLAH changed the Qibla to the Kaaba in Mecca. This shift was an effort to distinction the true believers from those who were simply in the company of the believers for some benefit besides the worship of ALLAH (mostly amongst the former Jews and Christians). From that point on, Muslims were to pray towards the sacred mosque (2:142-146). But the point is that Jerusalem served as a point of worship, just as the Kaaba does now. Yet no one accuses Muslims of once worshiping the city of Jerusalem. The Kaaba is but a tool to worship God, just as the moon is. Those from western society may not know that some use the lunar time system, instead of the solar time system. So when they hear that Muslims use the moon to determine when to fast or pray, it conjures up thoughts that Muslims must worship the moon.

The numerous flags with the star and the moon help to fuel this idea. But claiming that Muslims worship the moon is as credible as saying the entire western society worships the sun because their every action is scheduled by the sun's activity. The claim that Muslims worship the moon is completely unsubstantiated, but often offered as proof of the invalidity of Islam. Arabs, as well as their Hebrew cousins [which include Jesus (pbuh)] use the moon to tell the time. They do not worship the moon in any form or fashion. And the symbols on the flag have the same bearing on the faith of Islam that the stars and stripes have on Christianity. Absolutely none. The moon and crescent have no religious significance, as it was adopted by Muslim countries from the dream of the founder of Ottoman Empire, Uthman, 800 years after the death of Prophet Muhammad (pbuh).

The Arabs despite their worship of a multitude of gods, even before the birth of Prophet Muhammad (pbuh), held ALLAH as the supreme deity. ALLAH was viewed, as the Hindus view the Brahman, above description. And like the Hindus, they allocated inferior deities to bridge the gap between them and the supreme God. But there have been some Christian opponents of Islam, who suggest that the Arabs called one of these lesser gods, ALLAH. Of course, this is unsubstantiated and refuted by Muslim scholars who prove the moon god which they are referring to was actually called Sin, not ALLAH.

But even if their claim is true, they shoot themselves in the foot, when they say that ALLAH is but a contraction of AL-ILAH which is "the God" in Arabic. They have to dissect the word "ALLAH" to have any point to make, because as I have said Arabs have been calling the supreme God, ALLAH forever. Even Arab Christians called God ALLAH before Prophet Muhammad (pbuh) brought Islam. It becomes obvious that the generic word for god, "ilah," could have been used for every single god that they had. So they play a sad game of associating the word "ilah" with the Canaanite god "Baal." The first problem that they have is Baal was the sun-god, when they said ALLAH is the moon-god. The second problem that they have is that "ilah" is related to the Hebrew word "el," which is used in the Bible for the Hebrew God. This means that the word used for God in the Bible is subject to the same criticism as the word for God in Arabic, i.e. they too worship the moon-god (or sun god). And a third problem is that in the mythology of Baal the sun-god, his father was named "EL." In fact, the words "Baal" and "el" were interchangeable until a rift came between the Jews and the Canaanites.

Also, the polytheistic Moabites used Yahweh or Jehovah as the name of God, and even early Jews gave Yahweh, a wife name Asherah. If the discrepancies of people of the past, including Israelites, do not discredit the validity of the God of the Jews and Christians, then the discrepancy of the past Arabs have no bearing on the God of Islam. Furthermore, no Muslim worships any earthly or heavenly body. This point is brought home by the Qur'an itself.

41.37 Among His Signs are the Night and the Day, and the Sun and the Moon. Do not prostrate to the sun and the moon, but prostrate to Allah, Who created them, if it is Him ye wish to serve.

An interesting note is that the Aramaic word "alaaha" and the Hebrew words "elah" and "eloah" all mean God and they all sound strikingly similar to ALLAH from Arabic. In the movie, "The Passion of Christ," you might notice the similarities when Jesus (pbuh) speaks of God in Aramaic. Perhaps if some were a bit more careful, they would not smear a name for God used by their own prophets and/or their Lord and Master.

MISINTERPRETATIONS OR MISTRANSLATIONS OF THE QUR'AN

It is an unfortunate fact that there have been many people who have misinterpreted the meaning of the Qur'an and they have performed some horrific acts because of this misunderstanding. There are also mistranslations of the Qur'an which cause some difficulties, some of which I have discussed in this book. In view of these mistranslation and misinterpretations, some have suggested to get rid of the Qur'an. They feel that because people kill themselves, and others, because people are intolerant, because women are oppressed due to these difficulties that the Qur'an is at fault. They feel that eliminating the Qur'an eliminates the problem. These are the same people who say elimination of religion, will eliminate divisiveness, intolerance and even wars.

Many Americans believe that the principles of democracy and the Constitution of America have been breached in today's times. Fighting preemptive wars against the will of the majority of Americans, manipulation of the voting system and torture, all violate the principles by which this country was founded. Those who perpetrate these actions perhaps sincerely believe that they are doing what is right according to the ideals of democracy and the Constitution. In order to rectify their violation of the Constitution, is it best to eradicate the Constitution?

More people have died at the hands of those who hold a differing political view than of those who hold a different religious view. The two world wars, the Civil War, the American Revolution, the French and Indian War, the Vietnam War, the Korean War, and the two gulf wars had absolutely nothing to do with religion. Most wars are in pursuit of territory and dominance, and to spread one country's political agenda throughout the world. People criticize religion for spreading through violence, when the land that they live on, and the government system that they established domestically and abroad is most often acquired through violence or the threat of violence. As I write this book, President Bush is accused of spreading democracy at the point of the gun on the Muslims of the Middle East by his own press secretary, Scott McClellan, who resigned due to this practice and others. If this allegation is true, then it is quite hypocritical for westerner society to criticize Islam for a past practice that they are implementing in the present. If it is false, then it is a shining example of how justifiable actions can be misinterpreted, misconstrued, misunderstood and misrepresented. Whatever the answer is, this does not damage the validity democracy, nor does terrorism damage the validity of Islam.

This is a human problem. And as long as there are humans, there will be these problems. The elimination of the Qur'an or religion will not solve the problems facing man, especially because in them is the solution. Just as a man has morals without religion, he is immoral without religion. It is untenable and impractical to call for the ban of any book or document because it can be misconstrued. It is the interpreter's error not the author's. So the interpreter must be held accountable for their misunderstanding. And those who know the proper meaning have a responsible to clarify all possible misunderstandings.

If you believe that suicide bombing is ALLAH'S or Prophet Muhammad's (pbuh) fault, then you should also believe it is the fault of the authors of the Geneva Convention for the torture in Guantanamo Bay, Cuba.

EARTH LIKE A CARPET

71.19 And Allah has made the earth for you as a carpet (spread out)

It has been suggested by some that the Qur'an describes the earth as being flat. The verse above is used to illustrate this point. But there are two major problems with this claim. First of all, this verse does not say that the earth is flat. This is their misunderstanding. And secondly, there is a comma at the end of this verse. It appears that the thought in this verse is continued into the next verse. Let us first examine what the verse really says.

The verse gives the analogy of the earth as carpet. It takes a stretch of the imagination to conclude that this means the author of the Qur'an thought the earth was flat. If I say "your head is like a basketball," it doesn't mean that I can bounce and shot you head in a basket. Obviously, I am saying your head looks like a ball, not that it has the function or texture of the ball. In like manner, the earth is spread out over its core like a carpet is spread. Thus, ALLAH is saying that there are levels to the earth, which is a scientific fact. Also, the analogy is pertaining to the ground covering the earth, just as the analogy of the basketball and someone's head is only about the shape. It is not necessary for their head to have 6 ridges around it and be full of air, or for the earth to cover a flat surface to be true. The earth must only cover a surface to be true.

"Can a carpet be placed on a round object?," I once asked someone on an message board specifically geared against Islam. He replied, "Yes. But it would be very difficult." To which I said, "I would assume that it is difficult for you to spread a carpet over a round surface. It is even more difficult for you create the universe. But the being that created the earth and the universe hasn't got the same limitations as you do."

Indeed God gives us reasoning. That is, if he declares the earth to be round (79:30), then he says the ground is laid out like a carpet, logic would tell us that the carpet covers the round ball. Is this too much to understand? If I say paper is spread around a ball, will you insist that I am saying a ball is flat? Wrapping paper is normally formed around a present to be square. But if I wrap a basketball up, does that mean that the ball is square? NO. Can you wrap a circular basketball with wrapping paper? The answer is yes. The point that I am making is that this verse does not describe the shape of the planet at all, only that the surface is cover by earth. This brings me to the second problem. The thought of verse 71:19 is incomplete. The Qur'an continues:

71:20 That ye may go about therein, in spacious roads.

This is a crucial part of the subject, which is conveniently omitted by those against Islam. The verse that follows makes it crystal clear that the earth mentioned is the land, not the whole planet. This would easily be seen by those not clouded by prejudice. Seeing that the ground is flat, describing its layer as a carpet should be no problem especially since this verse doesn't talk about the bodies of water around the land. The problem is that people don't read everything about the topic in discussion and make claims which are faulty. This is a perfect example. And there are plenty of verses in the Qur'an which corroborate my explanation that this verse is speaking specifically of the land.

15:19 And the earth We have spread out (like a carpet); set thereon mountains firm and immovable

20:53 "He Who has made for you the earth like a carpet spread out; has enabled you to go about therein by roads (and channels)

51:48 And We have spread out the (spacious) earth: How excellently We do spread out!

78:6 Have We not made the earth as a wide expanse,

78:7 And the mountains as pegs?

For those who would insist that this is about the planet, I have shown that even their false interpretation of the verse holds no weight because carpet and paper can cover a round object.

ANSWERING PRAYERS

Suppose you are in great need of money and you fiercely pray to God for this money, yet he does not answer your prayers, is this reason to doubt the existence of God? There are people who consider that no answer to your prayers means that there is no God. The first point to be made here is that people misunderstand the purpose of prayer. Prayer's primary goal is to worship God, not to provide opportunities to ask God for favors. Prayer in Islam is not a means to obtain material gain. Some religious people are like the Jews of Jesus (pbuh)' time, wanting earthly gain from God. But like Jesus (pbuh), Muslims offers them heavenly gain. Eternal success, not temporal success. So in Islam, prayer is giving, not asking. Giving of yourself, of your time and of your mind, in exchange God gives of himself. It is possible that God gives you earthly gain, but it is a promise that he exchanges your prayers for heavenly gain. And of course, any earthly gain you receive is but a test to see if you will still remember God, just as every loss is. This misunderstanding of the main purpose of prayer as asking for things is the reason a rich person may not pray to God and why poor people come to the places of worship in droves. All should come to worship God.

Secondly, the response or non-response to a prayer cannot disprove the existence and evidence for the First Cause. You can only deduce from your unanswered prayer that the First Cause or God did not answer you, not that he does not exist.

The third point is seen when we consider people's wishes and whether they are always granted. Do you grant your children their every wish? No. Some wishes that they have, you may grant them immediately and without hassle and other wishes, you make them strive for. Some wishes you grant them without them even asking. And others wishes, you do not grant at all. As their parent, you know best whether they can attain their goals themselves, and whether their goal is ridiculous or harmful to them. So you decide which wishes to grant and others which are not be granted. God grants his blessings in the same manner. It is his wisdom, which determines how pertinent a matter is, and whether your prayers are to be fulfilled or not.

CONTROVERSIAL SUBJECTS

WHY IS THERE EVIL IN THE WORLD?

The question "why is there evil in the world" is a frequently asked question. It is normally a concern that bothers the theist and it is a question posed by the atheist and agnostic. It is a question of God's existence. From the standpoint of the FIRST Cause setting things into motion, God's existence is very conceivable, but why does this God allow sin and evil?

First, we must admit the existence of right and wrong and good and bad. It is a good thing to help someone in need, to help an elderly person cross the street safely. And it is bad to rob an innocent person. These things are universally accepted as the right and wrong things to do. So whether God exists or not, there is still right and wrong. If we take the stance that there is no God, then what we are left with is man's free will to do something right or something wrong. This free will is presence only in man. Animals are bound by nature, not by free will. The cat will not one day decide to never harm another mouse. His nature is to be the predator of the mouse. It is out of his control. Therefore, it is not wrong for him to kill and eat a mouse.

If we are but evolved animals, then our every action is an act of nature and as such it cannot be deemed right or wrong, like any other animal. Some have theorized how morals and ethics were developed in mankind during the evolutionary process. But this does not negate the facts that if there is no provider of our morals then our actions, whether perceived as moral and immoral, are our nature. And as our nature, they are not subject to scrutiny or litigation. Robbing a bank and feeding the poor are equally worthless and meaningless actions, done by human animals.

Nonetheless, man's nature is to decide the proper course of action in any given circumstance, thus he is obligated to discern right from wrong. He can choose to do right and reap the benefits of it or he can do what is wrong and face the consequences. But man's propensity to do good or bad has no bearing on whether he was created or not. His decision to do evil does not disqualify the existence of God. So the atheist and agnostic are actually questioning the goodness of God. They mean to ask, if God is good, then why does he allow evil? The answer to the question, "why is there evil in the world?" is the same as the answer to "why is there good in the world?" If we are to conclude that God is evil because he allows sin into the world, then what are we to say about a God who allows an abundance of good into the world, also? The answer is that God gives man free will and sometimes he chooses good and other times he chooses evil. So, the person responsible for the evil of this world is in our mirrors.

Some might ask, "Why does this just God not intervene and cure the ills of humanity? If a person is about to mug an innocent person, why doesn't this God stop him? When a wealthy person spends his money frivolously, why does God not make the rich person give his money to the needy?" Again, it is free will, which includes personal accountability and responsibility. The person who insists that God is to blame for our bad deeds would not concede that our good deeds are to be accredited to him, as well. Their line of questioning is nothing but an attempt to pass the buck. Man wants to take credit for his good deeds and take no responsibility for his bad decisions and deeds.

OUR FINAL DESTINATION

10.56 It is He (Allah) Who giveth life and who taketh it, and to Him shall ye all be brought back.

OUR FINAL DESTINATION

RESURRECTION AND JUDGMENT

The most celebrated day of anyone's life is their birthday. No one ever forgets their own birthday. There is but one way all 6.8 billion people on earth came into being. However there are countless ways that one leaves the world. Very few people contemplate their death day, yet it is an unequivocal fact that YOU WILL DIE!!! It is only one day and no one knows when it is coming, but you have to prepare for it. If a Muslims say he will do something in the future, he is sure to add "INSHA ALLAH" which means "if ALLAH wills." He knows that it is entirely up to God whether you see tomorrow or not, so this phrase keeps him in constant remembrance that he should do all that he can for God today. The end of life's test is inevitable. And if you have ever taken a test with a timer, you know the importance of reading and following the directions. And you are graded on what you completed on the test.

As it is in every civilized nation, there is a system of judgment for mankind in Islam. In the judicial system on earth, a man is innocent of a crime until he is proven to be guilty. Before that, it is established that there is probable cause to investigate this person, in the first place. As the Qur'an asserts some suspicion is a sin (49:12), you should consider a person to be just until it is proven otherwise (49:6). Of course, this system is put in place to eliminate human error, like suspicion without just cause and the presumption of guilt. But in these court cases you will not see a judgment rendered on the good deeds done by the defendant. This kind of judgment is done by God. He does not concentrate solely on the wrong you have done, but on ALL that you have done.

The memory of man is astounding. It can be triggered by a sound, a smell or the sight of something familiar. Of course, this means that our memory is stored. And why are things placed in storage? Because they are still important to us, they still have use and one day they will be retrieved. Everything that we have ever thought of and everything that we have done is in storage. So everything that we have done is of importance and one day it will be retrieved.

Islam Is The Truth

On the Judgment Day or the last day, every person will be called to account for every action they have done, no matter how big or small. He will be rewarded for every good deed done. In fact, his reward for these deeds will be excessive, it may be doubled, or even 10 times as much as the deed deserves (27:89.4:40, 6:160), whereas the evil deeds will be punished as it is just due (6:160). Every evil deed done will be punished, if it is not repented for or erased by your righteous deeds (11:114). Amazingly, this formula doesn't work in reverse. No evil deed will erase a good deed done, supposing that your intentions were good also. ALLAH will NEVER ignore your good deeds (47:35). Can anyone deny the mercy of ALLAH? His mercy is endless.

He first gives man free will to choose his destiny. Then he gives him guidance upon guidance. He instills in man a conscience, and then he continuously sends prophets and revelation to instruct man. He gives man a multitude of righteous deeds and methods to worship him, in contrast to a relatively short list of what is to be shunned. He rewards these righteous things and provides numerous ways to clean your slate from your wrong doing. These slate cleaners include charity, prayer, fasting, repentance, and reversion. He paints you the path to success, and places you on the right road. And he erases all your backwards steps, with your intentions to move forward. For those whose lifetime of good outweighs that of his evil deeds, the reward is Paradise. For those who, despite all these opportunities, live a life which is characterized by sin, he will be rewarded with hell.

Even after death in the grave, the soul of man will be conscious of his behavior on earth. Some will wish to increase their good deeds.

23:99 (In Falsehood will they be) Until, when death comes to one of them, he says: "O my Lord! send me back (to life),

23:100 "In order that I may work righteousness in the things I neglected." - "By no means! It is but a word he says." Before them is a Partition till the Day they are raised up.

OUR FINAL DESTINATION

23:101 Then when the Trumpet is blown, there will be no more relationships between them that Day, nor will one ask after another!

The trumpet here is in reference to the sign of the end of the universe as we know it and the beginning of the Day of Judgment, where every deed and action done by man will be rewarded, punished or forgiven (3:30). I have suggested that time is a stopwatch, which God began at the beginning of the universe. Now is the time for the "stop" part of the watch. And God only knows when it will stop.

46:3 We created not the heavens and the earth and all between them but for just ends, and for a Term Appointed.

On this day, every soul that has ever lived will be reborn to stand trial for their deeds. This rebirth is referred to in the Qur'an as ALLAH repeating creation (10:4, 21:104). The verses mentioning this rebirth often scoff at those who would doubt the coming of the Day of Judgment. It asks, "Does man think he will not be called to account for his actions?" (75:36) and "Can not the one who created everything, create everything again?" (29:19-20)

2:28 How can ye reject the faith in Allah?- seeing that ye were without life, and He gave you life; then will He cause you to die, and will again bring you to life; and again to Him will ye return.

While man is living his life, there are angels appointed by God to record every action done by him (43:70, 50:17-18). But the angels record every ACTION, not intention. It is God who knows your intentions (50:16) and he will call you to account for your sins and only YOUR sins. Every man must take responsibility for his own actions

(6:164, 29:12-13, 94:5-6). Just as man is proud to accept reward for his righteousness, he should be brave enough to accept the consequences for his misdeeds.

On this day, God will gather all of mankind and all will testify that he is LORD (7:172). And the angels will bring forth the book of the deeds of each person and that person will read the book of his/her deeds (17:13-14, 18:49, 45:28-29). So ALLAH provides the perfect witness for the case. You! In this trial, you will testify for and against yourself (24:24-25). The Qur'an says you will not be wronged in the least of the Day of Judgment (36:54) because the actions and intention are so meticulously recorded and the witness is more than an eyewitness but the sole participant. If man can use his memory, history books, photographs and cameras to illustrate fragments of the past, then is it outlandish to believe that God can illustrate your entire history? And your actions will be weighed like a scale by ALLAH to determine if your righteousness exceeds your wickedness or vice versa (23:102-103).

And the Merciful, Loving God even grants man opportunities on the Day of Judgment to eliminate some of his sins. First of all, he takes your environment into account when he judges. If your environment makes one subject to iniquities and you are unable to avoid it or escape it, ALLAH will forgive you of your sins.

4.97 When angels take the souls of those who die in sin against their souls, they say: "In what (plight) Were ye?" They reply: "Weak and oppressed Were we in the earth." They say: "Was not the earth of Allah spacious enough for you to move yourselves away (from evil)?" Such men will find their abode in Hell,- What an evil refuge!

4.98 Except those who are (really) weak and oppressed men, women, and children - who have no means in their power, nor (a guide-post) to their way.

OUR FINAL DESTINATION

4:99 For these, there is hope that Allah will forgive. For Allah doth blot out (sins) and forgive again and again.

In these verses, ALLAH says there is hope that he will forgive you. The phrase "there is hope" is also translated as "maybe" he will forgive. This is in order to keep man from using his environment as a crutch and an excuse to sin. Islam encourages Muslims to fight oppression, or leave the situation if nothing else. Of course, if you are unable to leave in this situation, you and ALLAH know your intentions and his nature is to forgive repeatedly. And ALLAH will not punish a person if he is seeking forgiveness (8:33).

God also allows for intercession of man's behalf (19:87, 20:109). The Prophet Muhammad (pbuh) can ask God for forgiveness of man. But the prayers of Prophet Muhammad (pbuh) for those who stand on the side of Muslims but are actually the Muslim's enemy will fall on deaf ears (9:80). Along with Prophet Muhammad 's (pbuh), angels pray for the forgiveness of all mankind.

42.5 The heavens are almost rent asunder from above them (by Him Glory), and the angels celebrate the Praises of their Lord, and pray for forgiveness for (all) beings on earth. Behold! Verily Allah is He, the Oft-Forgiving, Most Merciful.

When you realize that Prophet Muhammad (pbuh) never said anything on the subject of religion that was not directly from God and that angels are totally obedient to God, it is clear that their intercession and prayers for forgiveness are not their own, but more blessings from God. It is God who is giving man every excuse to be forgiven.

Despite all the favors given to man, there are still some people whose sins outweigh their righteousness. They will be handed the record of their deeds called "Sijjin"

(83:7-9). They are called the companions of the left hand (56:41). Those whose righteousness deeds hold more weight than their evil deeds will be handed the record of the righteous called "Illiyyun" (83:18-21) and identified as companions of the right hand (56:27) and the most righteous will be called the Foremost (56:10-11).

HELL

67:6 For those who reject their Lord (and Cherisher) is the Penalty of Hell: and evil is (such) Destination.

67:7 When they are cast therein, they will hear the (terrible) drawing in of its breath even as it blazes forth,

67:8 Almost bursting with fury. Every time a Group is cast therein, its Keepers will ask, "Did no Warner come to you?"

67:9 They will say: "Yes indeed; a Warner did come to us, but we rejected him and said, 'Allah never sent down any (Message): ye are nothing but an egregious delusion!'"

67:10 They will further say: "Had we but listened or used our intelligence, we should not (now) be among the Companions of the Blazing Fire!"

67:11 They will then confess their sins: but far will be (Forgiveness) from the Companions of the Blazing Fire!

The Qur'an gives some of its most vivid images in its description of hell and its punishment for those who prefer sin and evil over virtue and righteousness. It describes people thrown into hell wearing chains and shackles (25:13), it describes the torment of a blazing fire (51:13) and it mentions what those who abide in hell with be eating and drinking.

88:1 Has the story reached thee of the overwhelming (Event)?

88:2 Some faces, that Day, will be humiliated,

88:3 Labouring (hard), weary,

88:4 The while they enter the Blazing Fire,

88:5 The while they are given, to drink, of a boiling hot spring,

88:6 No food will there be for them but a bitter Dhari'(thorn-fruit)

88:7 Which will neither nourish nor satisfy hunger.

Probably worse than the companions of the left hand's diet is the fact that they will be able to see the rewards of the companions of the right hand and the Foremost. They will even be able to communicate with them.

7:50 The Companions of the Fire will call to the Companions of the Garden: "Pour down to us water or anything that Allah doth provide for your sustenance." They will say: "Both these things hath Allah forbidden to those who rejected Him."

There will be a partition between the two places, similar to what the gospel records Jesus (pbuh) mentioning in his story of the rich man and the beggar, Lazarus (Luke 16:19-31). The rich man flourished in this life, perhaps at the expense of the beggar, but the tides had changed. The rich man chose not to help the beggar, whereas the beggar now can't lighten the punishment for the rich man. And as in the Qur'an, the rich man in Jesus' (pbuh) story, who is in hell, wishes that he could relive his life in the manner prescribe by God through the prophets. Thus hell is a place full of the regret. It is also a place filled with those who play the blame game. People will blame each other for the predicament that they are in (7:38). They will live in a state of regret and unaccountability and anguish, thus the Qur'an says they will neither live nor die (87:12-13). Finally the most painful punishment is neglect, the neglect of God. Just as the sinner ignores the light of ALLAH while he is alive, he is shielded from Allah's light in hell.

83:15 Verily, from (the Light of) their Lord, that Day, will they be veiled.

But as a God of graciousness, ALLAH wishes to hinder man from the path of unrighteousness and the destination of this great punishment. Thus he gives man a taste of the penalty to come in this life, in order to teach him that this is not the path that he wants to take. Again ALLAH tests nations with suffering, with adversity, with oppression in order to teach them a lesson of humility (6:42, 7:94) and he does the same with each person individually, and especially those who are heading on the wrong path.

32:21 And indeed We will make them taste of the Penalty of this (life) prior to the supreme Penalty, in order that they may (repent and) return.

ALLAH wants man to return to his initial state of Islam, thus he gives him every opportunity to change his ways. But it is man who chooses his fate. If he does not heed the warnings, if he does not use his intelligence, if he does not feel remorse for sin, if he does not fell compassionate for those less fortunate, if he does not take advantage of the innumerous blessings and mercies bestow upon him by his creator, it is no one's fault but his own. The Qur'an gives great details of the torment of hell. It is similar to the methods used in "Scared Straight," a program in which inmates describe the harsh realities of prison to deter at-risk teens from further pursuing a life of crime. Most of the teens take heed to the warning. But there are others who disregard the advice and warning of others. They disregard the description of the prison's horrible conditions. They continue their bad behavior at all cost to themselves and others. This is why the Qur'an says none but the MOST WRETCHED of people will go to hell (92:15).

29:55 On the Day that the Punishment shall cover them from above them and from below them, and (a Voice) shall say: "Taste ye (the fruits) of your deeds!"

Hell is described as a reward for the behavior you exhibited in this world. It is an evil reward for the evil done (30:10). This is karma in truth. This is what you have earned. Should one who has wreaked havoc and mischief on the world be given peace and serenity? Would he even appreciate peace and serenity? Is there any society which does not agree with punishment for crime? A criminal set free in Paradise would commit crimes as he did on earth. And the confrontation of hell will cause them to regret their actions, like the sight of prison for one just convicted cause him regrets. But this is not the retribution for their actions. Their retribution lies inside the walls of the prison and the walls of time. Yet there are criminals who consider prison to be a second home. Strangely they become accustomed to prison life. Unfortunately for those in hellfire, there is no chance of growing accustom to the fire of hell because this punishment is too severe to become acclimated to (4:56). And would a criminal cease committing crimes if he was not punished? Probably not.

35:37 Therein will they cry aloud (for assistance): "Our Lord! Bring us out: we shall work righteousness, not the (deeds) we used to do!" - "Did We not give you long enough life so that he that would should receive admonition? and (moreover) the warner came to you. So taste ye (the fruits of your deeds): for the wrong-doers there is no helper."

As for those who hinder others from the path to Paradise, their punishment is doubled (11:19-22, 7:38, 16:88). Persuading someone to do evil is worse than doing evil yourself in the sight of ALLAH. It is as if your evil thoughts are giving birth to evil in someone else and you are a harvester and breeder of evil. Also, hell has different levels and degrees of punishment as described in the Qur'an (4:145). It has 7 gates and they categorize the sinners (15:44). This is in order to give the proper punishment for the appropriate crime. Adolph Hitler is not on the same level of sin as the average mugger. Therefore his penalty should be far more severe than that of a mugger. Satan has encouraged and suggested that man do all sorts of evil deeds. Though the decision is ultimately up to man, whether he ignores or accepts satan's advice, it is satan's intention to lead man astray. So he is the greatest of those who hinder from the path of ALLAH. And as Allah has promised, those who hinder others from the straight path will lose the most in hell (11:22).

It has been argued that it is illogical and impractical to punish a man for an infinite amount of time for a finite life of crime and sin. There are a couple problems with this argument. The first is that most crimes take a short amount of time to commit, yet they can be punished for years. A man robs a bank. It may take 10 minutes, but his punishment could be 20 years or more. A man kills another person or hands over government secrets. Both could be perpetrated in a matter of minutes, yet the penalty for such an offense could result in the loss of their life. Thus a momentary action can result in a punishment that has no ending. Even if the punishment is not death, but imprisonment for the rest of your life, the punishment remains without an end. An atheist who is for the death penalty and one who is for life in prison are almost one in the same. One wishes to expedite death, while other wishes the criminal a lifetime of punishment, then death by natural causes, thus never gaining relief from punishment.

OUR FINAL DESTINATION

The second point to be made is the assumption that hell is infinite. The duration of a person's time of hell is better described as indefinite, than infinite. The Qur'an often mentions the torment of hell to be forever, but this may be used as another measure for deterring man from sin. Along with the horrid images of hell is the idea that it is a never ending punishment. But the Qur'an also says that the people of hell will dwell therein for AGES (78:23). As in other references of time in the Qur'an, this is in respect to man's perception of the time spent in hell, thus it is relative. Hell may seem to last forever due to man's disposition inside of it, but it may very well just be a very long time for him. To add to this notion, on at least two occasions, the Qur'an says they will dwell in hell forever, EXCEPT as ALLAH wills (6:128, 11:107). There are perhaps some who deserve everlasting punishment and others who deserve relief from the punishment. The possibility that one can dwell in such a place without release is what is meant to keep man from following this path. But Allah has left the slight chance for relief, but who wants to take that chance?

The fact that hell has different degrees and levels, might also be an indicator that hell is not literally forever, or not forever for everyone inside of hell. If there is a lowest level and a more harsh degree of hell, then there is a highest level and the least harsh degree of hell. In the prison system, there are the most dangerous offenders and those who are less dangerous. Obviously, the least dangerous is closer to relief than the most dangerous prisoner is. And the least dangerous offender is more likely to be considered for release. This would explain the verses of Chapter 7 which illustrate the life of hell and ironically interjects the probability of such a person to enter paradise (7:38-41). Though it pronounces the improbability of such an event happening, considering all the benevolence given to man while on earth, it is not impractical or impossible for God to do.

According to traditions attributed to the Prophet Muhammad (pbuh), there will be Muslims who go to hell, but no one who believes that there is no God but ALLAH and that Muhammad is his messenger, will remain in hell. Most Muslims believe this tradition to be valid and it is actually a claim which helps substantiate the notion that one's stay in hell is indefinite, not infinite.

PARADISE

4:124 If any do deeds of righteousness,- be they male or female - and have faith, they will enter Heaven, and not the least injustice will be done to them.

The great benefit of believing in ALLAH, praying, fasting, taking the pilgrimage and giving charity is the final destination of PARADISE. It is an oasis, a utopia full of perfection. Exactly what a righteous person would want on earth is what he will gain in Paradise, except everything will be unimaginable better. He is rewarded for his hard work, perseverance, patience and self-restraint. In the Qur'an, admittance into PARADISE is called SUCCESS (2:4-5, 9:88, 23:1). Man is either lost in hell or he is successful in Paradise. And ALLAH gives the righteous a taste of this success in this world and all of it in the next (16:97).

The gifts of Paradise will be in similitude with things man has experienced of earth (2:25). Paradise is most often mentioned as having great "gardens, beneath which rivers flow." It also contains at least four free flowing springs (55:50, 55:60). There will be no excessive hot or excessive cold weather (76:13). And those who live in Paradise will be afforded great palaces or mansions.

39:20 But it is for those who fear their Lord. That lofty mansions, one above another, have been built: beneath them flow rivers (of delight): (such is) the Promise of Allah: never doth Allah fail in (His) promise.

These mansions will be furnished with reclining silk couches (55:54) and green cushions and beautiful carpet (55:76). The righteous will have clothing of green silk and heavy brocade (76:21). They will be adorned with bracelets of silver (76:21) and gold (18:31) and pearls (22:23). They will be reclining on thrones raised on high (18:31, 88:13), and served food on trays of gold (43:71) and drinks from crystal-clear vessels of silver (76:15-16). Though they will be reclining, they feel no fatigue (15:48). The best of everything is in their midst. Fruits of all kind (44:55) are hanging from lote-trees without thorns (56:28-29) and they are at the Muslim's very fingertips (69:23). The Qur'an draws images of someone getting his comfort from the shade of these abundantly fruitful trees (56:30). But there is more than fruit in Paradise. There is also the flesh of fowls or any other meat that is desired (52:22). As well as rivers of honey, milk and wine (47:15).

Because Islam denounces the assumption of alcohol, the consumption of wine in heaven has drawn some criticism. As seems to be the case most often, those who bring these criticisms do not read the entire Qur'an to get the full understanding of the topic in question because if they had, they would quickly see that the Qur'an takes great pains to explain its usage and the definition of the wine given to the righteous in Paradise. As I have written earlier in this book, the reward for good from ALLAH is the like thereof.

55:60 Is there any Reward for Good - other than Good?

Therefore when the Qur'an says man receives all that he desires, that is all the good that he desires. It is illogical to think that a man who abstained from intoxicants on earth or at least believes in abstinence of intoxicants, is intoxicated in Paradise . The Qur'an makes it clear that the wine in Paradise is not an intoxicant on numerous occasions.

37:45 Round will be passed to them a Cup from a clear-flowing fountain,

37:46 Crystal-white, of a taste delicious to those who drink (thereof),

37:47 Free from headiness; nor will they suffer intoxication therefrom.

56:18 With goblets, (shining) beakers, and cups (filled) out of clear-flowing fountains:

56:19 No after-ache will they receive therefrom, nor will they suffer intoxication

76:21 Upon them will be green Garments of fine silk and heavy brocade, and they will be adorned with Bracelets of silver; and their Lord will give to them to drink of a Wine Pure and Holy.

83:25 Their thirst will be slaked with Pure Wine sealed.

Strangely enough, the criticism of the wine of Paradise is most often from Christians, who believe that Jesus (pbuh) turned water into wine for others to drink (John 2:1-11) and who is believed to have drank wine himself (Luke 7:34). I do not recall Jesus (pbuh) ever mentioning that this wine was pure, holy and non-intoxicating, as the Qur'an does. But I do recall Jesus (pbuh) recorded as saying he will not drink wine until he drinks it NEW with his followers in HEAVEN (Matthew 26:29). It seems Jesus (pbuh) spoke of a different kind of wine to be served in heaven, just as the Qur'an states.

Upon arrive into Paradise , the believers will be greeted at the gate by angels.

13:24 "Peace unto you for that ye persevered in patience! Now how excellent is the final home!"

The Qur'an says this is a place where man will die no more, but live (37:58-59). ALLAH will extinguish the anguish of your heart (7:43, 15:47). There are no more feelings of fear or sorrow (2:62, 3:170). You are far removed from your sad and angry feelings. There is no enmity between you and others. You are in a state of happiness, peace and security (15:46-48). Paradise is where you escape from foolish, vain, malevolent, or dishonest talk (78:35, 88:11). You will only hear believers saying "Peace! Peace"(56:26) and giving good conversations (37:50). And these believers are both men and women.

Because of the great misrepresentation of Islam to others, it has been assumed by many that Paradise is only a place for men, yet there is no guaranteed of man's acceptance into Paradise unless he is martyred. Fortunately, the Qur'an eradicates such misconceptions.

9:71 The Believers, men and women, are protectors one of another: they enjoin what is just and forbid what is evil: they observe regular prayers, practise regular charity, and obey Allah and His Messenger. On them will Allah pour His mercy: for Allah is Exalted in power, Wise.

9:72 Allah hath promised to Believers, men and women, gardens under which rivers flow, to dwell therein, and beautiful mansions in gardens of everlasting bliss. But the greatest bliss is the good pleasure of Allah: that is the supreme felicity.

This is a clear path to Paradise for believing men and women. I often hear Christians query Muslims about their certainty of entering heaven. Paradise is a promise from God, for your belief and for the fruits of your labor. Of course, it is not as simple as declaring that you believe in a particular person as God and a particular event like the Resurrection. Though the Christian and Muslims perspective on these issues vastly differ, Muslims do believe in the Supreme Being and they do believe in a particular event, God sending revelation to man, but declaration of belief is not enough in Islam. You must demonstrate your belief in God. If you truly believe in God, you will be righteous. This is why the Qur'an speaks in general terms about those who will inherit Paradise or hellfire. It says that believers will go to heaven and disbelievers will go to hell. Because generally speaking, those who are believers will be righteous and disbelievers will be sinners. It is obvious that this is in general terms. If it were definite, there would be no need for JUDGEMENT and due process (witnesses and testimony). But the Muslim that follows the tenants of Islam can assert that he is GUARANTEED Paradise according to God's promise in the Qur'an.

And Paradise has ranks and levels just as hell does. A person is ranked according to how hard and how much he strove and persevered in the cause of ALLAH. One who gives more of himself is rewarded far greater than one who did the minimum amount required. A person who gives 10 percent of his wealth in charity deserves more than a person who gave 2.5 percent, even though the latter is by no means in error. And this is also dependent upon how much one can afford to give. A poor person, who gives 2.5 percent to help others, has sacrificed much more than a millionaire who gives 2.5 percent. Thus the former is rewarded more for this sacrifice. And again, we find in the gospels of Mark (12:41-44), that Jesus (pbuh) endorses the same sentiment as the Qur'an puts forth.

4:95 Not equal are those believers who sit (at home) and receive no hurt, and those who strive and fight in the cause of Allah with their goods and their persons. Allah hath granted a grade higher to those who strive and fight with their goods and persons than to those who sit (at home). Unto all (in Faith) Hath Allah promised good: But those who strive and fight Hath He distinguished above those who sit (at home) by a special reward,

4:96 Ranks specially bestowed by Him, and Forgiveness and Mercy. For Allah is Oft-forgiving, Most Merciful.

Those who strive the hardest are called the "foremost." They are those who are nearest to ALLAH (56:11) and the highest ranking (9:20). The Qur'an says that the foremost group will consist mainly of the early generation of Muslims, with a few from later generations (56:13-14). And the Muslims who are not ranked as highly will be in the lower level of heaven. They will be the companions of the right hand (56:27). This group will consist of many of Muslims from both the early and the later generations. So it is every person's duty to be a companion of the right hand, but it should be every Muslim's goal to be with the FOREMOST.

The greatest gift that the righteous believer will get is that he will see the glory of ALLAH. This is what man since the beginning of time has imagined. Man has been forever fascinated with the image of God. To such an extent that he almost compulsively manufactures his own image of God. The reason idolatry exists is because of man's obsession with seeing God. Subconsciously some know that what they construct or who they exalt to be God, whether it is a man, or animal, is not God, but man continues his idolatry. Muslims know that ALLAH is nothing that we can imagine, but this does not quench our thirst. Just as the mighty messenger of God, Moses (pbuh), wanted to satisfy his curiosity, so too does every Muslim. But just as Moses (pbuh) became a believer, when we became believers we were content to wait for this magnificent gift. It is said "good things come to those who wait." It can also be said that "The greatest thing comes to Muslims who wait."

75:22 Some faces, that Day, will beam (in brightness and beauty);

75:23 Looking towards their Lord.

The momentous event of grasping the glory of God is a great experience. So too is all the pleasures of Paradise , but what is an experience without others to share it with. Those who you care most about are also those whom you would like to be present with you. In Paradise , there are similarities from this world, in food, drink, clothes, trees, rivers and so on. There is also the same need for companionship. Some religions have no companionship in heaven, but this is not the case in Islam. Those in Paradise will have their pain and suffering taken away, but not their memory. People in heaven and hell will discuss events that occurred here on earth.

What would you remember most about this life but the relationships you shared with your family and friends?

13:23 Gardens of perpetual bliss: they shall enter there, as well as the righteous among their fathers, their spouses, and their offspring

52:21 And those who believe and whose families follow them in Faith,- to them shall We join their families: Nor shall We deprive them (of the fruit) of aught of their works: (Yet) is each individual in pledge for his deeds.

43:70 Enter ye the Garden, ye and your wives, in (beauty and) rejoicing.

And for those who are not married, they will be joined to Companions. The word used in the Qur'an for these companions is "houris." They are characterized as having wide and lovely eyes (52:20), they are virgins and of equal-age to the believer (56:36-37), good, beautiful (55:70) and pure (3:15). They have been often described as only being female, when the Arabic word, "houris," just like the word companion or spouse, can be either male or female.

I have often seen Islam ridiculed on the account of the companions in Paradise, as well as those who will be reunited with their spouse, for thinking of Paradise in sensual terms. This is quite comical in my view. One of the greatest gifts God gave man is love and companionship. Why would he revoke this gift when rewarding his devotees for eternity? Would not a loving God provide more love in Paradise? The relationships continued or established in Paradise are actually a great tool to help propagate Islam.

OUR FINAL DESTINATION

"If you want to live happily ever after with your wife and family in Paradise, become a Muslim."

I have mentioned a few things which both the Qur'an and the words of Jesus (pbuh) as recorded in the gospels of the Bible agree on pertaining to heaven, but they differ with regards to companionship in heaven. Jesus (pbuh) says you will not be married anymore in heaven (Luke 20:35). This is interesting, because when you read Jesus' (pbuh) story of the rich man in hell and Lazarus the beggar in heaven, it is clear that both people recognize each other from their time on earth. And though the rich man is in the torment of hellfire, he still feels compassion towards his brothers who are still on the earth sinning (Luke 16:27-28). If you feel compassion in the midst of punishment, it is reasonable to believe that those in heaven will also feel compassion, especially when they recognize a loved one. In this instance, Jesus' (pbuh) words are in accordance with the Qur'an, that there exists love and compassion for others in the hereafter. It should also be stated that Jesus (pbuh) is said to have compared Heaven with the courtship that one man might have with 10 virgin women, 5 of which he marries (Matthew 25:1-13). Thus the Bible is conflicted on Jesus' (pbuh) position on companionship in heaven.

The problem in Islam arises with the notion that those who are martyrs will receive 72 virgins in Paradise. There are a number of problems with this idea. The most glaring one is that this claim is nowhere to be found in the Qur'an. The Qur'an say one who dies while striving in the way of ALLAH will enter Paradise. It also says there will be companions in Paradise. This is somehow joined together and Paradise has become an abode for a man with a harem of women at his disposal. But this is a forbidden act on earth, how exactly would it be permissible in Paradise? What then is the difference between a sinner and a saint, if the saint waits his lifetime to forever indulge in the acts that a sinner performs on earth? The difference would only be the patience of the saint over the sinner. Fornication is fornication wherever you are. And sex becomes the motive for getting to Paradise. Clearly the Qur'an says you will be united with you wife in Paradise, if she is a believer. And "houris" are for those without a wife or husband and no one needs 72 of either.

It is obvious that this idea was conjured up by a man to encourage other men to fight fiercely for the cause of ALLAH and for the abundant pleasures of the hereafter, because no chaste woman wants 72 companions. This is another example of the manipulation of Hadiths. Someone put their own words on the lips of Prophet Muhammad (pbuh), which is unsubstantiated by the Qur'an and in contrast to the moral code of Islam. Nonetheless, believing men and women should be happy to know that ALLAH will provide all with love and companionship in his utopia.

And unlike hell, there is no ambiguity about the duration of the righteous Muslim's stay in Paradise . These great gifts for Muslims will NEVER COME TO AN END (84:25). In Paradise , this no need for sleep and no sense of fatigue or weariness for its inhabitants. And "they will never asked to leave" (15:48). In the Qur'an, ALLAH says that the decision is solely ALLAH'S as to whether a sinner will leave hell. He also says this of those in Paradise, but he adds reassurance for the believers that theirs is a "gift without break" (11:108). He leaves those in hell some hope of departure, but he leaves the Muslim no chance of departure from his state of bliss.

THE HEIGHTS

7:46 Between them shall be a veil, and on the heights will be men who would know every one by his marks: they will call out to the Companions of the Garden, "peace on you": they will not have entered, but they will have an assurance (thereof).

7:47 When their eyes shall be turned towards the Companions of the Fire, they will say: "Our Lord! send us not to the company of the wrong-doers."

The Heights is a place in between Paradise and hell, in which people are gathered. But who are these people? Some suggest that this is a place in which the Prophets of God are. That the Prophets are communicating to both parties in the afterlife. But the Qur'an says Jesus (pbuh) and John (pbuh) both prophets of God, will be amongst those "nearest to God" (3:45, 3:39). If they are not in Paradise, then they are not the nearest to God.

It is clear that all people have been judged and rewarded or sentenced at this time, because the people of the heights are communicating with those in each place. Thus they too have been judged. But what is the verdict? It seems to be a place for those who are not righteous enough for heaven nor wicked enough for hell, because they ask not to be sent to hell and they have aspirations of entering heaven. They are like the person who is given community service in court. After he fulfills this obligation, he is free. So not only are there ranks and levels in the hereafter, there is also a place for those who live in the gray area to attain the pleasures of ALLAH. This place might also signify that hell is temporal and that paradise is the ultimate goal of the hereafter, since some are able to enter this bliss after their judgment.

If Islam is the correction and completion of other faiths, then perhaps the Hindus' and Buddhist' understanding of reincarnation is explained in the circumstances of those on the Heights. Perhaps the reincarnation that they speak of, in which a person is rewarded or punished for his life by being promoted or demoted in his next life and the ultimate goal "Nirvana," is actually one's life and death on earth and their struggle in the hereafter to reach Paradise. How great, how merciful, how forgiving, how loving is a GOD, who goes out of his way, over and over again, to see that man is exalted to his true place amongst creation?

THE CONCLUSION

After reading this book, ask yourself why has Islam been so erroneously represented? If Islam were so evil and so backwards, no assistance would be necessary to discredit it. Yet it can be seen in this book that many of the problems people have with Islam are due to purposeful misrepresentation of Islam. This problem is only magnified by those who misunderstand Islam and teach their misunderstanding, whether they are Muslims or non-Muslims. But when studied objectively, it is clear that Islam is the truth. The truth that is to be understood, not just felt. It is to be intellectualized and rationalized. It is a building block. Truth compounded upon truth. Proof compounded upon proof. Thus it is cemented in your mind. It is not just a feeling that nests and rests in your heart, because feelings can fade. This is a house of straw or a house of cards. But the house of brick is practically impenetrable because its foundation is LA ILAHA ILALLAH. MUHAMMADI RASULULLAH.

Despite the differing views that Muslims have, we must always seek these words as our common ground. Belief in these words and the words of the Qur'an is what truly makes one a Muslim and a mu'min. And there is no Muslim who is at odds about these things. Many Muslims may disagree with my perspective on certain issues in this book and that is fine. There is probably no book that I have read which I agreed whole-heartedly with except the Qur'an. But I have discovered great truths reading and investigating the words and works of Muslims and non-Muslims. Muslims must learn to live in harmony with other Muslims and non-Muslims who do not share their views. They must learn to live with those who detest Islam.

Abu Lahab was a man who detested Prophet Muhammad (pbuh) and Islam. He propagated against every word that the Prophet (pbuh) spoke. At any given time, the Prophet (pbuh) could have extinguished his opponent's voice, but he did not. And

THE CONCLUSION

he did not for the same reason that Muslims should not get beside themselves in response to slander or ridicule. That reason is that "TRUTH STANDS OUT FAR FROM ERROR." If we understand Islam, we should know that no matter what the argument or opposition is, it cannot stand up to Islam. There is no need for violence. The truth hurts those who speak falsehood more than any weapon that can be made. Truth affects their hearts and minds.

21:18 Nay, We hurl the Truth against falsehood, and it knocks out its brain, and behold, falsehood doth perish!

Instead of combating people for their ideas, combat their ideas. Compare and contrast their ideas to Islam. And no matter what the -ism is, Islam will Prevail. Propagate the religion of Islam. We know that there is a ton of misinformation on Islam, so it is our duty to teach true Islam. You see, truth hurts, but truth also heals. Tell everyone to come to their good. Come to the truth. Come to Islam.

48:28 It is He (Allah) Who has sent His Messenger with Guidance and the Religion of Truth, to proclaim it over all religion: and enough is Allah for a Witness.

NOW YOU KNOW THE TRUTH!!!

FOR MORE INFORMATION:

The Holy Qur'an by Adbullah Yusuf Ali, Muhammad Marmaduke Pickthall, or M. H. Shakir

The Noble Qur'an by Drs. Muhammad Taqiud Din Halali and Muhammad Muhsin Khan

Learning from the Qur'an by Harun Yahya

Dialogue with an Atheist by Dr. Mostafa Mahmoud

Evolution Deceit by Harun Yahya

The Holy Bible (NKJV or RSV)

In the Shade of the Qur'an by Sayyid Qutb

Understanding Islam by Yahiya Emerick

The Koran for Dummies by Sohaib Sultan

The Bible, the Qur'an and Science by Maurice Bucaille

How to Tell Others about Islam by Yahiya Emerick

Miracles of the Qur'an by Harun Yahya

Malcolm X by Alex Haley

Al-Qur'an the Miracle of Miracles by Ahmed Deedat

The 99 names of ALLAH by M.I. Siddiqi

The Qur'an and Modern Science ~ Compatible or Incompatible by Zakir Naik

The Amazing Qur'an by Dr. Gary Miller (Abdul-Ahad Omar)

If I Should Speak by Umm Zakiyyah

The Choice, Vol 1 & 2 by Ahmed Deedat

Thinking About God by Ruqaiyyah Waris Maqsood

No god but God by Reza Asian

Al-Islam in America by Zavia Books

ABOUT THE AUTHOR

Mr. Campbell was raised attending both the Christian Church and the Muslim Mosque. He was always inquisitive about religion. Around the age of 14, he decided that Islam was the path for him. However, he was rather secretive about his belief due to the negative perception many had of the religion. When Islam became the topic of any discussion, he maintained the Islamic sympathizer role as the son of a Muslim, while being careful not to be identified as a Muslim himself. The stigma surrounding Islam and Muslims only intensified throughout the years, but so too did his desire to announce to the world that ISLAM IS THE TRUTH. Throughout his life, he had engage others in discussions on religion and a little over three years ago he realized that the issues that were raised in debate and in dialogue were issues which warranted extensive details, evidence and explanations. Drawing from all the books, lectures, and debates he come in contact with, and all the talks with Muslims, Christians, Jews, Hindus, atheists and agnostics, he set out to write one book which would convince all of the truth about the God of the universe. This one book blossomed into eight books which are written with the primary goal of proving the validity of Islam. It is with his sincerest effort that he wrote these books, with the hope that all readers will set aside their preconceived ideas and have an open mind.

BOOKS BY THIS AUTHOR INCLUDE:

"ISLAM IS THE TRUTH"
"JESUS WAS NOT CRUCIFIED"
"THE JEWISH TORAH IS NOT THE WORD OF GOD"
"THERE IS NO TRINITY"
"25 MYTHS ABOUT ISLAM"
"GOD THE IRRESISTIBLE"
"FAQs ABOUT ISLAM"
"WHAT GOD SAYS ABOUT JESUS"

FOR INFORMATION ON PURCHASING THESE BOOKS LOG ON TO
WWW.ISLAMISTHETRUTH.ORG

Made in the USA
Middletown, DE
27 November 2021